Positive Flow Parenting

By

Lawrence Vijay Girard

Fruitgarden Publishing

P.O. Box 271570 Las Vegas, Nevada 89127

"Information and Inspiration for Living in Harmony with Life."

First Printing 2002

DEDICATED

To Bhavani
who shares with me
the gift of twins.

To Kai and Sabari
who have enriched my life
beyond measure.

To Swami Kriyananda
who has lovingly guided me
in the ways of the positive flow.

Contents

1

The Adventure of a Lifetime

There is nothing in life quite like the thrill that flows through body, mind and spirit when you first see and hold your newborn child. Months, possibly even years of effort have culminated in this miraculous moment. A soul from beyond the portals of this world has come to share the adventure of life with you. It is a new beginning, a fresh start, an opportunity for both parent and child to reach forward toward the fulfillment of life's purpose.

When my twin daughter and son were born I was bursting with the exaltation of the moment. I was completely overflowing with the joy of their physical presence and the added good fortune of having a boy and a girl in one fell swoop! Yet, as I look back at that time I realize that with so much energy having been put into the birth of the twins I had never thought much about parenting. The fact that I was going to be a father had never translated in my mind to me being a parent.

What qualifications did I have to be a parent? Are we all imbued with natural instincts for raising our young like animals in the wild? How is it that I could have gone through so many years of school as preparation for entering society and the work-place and I had never once talked to anyone about what it would be like to be a parent and raise a child? Was I supposed to

1

raise my children the way my parents raised me? If so, how did they raise me? Did they follow some kind of plan? How did they make decisions about what to do in any given situation?

In a close family parents and grandparents can help guide new parents. But in our society today we aren't guaranteed that others will be around to help us. And besides, does the fact that a person has been a parent automatically mean that they are good at it? Common sense tells us no.

Consider the millions of people that drive cars on the roads each day. Experience tells us that some drivers are better than others. At least all drivers take a test to prove a basic understanding of the skills necessary to drive safely. Compared to the complexities of parenting driving is a piece of cake. How is it that we can expect ourselves to be good parents with no training?

I am not suggesting that everyone should take a test before being allowed to be a parent. But it does make sense that we shouldn't leave such an important subject to chance. Taking the time to prepare ourselves for success in any life endeavor would be considered a wise action. Let's take the time now to consciously explore the realm of parenting.

It is the most natural thing in the world for a new parent to think: What do I do in this situation? What do I do in that situation? The western mind would be very happy if it was given a long list of do's and don'ts to memorize. We can't help thinking that if we read enough books or go to enough classes we will be educated well enough to do a good job. There are many good books on parenting that try to help people from this point of view. I am going to share with you a different approach.

Positive Flow Parenting is about growing beyond lists and the opinions of others – including my own. It is discovering from your own direct experience a way to face all of your life challenges: including those pertaining to parenting. The greatest truths in life are not found outside of ourselves, but can be discovered within the heart of each person's own being. We are going to explore an inner source of creative wisdom that will be able to guide us at every step of the way.

Not long after the birth of the twins I was taking one of them – I won't say which – to the counter for our first experience in diaper changing. I felt confident. Earlier I had laughed about what it would be like. Now there was a living, breathing child in my hands, wholly dependent on me. I moved carefully. As I lifted my little one onto a fresh diaper I was met with an inevitable, yet shocking experience: unwanted bodily wastes began to issue forth. To my horror, when I realized what was happening I had to fight the urge to let go while the blessed one was still being held up in the air!

Thus from day one, parenting is fraught with the unexpected. And when we consider the countless ways that life will challenge us, not only physically but intellectually, emotionally and spiritually, parenting does seem a daunting task. It is a little like trying to assemble something that you have brought home in a box that says: Detailed instructions included. Only for some reason we can't find the instructions, so we have to figure it out for ourselves.

Let's think about this for a minute. What if there was a universal manual for raising children? What would it be like? It would certainly need to be printed in every language of the world. It would have to include detailed instructions on every mental, physical and spiritual factor as they applied to each individual person in any given situation. Of course that would make it pretty thick! It might take a whole lifetime just to read it. To say nothing of how big and heavy it would be! And what about people who can't read?

No, a manual is not the answer. How about interactive video? No, too technical. And besides, this system would have had to be put in place before video was invented. God must have thought this out. It has to work for everyone, everywhere.

3

It needs to be portable so you can have it on site at all times. It must be individual so that it provides guidance for each and every person. It would need to be flexible, so that changes in circumstances can be taken into consideration.

Does this seem like idle thought? Worthy of a good laugh before heading back to the real world?

Let's look at nature for a moment. The planet earth is spinning through space balanced just between racing off into the galaxy and crashing into the sun. On the surface, millions of species of plant and animal life are interacting with each other in a delicate balance. Each day untold numbers of species are born into this world while others are forever lost. Many people think that this world is just matter, physical, what you see is what you get. Yet it has been scientifically proven that underneath matter, activating our world, is an invisible force called energy. Some scientists are now saying that guiding this underlying universal energy is universal consciousness.

This might seem like a new and fantastic idea to some people, but as it happens, our scientists are only now discovering the underlying components of life that have been known by the sages of India for thousands of years. Western science is not discovering new truths, but only becoming aware of the laws of life that have always existed.

What, you might ask, does this have to do with parenting? Let me share with you the most amazing truth. The Creator of life did provide instructions, not only for parenting, but for the basis of how to live life itself, of which parenting is just a part. It isn't a book that you have to read and memorize each day or year as updated versions come out. Yet, it is always up to date and correct for each and every moment of our lives – no matter what is happening. It is available to each and every one of us at no charge.

4

But, there is one little catch.

You see, as a practical matter, if God was to broadcast out loud instructions to everyone there would be such a horrible noise that no one would be able to understand anything. If you did hear some particular instructions, how would you know they were for you and not your neighbor? What about those people who don't want to know what God has to say? Should it be shouted out anyway? What about those who don't believe in God?

There are certainly many reasons why the Creation is set up the way that it is. No matter what those reasons might be, the end result is that we have to want to hear what God has to say to us. It is God's nature never to impose on us; otherwise we would be automatons. So we must activate our ability to hear His/Her guidance for us by learning to attune ourselves – like a radio receiver – to the guidance that is always available to us. The process of learning to hear this inner guidance is very much a part of what we will be exploring in the coming chapters.

Why can't we hear it all of the time? Because it isn't outside: It is inside. We live in a world that convinces us that understanding about life comes from the outside. It is like we all come from Missouri, the "show me" state. We believe that something is real only if we can experience it through our senses. As long as we are busy looking outside ourselves through the senses, we will only capture glimpses of our Creator who remains hidden in the beauties of the sunset, the power of a hurricane, the scent of the gardenia or the loving embrace of mother and child.

The really exciting news is that if we turn within we can perceive through direct intuitive perception God's loving presence and guidance. This inner relationship is the source for finding the solutions to all life challenges: including the daunting process of parenting.

"All right," some will ask, "What religion is this?"

Let me be absolutely clear. This is not about religion. It isn't about this church or that temple. It is not about what God's correct name is. It isn't about dogmas or affiliations of any kind. You don't have to take anyone's word for anything. You don't even have to believe in religion or God. This is about your own direct personal perception of a truth. A truth that you can consciously connect to within your own self. All you have to do is be willing to see truth for what it is; which is the way a scientist does.

If we want to increase our chances of being good parents we need to root our understanding of how to achieve that goal on the broadest possible realities. Many people rely on their own experience of growing up for basic parenting guidelines. To that they add cultural or religious traditions. Social and economic conditions will also play a part in how things go. Why not add to the possibilities by seeking to align our efforts with the central truths that make life itself? Life is like a flowing river. We can wander by the rocks in little whirlpools of separateness or we can enter the mainstream, a positive flow of divine wisdom, love and joy.

Much has been written through the centuries about the spiritual nature of life, its true reality as a manifestation of Divine Consciousness and that each of us must choose a path in life that will lead us closer to or farther from a growing awareness of Spirit. Some people conclude from all of the various descriptions that no one can agree on what is going on! But if you look closely at the writings of those who have personally realized the truth of their relationship with God, the saints of all religions, you will find an incredible similarity no matter what country, language or time.

The most basic of the discoveries that saints have made is that God does exist. And that the purpose of life is that we should grow in our own awareness of that truth. As if that weren't enough, the saints add that each one of us as a soul, is a part of God. We are not separate, but a part of the whole. The only reason we aren't aware of our oneness with God is that we have let ourselves identify more with the outward Creation through the senses and emotions than with the inner realities of the soul. They then say that the spiritual path is simply the process of remembering what we truly are: Spirit.

What is God? Everyone pretty much agrees that you can't describe infinity, omnipresence, omnipotence, etc. Poets of every age have tried to capture in words, glimpses of the Divine. Some of the clearest descriptions of God come from India. God is described as: Satchidananda – ever existing, ever conscious, ever new joy. The great yoga master Paramhansa Yogananda spoke of the experience of oneness with God in his poem *Samadhi*. He describes the complete union with Spirit as "enjoyable beyond imagination of expectancy."

This description reminds us that our limited minds can not grasp the incredible scope of God and the Creation. What we need to do is expand beyond the confines of the mind and let ourselves experience depths of joy and under-standing that we instinctively know as souls must be there, but have heretofore alluded us. The thing that we need to keep in mind is that this expanding process happens on the inside, not the outside.

We each have, in the very way that we are made, a connection to Infinite Spirit within us. Through our inner connection to Spirit we will find the guidance that we need in order to creatively address every challenge of life and parenting. Spirit is the source of all happiness. Spirit is the central solution to all situations. Living in and with Spirit is the heart of *Positive Flow Parenting*.

In order to understand how we can use our connection to Spirit as a source for our efforts in life and parenting, it will help if we have a feel for how the Creation is made and where we, as souls, fit in to the big picture. The cosmology of Spirit is certainly a larger subject than we can cover here, so I am going to share a very brief overview. Keep in mind that while you don't have to agree with this view of the way life is made in order to benefit from the *Positive Flow Parenting* approach, these ideas will help you to see how we are trying to align ourselves with the way life is made.

God, or Infinite Spirit, is an infinite consciousness of joy, peace and love that exists beyond the Creation. When God decided to make the Creation it was from this ocean of consciousness that all life sprang forth. The Creation was manifest in three overarching stages: the Causal Plane, the Astral Plane and the Physical Plane. These three layers of the Creation are superimposed upon one another. The key to understanding how the Creation fits together is to understand that Spirit is: Center everywhere, circumference nowhere. So life springs forth from literally....everywhere.

The Creation is at its root an ocean of consciousness or ideas. This is the Causal Plane. The focusing of infinite consciousness into the specific ideas that form the Creation as seemingly separate from Infinite Spirit is where the soul, individualized spirit, is created. The soul is a part of Infinite Spirit that has limited its awareness to the Creation. It is like a wave on the sea that thinks of itself as a wave – limiting its awareness – rather than being identified with the whole ocean as its reality.

Cloaking these ideas of limitation is the next stage of the Creation, the Astral Plane. The Astral Plane is where the Creation takes on the garb of light and energy. The astral body radiates light and energy that reflects the qualities of consciousness that make up the current awareness of each soul. The astral world is where the concepts of heaven and hell find their reality. This is where souls come from when they enter this world and where most souls go to after their sojourn in this lifetime.

Finally, in the most limiting part of the Creation, the physical plane, the causal and astral forms are covered with a physical body. This is the universe of matter and this physical body is incredibly limiting. It is akin to being a prisoner in a very small cell. Our predicament is that we have become so identified with our physical body we think that it is what we are. Fortunately, as we will discuss in more detail later, this physical realm is also where we can make much progress in our efforts to reawaken the memory of our reality as Spirit.

As the result of the way God made the Creation we can see that we have three bodies: ideational (causal), astral and physical. They are connected in ways that we cannot perceive with our senses, but as a soul we are always connected all the way back to our source in Spirit. What keeps us connected? Simply put, it is God's Love, like a magnet, always trying to draw us back toward our home in Spirit. What keeps us from being drawn back into God's Love? Our desires. Like a veil, our desires keep us tangled in the web of separateness until we eventually realize that they will never satisfy us. Only complete reunion with the infinite awareness of God's love and joy can ever satisfy us completely.

So how do we get out of this mess?

This is where we turn back to the examples of the saints. What are the qualities that they manifest as the result of their efforts? These qualities might be called the natural state of the soul. Each person if stripped of their self-involved likes and dislikes would naturally manifest a unique positive expression of the Divine, just as the saints do. What each of us needs to do is awaken within ourselves the same universal soul qualities that the saints express.

Does all this mean that we must become saints before we can be good parents? No. But it wouldn't hurt! What it comes down to is that if we want to be successful in any area of life it is helpful if we know what the rules are. That will tell us how we can

9

be successful. Once we have a view of the playing field we can develop skills, formulate strategies and consciously move forward with a realistic view of what we are trying to accomplish.

Many people leave parenting - like much of their life - to chance. They go where the wind blows. They follow the crowd. One of the interesting things about the saints is that they invariably do not follow the crowd. They strike out and seek new understanding. Often they are ridiculed for their ways, but they are adventurers seeking new heights. They are not willing to accept a humdrum existence. They push forward until they reach the ultimate goal: God.

Each one of us will need to muster that same determination if we want to achieve as much as possible in this life. There is no time to waste. Each day is a gift. We never know when it will be our time to return to the Astral World leaving untold tasks undone. Take each day wholeheartedly and embrace the opportunities that present themselves. Never forget, the positive forces of the universe are on your side. As a child of the Infinite we can rely on our Heavenly Father and our Divine Mother to sustain us, guide us and ever be with us.

The *Positive Flow Parenting* approach is based on the underlying principles that guide life itself. That is why we have just waded through some pretty deep stuff. We don't want to limit our efforts in parenting by the "modern" theories that change with each generation. We want to connect ourselves to the time tested truths about how life itself is made.

Just as all musicians use the same basic methods to play a wide variety of styles, once we have learned the basics of right living we can apply those same principles to parenting. Of course living life in the best possible way isn't something that a person becomes proficient at in just a few weeks. So as we move forward in our efforts we will always be learning new things, making lots of mistakes, pulling a few victories out of the hat, and most importantly, having the adventure of a lifetime!

2

Life in the Physical World

In order to understand more clearly our responsibilities as parents we must first remove the self-identification as "parent" and don our hat as "soul". As a soul we are given the opportunity in this physical world to improve ourselves until we can perfectly express the spirit that animates us. Unfortunately, the path to perfection is a long one – as we can see in our own selves, as well as in the world around us.

How is it that we are expected to achieve perfection in the short span of one life? What about those who live for only a few years? Or minutes? What of those who are physically or mentally challenged? What about those who live in luxury while others starve to death? Could a loving God create such an unjust world?

The apparent injustice in this world leads some people to denounce the existence of God. They say life is just an accident: the mere meeting of molecules that one day, like a lab experiment gone awry, exploded into a universe. Following that thought comes a belief that the only purpose to life – if there is one at all – is to get the most of whatever you desire for yourself. And that people who believe in God are just duping themselves because they don't have the guts to face up to "reality". There are also those who, while they do feel that God might exist, think that God is unapproachable: only to be known by a "chosen" few. They accept life at its face value, a physical and mental challenge to survive, and hope for the best when it is time to cash in at the end of life.

Interestingly enough, even without the fact that every major religion in the world has somewhere in its teachings a belief in reincarnation, our own western science is finding more and more evidence that leads to the conclusion that there is life after life. Studies of people that have been pronounced clinically dead, who came back to life after minutes or in some cases days, have led to a growing scientific proof that the soul goes on after the physical body is shed. A number of books with detailed descriptions of what these souls have experienced, beyond the limits of the physical body, have been published in recent years.

While it is not necessary to believe in reincarnation to grow spiritually or to be a good parent, a look at reincarnation can help us to understand the forces that are at work within ourselves and our children. Here is one way of looking at it.

Imagine a big broad window. The sunlight is able to come through it without any impairment. It is so clean and clear you can see right through the window to the beautiful scenery outside.

Now imagine that the same window is covered with dirt. Storms of rain and dust have conspired to cover its clarity with a thin coating of darkness. Now you can't see through the window so clearly. Your memory of the beauty on the other side of the window starts to fade. Sometimes it can happen that the window is dirty for so long that you can't remember what it is like to look through it.

So it is with the soul. Through incarnations the soul is cluttered up with the desires, likes and dislikes of many lifetimes. These desires disturb the clarity of our ability to perceive our true nature as Spirit. For most people it has been so long they question if there ever was any light in the first place.

It is important to remember that underneath the dirt the window is still as pure as ever. Once cleaned, it will shine as beautifully as the day it was made. No matter how far we have come from our home in Spirit the essence of our being is still pure Spirit. All we have to do is clean things up a bit!

Like returning to school in the fall, reincarnation provides the soul with opportunities to push forward without the burden of past failures. Temporarily forgetting the ups and downs of past lives we find a fresh environment in which to explore new possibilities. But, just like in school, even though we find ourselves in a new class with new clothing, we still bring the same old self with us. Hopefully we will be freshened up after a nice vacation in the astral world! Once here though, it is back to work.

A look at the process of electro-magnetism will help you to understand more clearly what I mean by bringing yourself with you into a new incarnation. When a wire is coiled around a piece of metal and electricity is run through the wire an electromagnetic field is created. The main factors that determine the size and shape of the field are the type and shape of the metal and the amount of energy that flows through the wire.

Thoughts and actions in this physical world are the metal. Different types of thoughts or actions would be like different types of metal. The coiled wire is our will. This is the conduit through which energy flows through us. The amount of energy that flows through our will to any given action or thought determines the amount of commitment we have given to that particular situation. The energy itself is neutral. It comes from God and can be used freely according to how well we have developed our ability to draw on it.

Carried in the astral body of each soul is a collection of magnetic vortexes that correspond to the likes, dislikes, actions, and reactions, which we have gathered through

13

many incarnations. On the surface it seems like it would be easy to deal with them. But once you get into it, like Pandora's box, things tend to get out of hand.

If you desire an ice cream cone, just eat one. There...the desire is gone! It seems so simple. But, consider what happens if you want an ice cream cone and you don't have the money? You become unhappy. What if you love ice cream so much that you eat it until you get sick? What if you love ice cream but you have diabetes and can't eat it at all? What if you go to the ice cream parlor and they don't have the flavor you want? Or they are closed? Or if you reincarnated into a time when there is no ice cream? What if you love ice cream so much that you come back in your next life as an ice cream salesman?

You see, one thought or desire, leads to another, leads to another, and on and on. And all we were talking about was ice cream! What about all of the millions, even billions of ideas, places, things to do, people to see, ways of life, types of bodies, and on and on?

This incredible mixture of past commitments of energy is carried with us into each new lifetime. Like seeds dropped last season, they lay buried in each person's astral body waiting to sprout when the right circumstances come along to awaken them. As an example. A person might go through their whole life without the desire to travel; never going far from their home-town. Then one day while rocking on the porch and reading the newspaper they see an advertisement they have never seen before. It says: Adventure in Tahiti! Suddenly, something sparks inside, some deeply buried vortex of energy that had been waiting for this chance to pop out. Then, like the genie in the lamp, the thought comes out of nowhere: Yes, I have always wanted to go there! It seems so natural.

Once these latent desires are awakened, what we do with them will depend on the strength of the desire and our current

14

state of consciousness. Small desires are usually not a big deal, but big ones can take incarnations to fulfill.

All of our tendencies from the past are not as deeply buried as that last example. Some people know from childhood what it is that they want to do in this life. Some even come with special talents they have developed over many incarnations – like Mozart. Others come with difficulties of many kinds. These also come from past actions.

These energies from our past color everything that we do in this life. All of our experiences are filtered through these inner fields of energy. As we live this life we are always receiving the results of our past actions and simultaneously planting the seeds of our future. Scientists say: For every action there is an equal and opposite reaction. The saints say: As you sow, so you reap.

Only once we are anchored in Spirit and free from attachments can we travel through this world untouched by the cause and effect law of duality. Until then, we must be careful that our actions lead us toward freedom rather than binding us to the tireless wheel of pleasure and pain, death and rebirth.

The energies that we have stored within us, our karma, are both positive and negative. From good deeds of the past we will reap positive benefits in the future. Likewise, from negative deeds of the past we will reap problems. This karma applies to all aspects of life: mental, emotional, physical and spiritual. Many people think they can find the roots of personality difficulties by exploring one's childhood. Certainly to some degree that is true. But it is also helpful to understand that many of our personality "quirks" are also rooted in our karma from past lives. The circumstances of our childhood were just the catalyst that gave those old energies an opportunity to sprout. Realizing that some of the things we face in this life can not be traced to a seeable source in this lifetime can help us to gain a broader perspective on our circumstances.

As personalities we are colored by the tendencies that we have brought from the past and the way that we have responded to our current life. As a soul, we are mostly untouched. Like the window that we talked about earlier, all of our good and bad actions from the past are like a thin dark coating that obscures our divinity. Underneath that coating our true higher nature is always waiting to shine through. This world's greatest gift is that it gives us the opportunity and the motivation to clean off the dust of the past and shine anew the window of our consciousness until the pure light of the Divine can flow through us without any impediment.

Along with the insight that these ideas bring to our understanding of the way we are made and the circumstances in which we find ourselves, is the light that it brings to bear on our position as parents. As souls, or individualized Spirit, we are all children of the Infinite. Through the intricacies of reincarnation it is quite probable that we will be parents of a particular soul in one lifetime and their child in another. If you think about it, it isn't all that uncommon for a parent to pause in a moment of confusion and wonder: Who is the parent here?

It would be helpful if, when we introduce our son or daughter as "my" son, or "my" daughter, we take the time to remember that these are not "our" children. We do not own them. They are children of the Infinite – just as we are – and we are only stewards. As stewards we hold a great responsibility. Our role is to do our very best for our charges as God's representatives.

There are many rewards to being a parent. There are also many sacrifices that need to be made. We must be prepared at times to lay aside our own personal desires and fulfill the sacred trust in which God has placed us. Remember, as we reap the rewards of our past actions through this special relationship we are also sowing the seeds for our future. Even better is to realize that the fulfillment of our highest desire, the desire to live in tune with God's Will for our lives, is fulfilled when we forsake our smaller self in the service of others. That doesn't mean that we let the little munchkins walk all over us! It means that we must always pay attention and do our very best.

3

Building a
Good Life

   While we are all unique, our uniqueness is built on a system that is the same for everyone. All souls are made by the same construction company – God. Let's use the example of building a home to see more clearly what we and our children are working with as we try to grow in this life. Keep in mind that parenting is a process whereby both parent and child are being challenged to improve. By working with and refining the qualities that will make us more perfect expressions of Spirit, we will understand better how to help our children do the same through their own lives.

   When you decide to build a home you must first find a site and develop a plan. In this case each soul is the site and God has provided the basic plan – which we've discussed in the last two chapters. Exactly how we implement our part of the plan and what custom features we add is up to us. The tools and the power are also provided by God: we have our bodies, our minds and the life sustaining energy that flows through us from within. Now we must do our part.

   The first thing to go up in our home is the foundation. Upon this all else will stand. As we know, the storms of life can be pretty fierce, so the foundation of our home must be strong. For the soul there is only one material that can withstand the stresses that life will bring to bear on us: Self-Honesty.

Self-honesty is the willingness to see things in life the way they actually are no matter how we feel about it. Whether we react to any given situation in life with happiness or sadness it is important that we don't cover up our true feelings. I don't mean that we have to announce them all of the time or wallow in feelings that aren't helpful, but we must be willing to honestly admit, "This is how I feel." Only after that can we move on to, "Now, what do I do about it?"

Self-honesty also means looking at our motivating impulses impartially and seeing them for what they are. When we have impulses and desires that we aren't proud of – we all have them – we don't want to excuse them by glossing over them with rationalizations. Without this basis of self-honesty we run a high risk that some circumstance in life will come along and knock down that which we have taken so much time to build.

There is a story told about a man who spent 40 years trying to get God's attention. He did endless austerities in order to prove his worthiness. On the outside he looked like the perfect devotee. But on the inside, as our story will show, he wasn't quite so perfect.

One day a messenger from God came to see the old anchorite. The messenger said to the anchorite, "God has told me to tell you that as soon as He is finished passing 25 elephants through the eye of a needle He will come to see you."

The old anchorite was completely devastated by this news. He jumped up saying, "That is the most ridiculous thing I have ever heard. I can't believe how I've been wasting all of these years." The anchorite then stormed off to town – presumably to make up for lost time!

Had the old anchorite been sincere in his search for God he would have realized that his goal was imminent for it certainly wouldn't take the Creator of the universe very long to

19

pass 25 elephants through the eye of a needle. But in the end, so close to his goal, imperfections on the inside of the anchorite kept him from attaining his goal. He looked strong on the outside, but he was hollow on the inside.

Stories like this can have many useful meanings. One has to do with our own personal search for God. If you aren't sure that God exists: admit it to yourself. Then, if you sincerely want to know the truth about the existence of God, do what you would do to get the answer to any other question: Ask. All of the saints say that if you call to God sincerely He will make His presence known to you. Why not put it to the test for yourself? Just remember, if God does exist He/She knows your heart, so you must call with complete sincerity. How long will it take to get an answer? We have ignored the Divine Presence for who knows how long? We must prove our desire to know Him through the intensity of our seeking and our willingness to receive the response that He gives rather than the response that we want or expect.

Another aspect of this story relates specifically to parenting. If your child spills grape juice on your new shirt it isn't very likely that you are going to be happy about it. So don't expect to feel happy. If you have developed an even minded temperament it won't be that big of a deal. But if you haven't, you might feel like getting upset. Rather than suppressing your feelings, acknowledge them – however ugly they may be – and then move quickly on to what you can positively do about them.

If we submerge our true feelings occasionally it isn't a big problem. But some people deny, deny, deny, until they can't stand it anymore. Then one day, like the fabled straw that broke the camel's back, something happens and they burst. As we build the house of our consciousness remember that self-honesty is the foundation that keeps everything else that we do strong. Without self-honesty we are building on quicksand.

The floor of our house must carry the weight of many activities. This represents our habits, our basic approach to life and the natural abilities that we have brought from the past. No matter what we do in life we are connected to our past by the ways of acting that we have previously cultivated. Our positive habits provide a strong platform from which much can be accomplished. Our negative habits, like a sagging floor, take the spring out of our step – making some tasks almost impossible. As we build our home strong positive habits will provide the best girders to support our efforts in life.

The walls and roof that surround our living space represent the personality that we show on the outside. If you take a moment you can imagine what you or someone you know would look like as a house. People with sharp personalities might have pointed spires. Softer personalities might be low to the ground or round like a geodesic dome. Some people seem like they must be made of brick, while others are made of straw.

The inside walls create the many rooms of various interests that we keep compartmentalized in our minds. Some of the rooms we enjoy and visit often. Other rooms are areas of challenge that we like to avoid. Some people seem like they must have endless rooms of interest and involvement while others have few rooms. People who are very withdrawn have few windows through which they can look out into the world. In some cases, they go so far inside that they wander for a long time in their own minds, never coming out to relate to the world in which they live. Others have so many rooms and windows that they can't seem to focus on any one thing at a time.

Balance is the key to this part of the house. We should strive as Buddha recommended, for the middle path. Whether it be aspects of our personality or of our activities, what we need to do is balance the opposites that this world presents to us. We should eat with enjoyment but not with greed. We should strive to do our best but not be attached to the fruits of our

21

actions. We should learn to focus our minds single pointedly, and yet, also leave time when we can mentally reach out without restraint.

The plumbing in our house is the physical body that we live through. If we don't eat right, keep it clean and take generally good care of it, we will have to call the roto-rooter man – otherwise known as doctors.

The wiring in our house represents our brain and nervous system which is powered by the life force that flows through our astral body to animate the physical body. Since the power source is Infinite Spirit and not your local utility company, you can always rely on it. There is no limit to the amount of energy that you can draw. The only limit is the fuse box that we install according to how much of reality we really want to experience. You see, sometimes we would rather watch cartoons then face Infinity!

Inside the house you will also find furniture and decorations. These are the various things that we have picked up from many incarnations, the odds and ends of our karma. Some of it is kept up in the attic or down in the basement and you have to search for it to find it, but it is all there.

Outside you will find the landscaping to be of interest as well. This is where we show how we feel about ourselves. Some fronts are stiff and formal while others are wild and disheveled. Sometimes people try to make the outside look different then they feel inside. If it is an attempt to get things cleaned up and moving in a positive direction then it helps. If it is an attempt at subterfuge then we get back to what I was saying about self-honesty.

The idea that we have built our current life from our past and are molding our future by our actions now is a very important one. It makes us responsible for where we are today instead of blaming others or our Creator. It also reminds us that we are the creators of our own future. Of course, if things aren't going very well in your life this might be a distressing thought. It isn't easy to take responsibility for the problems that we face in life. At the same time, if things are going well for you, you might be patting yourself on the back. One thing to keep in mind is that everything in this physical world is temporary. Pleasant is temporary. Unpleasant is temporary. Physical life itself is temporary.

You see, ultimately, we aren't trying to build the perfect house, the greatest all around personality that handles every situation in life perfectly or the best looking body that never gets sick. What we are trying to do is realize our oneness with Spirit, which is totally beyond the limits of the physical body and mind. But in order to achieve that goal we must use to the best of our ability the tools of body and mind to which we are currently associated.

Utilizing the best that is available to us in any given situation is what *Positive Flow Parenting* is all about. If the latest breakthrough in parenting put out by behavioral scientists is useful, then use it. If plugging directly into the wisdom of Spirit, which will take into account all of the factors that we have been discussing is available to us, then that's what we use. Finding what works and moving forward toward our goals, be they mental, physical or spiritual, is what learning to live in the positive flow of life is all about.

Oh yes, just one more thing about the electricity. When the power is withdrawn at the end of life the building must be vacated!

4

The Positive Flow

I can hear some readers beginning to grumble in the back. They are saying, "But what do I do when this happens? What do I do when that happens?" Well, that is what this chapter is all about. Like I said earlier, we aren't talking about what to do in "a" situation, but what to do in "any" situation. In fact, this is the way we want to live in every situation, which means most simply: all of the time.

I'm not talking just about a philosophy through which we can filter the needs of the moment – although that is certainly part of what we will be doing. More importantly, I am referring to an ability to consciously draw on the creative forces of life itself. This ability can find the practical solutions to all of life's circumstances, including things like: thumb sucking, bed wetting, getting along with others, practicing the piano, doing homework, choosing your friends, dealing with drugs, sex, finding a vocation in life, virtually anything that life will throw at us.

Is it going to be easy? Some of it yes, some of it no. Can it help right away? Definitely!

Will you instantly become a perfect parent? If you mean by that, "Will I avoid making mistakes?" The answer must be no.

But, if you realize that your child has been magnetically drawn to you because your inner energy patterns are magnetically compatible and that this compatibility offers just the opportunities that you both need to move toward your highest potential, then you already are the perfect parent for your child. Even if you aren't yet a perfect parent.

Remember when I mentioned the way God made the Creation with the Causal, Astral and Physical Planes? Let's look at it another way in order to understand what I mean by the positive flow. Let's compare the Ocean of Spirit – ever-existing, ever-conscious, ever-new joy – to an ocean, as we understand it in this physical world. God is the ocean. There are no waves, just a large expanse of water. God now decides – for reasons of His own – it would be interesting if there was a fountain on the ocean. So out of the depths of the ocean, up comes a huge rush of water into the sky. Now we have a fountain. The water goes up and when it gets to the top, as far as it can go from the surface of the ocean, it starts to come down. As it falls it interacts with the water going up, making interesting variations to look at. Once back to the surface the water again merges into the ocean.

The ocean, as God's Infinite Awareness, is the source of the Creation, yet it is beyond the Creation. The water rising up from the ocean surface is God's consciousness going out from its infinite source: first through the causal plane, then the astral plane, and finally the physical plane. As souls, or individualized Spirit, we are caught up in this rising stream of consciousness until we get so far from our source that we forget where we came from. We become identified with the Creation instead of with the Ocean.

Once we have gone as far away as possible we start the long journey back home. Because the flow away from our home in Spirit is so strong, rather than coming straight back to the ocean we tend to move forward a little, back a little, forward a

25

lot, back a little. This forward and backward motion goes on for a very long time until we finally reach our home in Spirit.

The water going away from Infinite Spirit toward limitation is the negative flow. The water moving toward the ocean and expanding consciousness is the positive flow. All of life is constantly in motion. It is in relationship to these two overarching directions of contracting consciousness (the negative flow) and expanding consciousness (the positive flow) that we can establish a value system that can handle the infinite variations of each person's life.

To complicate things even more, these flows of consciousness away from and back to the ocean of Spirit are intelligent and consciously active. The positive flow tries to help us realize our true reality as manifestations of Spirit. The negative flow tries to convince us that we are matter – a physical body with a personality. This is the universal battlefield that each of us stands on, where the forces of light and dark are doing battle within us and all around us.

Let's look at how these flows of consciousness affect us on a daily basis.

When we are tuned into the outward flow we are made smaller, more identified with the limitations of the mind and body. We think that the world of the senses is the only reality. We seek the fulfillment of our desires even at the expense of others. People living in the negative flow are described as selfish, self-centered, egotistical, etc. All of these labels indicate a contracting of consciousness. We even call these ways of acting small-minded.

The positive flow is one of expansion. As we come closer to our origin, Infinite Spirit, we become larger, broad-minded. Instead of thinking only of ourselves we want to give to others even at our own expense. Love becomes our way of life instead of hate or jealousy. We want to share instead of hoard. Joy replaces restless unhappiness.

26

When I use the terms broad-minded and small-minded I am trying to give you a directional sense of how this works. Our potential as expressions of Spirit is far beyond the concepts of mind: whether broad or small. In this sense being broad-minded doesn't mean simply being open to new ideas, but being identified with universal realities rather than the limited small-mindedness of the ego.

While these positive and negative flows of energy do battle within us we find that we are a mixture of positive and negative impulses. Sometimes we do good (things associated with the positive flow) and at other times we do bad (things associated with the negative flow). Eventually, when we realize our true Self as Spirit beyond the Creation the positive and negative fluctuations of this world will no longer bind us. Until we have reached our goal of Self-realization we are still affected by these polarities. It is a long road home. But remember, the biggest step along this path is that first step, the one that gets us going on our way. If we want to achieve victory we must take that first step. Then victory is just a matter of time as long as we keep pushing forward.

Let me explain what I mean by tuning in to the positive or negative flow. Spirit is center everywhere, circumference nowhere. This means that the doorway to infinity is hiding behind every atom of the Creation and even the spaces between the atoms. There is no place that we can go where Spirit is not. Why don't we perceive it? The most common reason is that we just don't try. After that, it is like an athlete who is out of shape and has forgotten how to use the apparatus of their sport.

The human form contains everything we need in order to contact Spirit. That is why the human form is so valuable and said to be at the top of the evolutionary scale. It is our inner apparatus for consciously connecting with Spirit that separates Homo sapiens from the rest of the animal kingdom. While our ability to consciously connect to the positive flow can be impaired through poor mental and physical habits, it can never be totally lost. In fact, it is happening to some degree all of the time whether we are aware of it or not. Every time we have a positive thought, a loving feeling, a joyful expression, we are reflecting to some degree the positive flow of life. When we express anger, selfishness, laziness or any other limiting quality we are expressing the negative flow.

While it seems like all of the positive and negative qualities of the mind and heart are our own; they are actually rooted in larger universal flows of consciousness. We express these larger flows through the instrument of our individual consciousness according to the qualities to which we have consciously or unconsciously attuned ourselves. This is how universal consciousness is stepped down through each individuals awareness.

Think of the way radio and television work. Each station is broadcasting a different type of programming. The individual stations represent different types of thoughts – whether they are soul qualities or specific intellectual information – that we each have available as a potential. It is only a potential until we actually tune the dial of our awareness to any particular frequency or vibration. Once we focus our attention we can express whatever is being broadcast on that vibration. We are only limited by the degree to which we have developed ourselves mentally, physically, and spiritually. Thus, if we want to feel peace, we should tune our awareness to the universal source of peace. If our concentration and intensity are sufficient we will tap into that peace and become aware of it.

It works the same way with specific areas of thought. Let's say you are a musician and are trying to write a song. Instead of just letting your fingers idly wander over your instrument, focus your mind inwardly with concentration. Ask the universe to flow through you. Consciously decide what type of song you want to write. Getting a specific vibrational quality clear in your mind will help you to draw a response. If you are good at this the song can come instantly. If you are new at it, it may take some time for you to develop your attunement. But it works!

This is the way that we can draw creative solutions into every part of our lives. Let's say you are a grocer and you want to set up a display in a way that will attract customers. At first you will draw on memories of previous displays. Maybe you will remember some classes that you attended in merchandising. If you leave it to those past memories you will end up with the same old display that everyone else uses. But if you release yourself from the past and open your mind to the possibilities of the moment by calling on your own higher Self – the positive flow of Spirit – you will draw new and fresh ways of doing the same old things.

Einstein received the theory of relativity in a flash of inspiration. His years of efforts had magnetically drawn to him this higher scientific revelation. In just a moment he suddenly saw clearly what he had been trying to understand for years. Having received that inspiration it still took him years to work out the details in a way that others could understand his discovery. Tapping into the positive flow of life doesn't mean we don't need to work hard once we receive inspiration!

The greatest creative minds in every area of human endeavor have attributed their insights to a Divine source. Invariably those who tap their inner, creative resources come to realize that in order to keep the inspirations flowing we must continue to expand our sympathies and understanding instead of contracting ourselves with thoughts like, "Aren't I great. I'm so creative. I thought up some good ones this time!" Egotistical pride in thinking that our little self is the source of any thought or ability is a classic ploy of the negative flow. It is inevitable that once we walk down that road we will lose that of which we are so proud.

29

In this world of relativity we are constantly looking for a definitive correctness that we can point to and say, This is right, that is wrong. The difficulty with our search is that there are few places in life where you can apply such strict forms of measurement. According to Einstein's theory of relativity the only constant in the universe is the speed of light. Everything else is in a constant state of flux.

The toughest area to put a firm definition to is human behavior. We can make generalizations like, it is right to love and wrong to hate. But is that right? Could there be times when hate or intense distaste is appropriate? There doesn't seem to be a definitive statement on the question of right and wrong in life that meets the requirements of every situation. The reason for this problem is that this world tries to support the impression of solidarity. The very nature of the physical Creation is to try and convince us: That which is true is solid, firm, unmovable, always the same. Yet, even nature herself belies this view in the very fact that everything physical is always changing: even mountains move!

Understanding that all of life is a flow rather than a specific time, place, thing, thought or action, is essential to coming to grips with a value system that takes into account life's variability. If a philanthropic person were to suddenly decide to make money only for himself you would think: That's too bad. If a lazy no good bum woke up one day and decided to go out and make money for himself you would probably think: That's great! For some people eating more sugar is a must, for others it means death: the same action, different results.

With these simple examples we can see that giving value to our thoughts and actions must be in relationship to the realities of our circumstances. We need to take into account the physical, mental, and spiritual aspects of every situation and then ask ourselves: Will my actions put me more in tune with the positive flow toward the Ocean of Spirit? Or will I find myself moving outward on the negative flow toward limitation and suffering? Attunement to these higher realities is the only firm ground on which we can base our decisions in life. All else is folly.

While there are broad guidelines that we can follow until we are proficient in contacting truth directly, our goal is to meet each moment of life with a sense of attunement to the positive flow rather than a list of rights and wrongs. Let's face it, there are some questions in life that we won't truly know our own answer to until we face that issue directly. I might say that I believe in non-violence, but if my family were attacked, how would I actually act in that moment of truth? Who can say beforehand how they will react to such a moment? The best that we can do is to practice living in the positive flow of life so that when the tough issues arrive we will be as prepared as possible. It is like anything else, the more you do it the better you get at it. What could be more valuable than getting good at being in tune with the positive forces of the universe?

5

Tuning In to the Positive Flow
Part 1

So now that we have a sense of what the positive flow is, how can we tune in to it? After all, it doesn't matter how helpful it might be if we can't experience it for ourselves. Just like in science, experience is the basis of what we are talking about. It isn't enough to think, "Yes, right on! This stuff is great!" We need to experience it for ourselves.

Let's see if we can use energies that we are all able to perceive right now as a starting point in our efforts to tune in to the positive flow. Try this. Sit upright in a relaxed position. Don't let your back touch the chair. Keep your feet flat on the floor and let your hands rest palms up on your thighs. Close your eyes and mentally relax. Watch the way your breath goes in and out of its own accord. Don't control your breath, just watch it. After sitting this way for a few minutes imagine that something terrible has happened in your life. Remember a tragic moment from your past or imagine one happening. Like an actor, get deeply into your emotions for a moment. Let your body take on any shape that seems to go with the unhappiness that you are feeling.

After a minute or two go back to watching the breath. Resume your relaxed upright position. Let your breath flow naturally of its own accord. Feel that with each exhalation you are releasing all negative emotions. With each inhalation bring in peace and harmony.

Now let's explore a happy feeling. Imagine that something fantastically good has just happened to you. Again, let your body react to the feeling. Don't be vague about your feelings of joy and enthusiasm. Let them be as real as possible. Try this for a minute or two.

You should be feeling pretty good right now. Let's look at what just happened.

If you actually participated in our experiment you will have found that watching the breath is mentally focusing and physically relaxing. Depending on how successful you were in your visualization of unhappiness your body might have slumped forward and felt drained of energy. Your body should have in some way reflected that you were feeling down.

Back in the upright position, as you watched the breath and released the negative feelings, calmness should have reestablished itself in your mind.

During your attempts to feel happiness your body should have felt upright and energized. The sides of your face might have lifted up into a smile. A general sense of well-being flooded your consciousness and you felt an increase of energy in your body. In fact, if you were totally into it, had someone burst into the room you might have jumped up and slapped them five!

No matter how much attention you gave to our experiment, I'm sure you can see the point that I'm trying to make. When we have any kind of feeling in life our bodies and minds follow those feelings by responding to the flows of energy that are created. These are the same for everyone: it is the way we are made. Even our language has taken this into account. When we are feeling good about life we are up, flying high. We can feel energy rising in the spine up into the brain. When we are unhappy we are low, downcast, depressed, and we feel a corresponding downward flow of energy in the spine.

Sometimes these energies are so persuasive that a happy person wants to sing or shout. You can burst out with sadness too, but tears bring cries of despair that lead to being drained rather than energized. It is hard to imagine a person walking off with a springy step after receiving bad news. Usually they dig their hands deep into their pockets, slump their shoulders and walk slowly with their head looking down at the ground.

These natural reactions to the movement of energy in the body give us a hint at how we can attune ourselves to the positive flow. The positive flow is inward toward the spine and upward toward the brain. The negative flow is downward in the spine and outward through the senses and negative emotions. When we do things that uplift us, enlighten us, we are doing things that are attuned to the positive flow. When we do things that drag us down, enslaving us to the senses and the ego, we are tuning in to the negative flow.

One of the ideas that we can extrapolate from this information is that if we can get our energy moving in the direction that we want to go, that will help to get our consciousness to where we want to be. You see, in the mind, reason tends to follow feeling. This means that our thoughts about any given situation will usually support how we feel about it. If we are upset the mind thinks thoughts that support being upset. If we are happy, we think happy thoughts. It is hard to think happy thoughts when you are sad and it is hard to think sad thoughts when you are happy.

If you want to be happy, act happy! At first you might think: Oh, I'm just kidding myself. But if you imagine what it feels like to be happy or remember a happy experience from the past, the energy inside you will start to flow in a positive direction. It is like going on a canoe ride. The stream of joy is always flowing.

Remembering, visualizing or affirming a joyful experience gets the canoe from the land into the water. Once in the stream we can leave visualization behind and experience the fresh new currents of joy on which we are now riding.

It is the same for technical information. By studying up on a subject we start to get the reference points that we will need to control our canoe in the water. But if we learn the basics of paddling on shore or just on the very edge of the stream and never reach out into the central flow, we will never tap our true potential.

To effectively tune in to the positive flow at will we must learn to control the mind. Let's look at how the mind works so we can harmonize with it. There are three parts to the mind: the conscious, the subconscious, and the superconscious. Each of these areas of the mind serve us according to how well we use them.

The subconscious mind is that which we associate with sleep and the tombstones of our past experiences. It is also a labyrinth of our positive and negative habits. While our experiences from this life are uppermost in the subconscious, our experiences from other lives can also be found lurking in this area. Our actions from the past have formed grooves in which we turn the wheels of our lives. Some of the grooves are positive patterns and others are negative patterns. When it is a negative pattern we think, "I'm in a rut." When it is a positive pattern we feel like we are on track or in the flow. Our subconscious habit patterns work a subtle, and sometimes not so subtle, control over our lives. Like a bank repository, here we will find the deposits of our past.

The conscious mind is like a train station. This is where all of our day to day activities take place. We keep a large baggage area available for storing the various tidbits of information that we have picked up. Important items are kept right up front, while less important things can be forgotten in the back. At the ticket counter we peruse the many possibilities that we can pursue in life. Sometimes it takes us a long time to decide what to do next! Out in the yard are the trains of the many activities that comprise our lives. The length of each train depends on the amount of interest and involvement we give to that part of our life. It can sometimes happen that we get so involved in one of our activities that we neglect others. That is when our switching yard duties can get us into trouble and one train crashes into another. There is a lot happening around here so we need to stay awake!

The superconscious mind is our direct connection to the creative flow of life. This is where we can drink the waters of any stream. No matter what your area of interest, like a universal encyclopedia, we can find the answer to any question, the solution to any problem. In fact, one of the big differences between the superconscious mind and the conscious mind is that the superconscious mind is solution oriented while the conscious mind tends to be problem oriented. The superconscious mind says, "This will work!" The conscious mind says, "Now let's think this out carefully; what about this, what about that?" In the meantime, the positive habits of the subconscious mind say, "Let's get to work!" While the negative habits of the subconscious say, "I don't want to think about it, let's go have a drink!"

Let's try another experiment. Sit again with your eyes closed and a straight relaxed spine. Watch the breath without restricting its flow. Once you feel calm and comfortable, turn your eyes downward and relax completely. Let all of your energy flow toward the floor. Feel yourself mentally sinking toward sleep. Do this for a minute or two.

Now quickly open your eyes. Look straight ahead and feel a surge of energy rising up your spine and straight out through your eyes. Focus completely on the world in front of you. Feel fully awake and ready. Enjoy this wakeful feeling for a minute.

Closing your eyes again, look slightly upward, drawing your gaze to the point between the eyebrows. You can even knit your eyebrows for a moment to get a sense of where you are looking, then relax. Feel that all of your inner resources are rising in your spine and shooting out your forehead like a beacon. Do this for a minute or two.

As you have probably figured out, these ways of focusing the mind correspond to accessing the subconscious, conscious, and superconscious mind. The value of the above exercise is to make you more familiar with the differences. Needless to say, we are all fairly used to accessing the conscious and subconscious, so let's talk more about accessing the superconscious.

Once again: What we are trying to do is tap into a flow of consciousness. Since the universal flow of creative thought comprises endless possibilities we must learn to tune our minds to a particular vibration that corresponds to what we are seeking. To do this, rather than just thinking thoughts, we must learn to feel them as well. Just as each type of food has its own taste, every type of thought has a certain vibrational feel to it. By immersing ourselves in the complete vibrational texture of a thought area we are more able to broadcast our need and perceive an answer.

The point between the eyebrows, also known as the spiritual eye, is the broadcasting area. We should feel that our whole being is rising up to this point and then reaching out to the universe. It can't be passive. It must be intensely focused, but not tense. With practice we can learn to relax as we increase our efforts.

The heart is the receiving station in the body. It is said that we can each find the center of the universe at a point of intuitive perception within our own hearts. Just like our physical muscles, our power of intuitive perception needs to be exercised if we want it to work well.

It is interesting that mothers often feel a natural intuitive connection with their children. Why do mothers feel it more often than fathers do? Mothers have the advantage of being vibrationally connected to the child because of carrying them in the womb. Certainly that can explain some of why a mother can recognize the vibration of their child more easily. But there is more to it then that. Woman's nature tends toward feeling, while man's nature leans toward reason. This doesn't mean that women can't reason and men can't feel! It just means that the male and female reference points tend to be in these directions. Men who develop their feeling nature are just as capable of feeling intuitively connect to their children as women. And likewise, women are equally able to express reason.

As we grow spiritually we are trying to balance our feeling and reasoning natures. Those who are good at broadcasting their thoughts must learn to relax and feel the response. People who are good at feeling the response need to learn focusing of the mind, clarity of thought, and the application of will. It is in the balancing of these areas that we will find our attempts to contact the superconscious mind most successful.

The focusing of our will activates the sending and receiving stations of the spiritual eye and heart. When we talk about will power, we are referring to our ability to say "Yes!" to life with enthusiasm and determination. This "yes" saying principle is very important for our success. You see, we only have two choices: yes or no. You might ask: What about passive, I don't care, it doesn't matter one way or the other? Passivity is actually part of the no saying principle. The way to make it positive is to think: Yes, any of these choices would be good. When we dabble in passivity or a lack of mental clarity, we are touching to some degree the negative flow.

The no saying principle can be very subtle. I'm not talking about the times when we say no with a positive understanding that the contemplated activity or choice is harmful. I'm referring to the kind of unwillingness that creeps in when there is a task that we would rather not do because we just don't feel like doing it or we just don't like it. It could be washing the dishes, mowing the lawn, lending a helping hand or taking the time to console a friend. We are also caught by the no saying principle when we think thoughts like: I can't do this. It is important to distinguish between can't and difficult or unpleasant.

Virtually every motivational exponent says that a positive, enthusiastic approach to life will result in the improving of every part of our lives. Can you imagine a speaker saying, "Be glum and things will improve!" What makes for a happy life anyway? A happy life isn't as much about what we achieve in the end, it is about the way that we live while we try to improve ourselves and others. If we bring a joyful, positive frame of mind with us to every life experience we will be well on our way to living in the positive flow.

6

Tuning In to the Positive Flow
Part 2

In all areas of life, experience is the greatest teacher. Theoretical knowledge of a subject is not the same as actual direct personal perception. At the same time, when we are first learning to do something new it doesn't seem very practical to invent things all over again, as if no one had ever done it before. Wouldn't it be a waste of time if every inventor had to start at the beginning and discover fire and invent the wheel all over again? It makes perfect sense that we would want to take advantage of the knowledge that has already been amassed on a subject before we strike out on our own into new territories. So let's look at what has made others successful in their attempts to live in the positive flow and eventually achieve complete success: Self-realization.

Like everything else in life, many different styles have been applied to man's attempts to achieve harmony with the positive flow of life. Underneath all of these attempts are the guiding principles that we have been discussing. Of all the techniques that have been used to increase the soul's awareness of our reality as spirit, the meditation techniques of yoga have proven to be the most successful. While it is true that these techniques are often associated with the styles of the country from which they originated, India, it has never been a part of the yoga teachings that you must follow any particular style. Yoga has always considered direct perception of truth – Spirit – as the unifying force in its centuries old tradition. Outward styles have always been left to the individual tastes of the practitioners.

Thousands of years ago great souls sought, just as our scientist today, to discover the underlying truths of life. Instead of looking outside through the world of the senses they searched inside their own selves. From these early explorers of consciousness has come a long tradition of techniques whose sole purpose are the achievement of Self-realization.

Although this isn't a book on meditation I would like to share with you a basic technique that will help you to start your own inner explorations. This is necessary because attunement to the positive flow is based on our ability to inwardly connect to Spirit within us. While meditation isn't the only thing that we can do to develop this inner relationship, it is certainly one of the most powerful.

There are four basic ingredients for success in any endeavor: energy, concentration, duration of effort and a proven technique. The reason I have listed a proven technique in the last position is that without the first three ingredients it doesn't matter whether the technique will work or not. And with the first three ingredients even a poor technique may bring success. At the same time, it doesn't make sense to put our efforts into something that isn't proven to work unless we are trying to break new ground. So when you shop for a meditation technique or techniques for success in any endeavor, check out its track record. If you can't find anyone for whom the technique has been successful, then like any off brand of merchandise: buyer beware!

Energy is the power with which all things get done. It doesn't matter if we are talking about things of a physical nature or things of a mental or spiritual nature. Nothing gets done without energy. Most people think that our energy comes only from the food we eat and the air we breathe. Science has told us that these chemicals are what sustain us. Jesus said, "Man does not live by bread alone, but by every word that proceedeth from the mouth of God."

The great master of yoga, Paramhansa Yogananda, explained that the "mouth of God" is the point at which the life sustaining forces of the universe enter our bodies and give us the power to breathe and eat. The corresponding physical body part is the medulla oblongata at the base of the brain. This is the "socket" that connects us to the cosmic life force. The medulla is also the negative pole – by polarity – of the positively charged spiritual eye. It is the movement of this inner energy in through the medulla and then up and down the spine that actually causes the breath to flow in and out of the body. When this energy is withdrawn the body no longer breathes.

When we can consciously draw on the universal forces through this point there is no limit to what we can accomplish. There are stories of saints from all over the world who have realized this truth and live solely by these inner energies, never eating food. If you find this hard to believe then I refer you to the life of Theresa Newman who lived in the last century in Konnersroth, Bavaria. She lived for over 40 years without eating or drinking. She could only swallow the tiny communion wafer that she received at church each day. She had fully realized the truth of Jesus' words. By living directly on the power of Spirit she was a living testament to the potential of all souls.

So do you now have to stop eating and live only on cosmic energy to be a good parent? Well, it wouldn't be as messy or take as much of our time as eating does, but it isn't very likely that many of us will be able to achieve this high state of inner connection in the near future. The important thing about this is that it is a very real potential. We accept so many limits in life just because we are skeptical that they are possible. Even when people who do amazing things are studied many people doubt the veracity of their abilities. A certain amount of caution in life is useful, but if it cuts us off from our greatest potentials maybe it would be better to be fooled occasionally then to live doubting everyone and everything. If we want to encourage our children in the thought that they can achieve any goal that they strive for we need to follow that same advice and believe that many forms of greatness can be achieved.

It isn't just saints who have tapped into this universal reservoir of energy. Many people in moments of crisis, when they just had to get something done have accomplished the impossible. People lift heavy objects, run great distances, climb or descend precipices, all of which they would never have believed that they could do these things, except that they felt an unseen power enter into their efforts and help them to succeed. Some explain these phenomena by pointing to hormones from the adrenal gland. Certainly adrenaline is a real chemical in the body. But these types of muscle stimulants can only do so much. How can a woman carry a piano out of a burning house all by herself? How can a man of ordinary size lift a large automobile off the victim of an accident? These people, in moments of need, suspend their conscious or subconscious objections to the possibilities and draw on their superconscious potential.

Hopefully we won't often need to go around lifting large objects in a hurry! But we will need to draw on momentous resources of energy to keep up with our children. The better that we get at tapping into our inner connection to the positive flow the more readily we will be able to draw on that inner source for energy and understanding.

In order to increase your own ability to draw on this inner source try this exercise. This can be done standing up or lying down flat on your back. To do this exercise we must first learn the double breath. The double breath is a short and then a long inhalation through the nose, followed by a short and then a long exhalation through the mouth. The exhalation out the mouth sounds like "ha, haaahhh." Unfortunately I haven't yet figured out how to describe the sound of air coming in the nose, but it has the same "in, innnn" rhythm as the exhalation.

What we are going to do is tense all of our body parts, simultaneously, while we inhale with the double breath. Then we will hold the breath for a count of three while we feel all of our muscles vibrating with energy. After that we will exhale with the double breath and relax the muscles. As long as there isn't a physical reason why you shouldn't do this, try it. Inhale with a double breath tensing the body, hold for the count of three, and then exhale relaxing the muscles. Try it two or three times.

While you practice double breathing with tension, try to imagine the energy coming into the medulla from its universal source and flooding your body and mind with energy. If you aren't sure where the medulla is, reach up with your fingers and find the indentation in the skull at the very top of the spine. Just inside at the top of the spine is the base of the brain. That is where the medulla is located. You can even rub small circles with your fingertips in this area before doing the exercise in order to be more aware of the energy coming in at this point.

This exercise is one of a whole series of energization exercises that were developed by Paramhansa Yogananda. Just as we have talked about drawing on the positive flow for inspiration and ideas this is one of the ways that we can draw on that same source for physical and mental energy. If you feel tiredness or tension in any part of your body during the day try using this exercise to release that tension and energize your body and mind.

Now that we have energized ourselves let's talk about the next stage: concentration. It doesn't matter how much energy we have available to us if we can't channel it in the direction of our goals. We have all met people who have boundless energy but can't seem to get anything accomplished. This lack of mental focus, or follow through, also keeps us from being able to attune ourselves to superconsciousness and the positive flow.

Here is another experiment. Close your eyes and try to think of nothing for one minute.

If you have already developed excellent concentration then the best that you were able to do is to simply be aware of the sensory information that is always flowing in to the brain through the five senses. If your concentration was less, you were caught up by thoughts about that sensory stimulation, wondering if you were thinking or just passively following a stream of thought until you suddenly realized that you were thinking.

No matter what we are trying to accomplish in life, without concentration we are doomed to mediocrity or failure. With the development of deep concentration we can bring to bear on any activity the resources of the universe.

Have you ever noticed that when you are mentally agitated your breath moves quickly? Conversely, have you noticed that when you are deeply concentrated the breath moves slowly? This natural phenomenon was explored by the ancient sages. They found that there is a subtle link between mind and breath. Through their inner experiments it became clear to them that the mind could affect the breath. Their next discovery – which is one of the great keys to cultivating our inner connection to the positive flow – was that the breath could be use to control the mind.

From this essential connection between breath and mind the science of mediation was born. Mediation can be defined as: inwardly focused single pointed concentration on a single quality or attribute of Spirit. Technically, the efforts and techniques that we use to learn mediation don't actually become mediation until we have become proficient at using them. In the beginning what we are doing is trying to meditate. Only once we have learned to intensely focus our attention inwardly can we actually begin deep mediation. Some meditation techniques are designed specifically for increasing our concentration abilities while others are for immersion in other aspects of the interior life.

We have already practiced the basics of a concentration technique in the last chapter. Oh, you don't remember? You weren't concentrating? Actually, I didn't call it that. We were exploring the differences between the subconscious, conscious and superconscious mind. Between our efforts to feel the differences we watched the breath. Did you notice what happened when you did that? Let's try it again now so that we can discuss it.

Sit up straight with your spine away from the back of your chair. Your feet should be flat on the floor. You can sit cross-legged on the floor if you want but it isn't necessary. If you are sitting on the floor use a small pillow to support the base of your spine. With a pillow it is easier to sit straight rather than being slouched forward.

With your eyes closed and palms resting upward on your thighs mentally release all thoughts of other activities. Take a few long deep breaths. Inhale through the nose and exhale through the mouth. Try to keep the length of the inhalation the same as the exhalation. Now, add a holding of

46

your breath after the inhalation. Make this hold the same period of time as the inward and outward flow of the breath. Don't strain, 6 or 8 counts is enough for now. So you will: inhale for the count of 8, hold for the count of 8 and exhale for the count of 8.

After six series of inhale, hold and exhale, just relax with your eyes closed and watch your breath without controlling it. Be sure that you aren't controlling the breath as it now flows in and out of the body of its own accord. You can watch the rising and falling of the chest or watch the air as it flows in and out of the nostrils.

To increase our focus and link of the mind to the breath we are going to add the mental repetition of a short phrase. This is called a mantra. One of the best mantras for this practice is the two words, Hong Sau. Hong Sau means, I am He or I am Spirit. It is an affirmation of our oneness with the Infinite. You can use the Sanskrit words, hong (rhymes with song) on the inhalation and sau (sounds like saw) on the exhalation. Or you can use the English words, I am, on the inhalation and, He or Spirit, on the exhalation. You can also use other words like, I am peace, I am love or I am joy.

While it is true that different phrases have different vibratory affects on us the important part of this technique is the development of concentration. Certainly it never hurts to add devotion to any technique. The expanding of the heart should be considered as a part of any spiritual practice whether it is specifically proscribed or not. But at this stage our largest efforts should be put into the single pointed linking of the mind to watching the breath.

Remember, we don't control the breath, we just watch it. As the breath flows in of its own accord we mentally say hong. As the breath flows out we mentally say sau. While watching the breath don't let thoughts intrude on your focus. If they do, gently dismiss them and return your attention to watching the breath and repeating the mantra.

Try to build up your practice of this technique of concentration to 15 or 20 minutes in the morning and evening. If you establish this as a regular part of your life you will find dramatic changes taking place within you. Your ability to focus your attention and your energy will noticeably increase. Even more valuable to you will be the peace and sense of well-being that comes with this process of inwardly connecting to the roots of your being. As the breath slows and the mind becomes still you will automatically be more able to feel the Divine Presence that is always trying to break through the barrier of our restlessness.

After you practice this technique sit for a few minutes and rest in the inward feeling of peace. It is in the silence after practicing techniques that we can develop an awareness of our intuitive connection to Spirit. This is the portal of consciously connecting to the positive flow.

For those just beginning in their efforts this will provide a starting point until you can explore mediation in more depth. Through the practice of meditation we are developing our most direct link to Spirit. While it will help us in our efforts to be good parents and successful in any outward endeavor, mediation's most valuable reward is an ever-growing awareness of our true nature as a part of God.

Of all the meditation techniques that I am familiar with the most effective is the Kriya Yoga technique that was brought to America in 1920 by Paramhansa Yogananda. The reason that the Kriya technique is so effective is that it works directly with the flow of energy in the spine. Through the conscious inward control of the energy in the spine we can in effect sweep clean the energies of our past karma that we carry within us. Through a technique like Kriya Yoga we have the potential to release ourselves from the seemingly endless cycles of physical birth and death in this lifetime. Without such a technique it takes much longer to advance spiritually.

So now that we have energized ourselves and begun to inwardly focus our minds with concentration lets add a most essential ingredient: persistence. As Thomas Edison said, "Genius is 1% inspiration and 99% perspiration." We will need to apply ourselves regularly with intensity if we want to achieve success in any of our efforts.

In the beginning it might seem a long uphill road to climb. The restless body and mind will intrude their serpent heads into your attempts to reach beyond them. There is also the factor of the negative flow. The negative flow will seek to distract you with thoughts of doubts or the entice-ments of other activities. While the positive flow is actively trying to help and encourage us, the negative flow is constantly throwing sand into the grease of our efforts. If you stick to a regular routine of practice you will find that your rebellious mental and physical companions will fall into line and behave themselves. I would also encourage you to seek out others of similar mind with whom you can meditate. Group support in your spiritual practices is extremely benefi-cial.

Learning to tune in to the positive flow isn't something that you will achieve instantly. It will take time and much effort. Along the way you will experience inspirations and little glimmers of your greater potential. In those moments you will know with a certainty like none that you have ever had before that you are a child of God and that you are now consciously homeward bound.

7

The Law of Magnetism

When I was a young boy I used to go miniature golfing at a course across the street from my father's office. I loved that last hole where you could win a free pass to play again if you got a hole in one. I used to think about that last hole a lot. My desire to get a hole in one was very strong. As you might guess, sure enough one day I did it. A hole in one...ahhh, that was a great day!

Do you think my desire to get a hole in one had any effect on whether or not I got one? A mathematician might say my desire caused me to play more often, thus statistically increasing my chances. A golfing expert might agree, adding that by playing more often I also increased my abilities through practice. In addition to those points of view a psychologist might say that my mental focus was increased by the intensity of my desire.

Who is right? They all are! Each of those factors can logically and correctly be connected to my success. Yet, if we leave our understanding of what happened with these three views we have missed a very important point; in fact, one of the main principles that makes *Positive Flow Parenting* work. It is the law of magnetism.

The law of magnetism is central to our ability to help ourselves and our children to live in harmony with the truths that we have been discussing. This principle will be invaluable in helping us to formulate specific strategies for dealing with any particular situation the might arise in life.

If a non-magnetized piece of metal is placed next to a magnet the piece of metal will become magnetized. The strength of the effect will depend on the strength of the magnet, the individual characteristics of the piece of metal and the length of time that they are in proximity. The stronger the magnet the greater the power it will hold over the piece of metal. The more the resistant the type of metal is the less it will be affected by the magnet. Also, the shorter the time of influence the less the affect will be.

This magnetic relationship has a direct correlation in every part of our lives. All of life is animated by energy. Energy is also what causes things to become magnetized. Therefore, everything in life is putting out some type of magnetic field. We aren't talking just about metal now. We are talking about everything: all types of plants, animals, places, things – natural or man made – activities, food, people and situations.

There are two basic powers at work with magnetism. The power to draw and the power to repel. The strength of either power is dependent on the amount of energy that is present. The greater the flow of energy, the greater the magnetism. Since all of life is energy, all of life is subject to the law of magnetism. The power to draw brings us our life experiences. It can also attract to us the solutions to those life challenges. The power to repel is the part of our magnetism that keeps things away from us. It could manifest as our defense against illness or the inability to obtain a desire. These two powers are by themselves neither good nor bad, they are neutral.

Each of us is a mixture of energies or qualities of magnetism. Some are strong while others are weak. Earlier we talked about the commitments of energy that we have gathered from past lives. All of those energies mixed in with what we have created from this life make up the sum total of our magnetism as an individual. As we live our lives it is more helpful to work on this more subtle energy/magnetism level than on the physical and mental levels alone.

For example. If we want to be physically healthy it isn't enough to eat the right foods and exercise. Certainly that will help. But we can add whole new dimensions to our efforts if we realize that it is also some part of our consciousness that is causing a lack of physical well-being. Years ago I knew a woman who was having health difficulties. Traditional doctors were unable to help her. She finally went to a practitioner of Ayurvedha, the ancient science of healing from India. The Ayurvedic approach to healing takes into account these subtler energies. Along with a daily dose of some herbs and exercises, my friend was proscribed the daily feeding of wild animals. As strange as that might sound to our western minds the end result was that she was soon cured of her problem.

When we see life in the light of these magnetic energies it makes sense that we would want to make our own personal magnetism as strong as possible. That is also one of the benefits of meditation. One of the things that mediation helps us to do is align our inner energies so that they aren't fighting against each other, thus weakening us. Magnets are strongest when all of the atoms are lined up with the same north/south polarity. When we have all of our inner energies aligned our ability to magnetically draw or repel – as the needs of the moment require – will be at its strongest.

The success that we achieve in any activity is directly related to the volume and focus of energy that we bring to bear on the situation. It is easy to see how this works physically. If you lean against a large boulder with the vague thought that maybe it will move, unless it is already poised to move, nothing will happen. But if you really want to move the boulder and apply all of your mental and physical strength, even if it is stuck, you may be able to move it.

On a deeper level, rather than seeing our efforts in life as having themselves resulted in the attainment of our goal, it is better to realize that our efforts result in the magnetic attraction of the desired result. Even though at times we can see a direct correlation between our efforts in this physical world – be they physical or mental – and the end result, the truth is that it is the underlying energies that cause things in this world to be accomplished. To see it otherwise is to think that the light bulb shines on its own power.

Jesus said, "If ye had but faith, ye could move mountains." Did he mean that if we had faith we could physically walk up to a mountain, pick it up with our hands and walk away with it? In the most esoteric way I suppose that is possible, but it doesn't seem very useful. When was the last time you needed to move a mountain? At the same time, many of the things that we face in life do seem as difficult as moving mountains. What two more daunting tasks can there be than perfecting our own higher selves and parenting a child? Jesus' statement points to the accessibility of the positive flow of Spirit, which when tapped can give us abilities far greater than a doubting mind can imagine.

As we learn to consciously tune in to the positive flow we won't have to just, "have faith". Through our direct experiences the belief that connecting to the positive flow might work will be transformed into true faith, which is based on knowing through experience and not just hoping.

Along with strengthening our magnetism we need to learn to read the magnetic patterns of life around us. The process that we use in order to do this is called attunement. Attunement is the fine art of reaching out with our inner awareness and touching the magnetic essence of a person, place, situation, subject, or in fact, anything. Through inner attunement we can actually perceive the central reality of any experience. In the spiritual life it is through attunement that we experience the joy, peace and understanding of God. In daily activity it is through attunement that we can understand and act in ways that will be most beneficial to ourselves and others.

When we are truly attuned to something, not just intellectually aware of its outward appearance, we will perceive its underlying magnetic essence – its vibration. Just in the same way that no two foods taste the same or feel the same, everything in life has its own vibration. Make it a habit to inwardly reach out and "feel" the vibration of whatever is around you. In this way you will learn to recognize different qualities of energies. You will be able to tell whether something is uplifting, activating or downward-pulling to your consciousness. Through this inner intuitive perception you will understand directly the qualities of magnetism that surround us all of the time.

This process of learning to recognize the vibrations of life around us is like learning a foreign language. It will take time to become fluent in this inward form of communication. But once we become proficient it will become second nature.

Attunement is how we actually connect with the positive flow. We align our vibration with the vibration of that which we want to understand. Then we open ourselves up to the creative potential on that wavelength. When we do this successfully our consciousness will be able to access the universal reservoir of information and understanding. This internal access won't be like falling into a well of information that we have to sort through in order to find the answers to our specific needs. It will be the awakening in our consciousness of an understanding that meets the specific requirements of the moment, according to who we are and what the situation is.

On a day to day basis, when we make a practice of living in the positive flow our whole perspective on life will change.

We will begin to see things that we never noticed before. These new observations will feel completely right, like a lost memory returning to the forefront of our consciousness. We may even wonder at times: Why didn't I see this before? Like a compass, these inner perceptions can guide us through the intricacies of daily life.

In the beginning we may not be consciously aware that we have started living attuned to the positive flow. We may just notice that we aren't as upset by difficulties or that the difficulties we had been experiencing are fewer. What is happening is that instead of fighting against the best flow for our lives we will have started going with the flow, thus lessening our struggle.

After a while we become more sensitively aware of what it feels like to be "in tune". Like a good dancer we will be able to move with the rhythms of our life without stumbling. That doesn't mean that there won't be some difficult passages. But when we live in the positive flow we are able to see them for what they are, stepping-stones to success, instead of barriers. We will also learn to improvise in ways that allow us to move gracefully through uncharted territories.

At times we may become aware that a place, person or activity just doesn't "feel" right. Remember, we feel these things in the area of the heart. The heart center is the receiving station. If we keep the heart calm we will be able to feel these inner messages. If we clutter ourselves up with emotions connected to restless thoughts in the mind we will find ourselves inwardly disconnected.

Many people have had a premonition or a hunch about something that is going to happen. These feelings can be positive or negative. What they are is a vibrational message about a situation. When you feel something like this listen to it. At first you might be fooled by your own desires which could lead you one way or another. With practice you will be able to tell the difference between guidance and personal preference.

Divine protection can come this way. So can the solutions to parenting.

As you begin to develop your inner relationship to the universe you won't necessarily find the heavens opening up before you. Hearing a heavenly voice speak direct guidance to you is certainly possible, but it isn't the most common way that people receive guidance. Most of the time you will find that your life just seems to move forward in harmony. You will find yourself in the right place, at the right time, more often than mere chance can explain. You can also find that new creative ideas will just pop into your mind with a clarity and conviction that commands your attention. There are countless ways that the creative presence of Spirit can subtly guide our lives.

Not only will you perceive these energies in your outward life but you will begin to feel the magnetic flows of energy within yourself. One of the ways that this can be felt inside is when your consciousness flows up the spine toward the spiritual eye. When you learn to connect this upward flow of energy to your listening center in the heart new possibilities will begin to present themselves. That is why yogis say that we should live at the spiritual eye. As the seat of spiritual awareness the spiritual eye is our connecting point to the positive flow.

When you start to feel this inner connection while you are meditating – or during any activity – try to let if flow through you rather than trying to hold on to it as a single feeling. We can't capture and hold these perceptions; we can only have them flow through us. Along with the pleasant vibrations and/or information that is specific to that experience will come the lingering positive vibrations that stay with us as our personal magnetism is raised through association with this higher flow of energy.

At first it is so novel to feel something actually happening inside ourselves that many people tense with surprise or enthusiasm, causing the experience to stop. With practice you will begin to realize that this inner connection is the soul's natural state and a consciousness of separateness unnatural. When you feel inwardly connected try to relax and flow along with the experience. This inner source of inspiration is inexhaustible. So if a thought or idea flows by before you have a chance to latch on to it, don't worry, another will be coming along to take its place.

Some churches discourage people from exploring these inner perceptions. The reasons run the gamut from simple ignorance about what is going on, to feeling threatened that if people can plug directly into Spirit, maybe they won't feel a need to come to church. Some will call these inner perceptions evil. Others will simply say that they are imagination. In the end, all of these negative views are self-serving. They purport to put an ultimate value on our own personal experiences. This has been the history of "Churchianity" but is not the view of the saints and sages throughout history who have been in intimate contact with Spirit. Ultimately it is only through each person's personal exploration of their own inner realities that anyone can truly know for sure what is real and what is not. Having an open mind tells us to accept the possibility that others may be right or wrong in their opinions. Common sense tells us that we must know truth for ourselves and not simply follow others blindly.

As a part of magnetizing ourselves in a way that will draw the response we are seeking we need to apply the time-honored practice of prayer. Prayer or "concentrated thought broadcasts" focuses the energy that powers the magnet of our consciousness to draw an answer from within. Just like a broadcasting tower the more energy and focus that we apply to the signal the farther it will reach. In this case the power goes toward drawing a response that is in tune with the signal that we are sending out.

Sometimes our broadcasts will be for a specific result and at other times a request that the highest truth be expressed. While our specific desires aren't always separate from what is in our best interest or the best interests of others, sometimes they are. So no matter what the purpose of your broadcast, be sure to stay detached and trust that the universe will respond in the most beneficial way.

While it is possible to get an instant response to your broadcast do not mistake the lack of a perceived response as a sign that your prayer wasn't heard. All prayers must be heard, for all things are a part of God. After you pray practice patience, acceptance and trust. The universe is your friend and the infinite wisdom of Spirit will guide the energies of your prayer to the best result even if you aren't consciously aware of what the result should be.

Prayer can also be like the friendly sharing of thoughts that goes between the best of friends. The idea of only talking to God when we want something doesn't seem like a truly balanced approach. After you meditate, sit quietly and share you deepest feelings with your Heavenly Father or your Divine Mother. Then sit in the silence and just enjoy the feeling of togetherness. It can be just like when you hold your infant in your arms. At that stage our children can't talk back to us but we know in our hearts they are receiving our love. Feel that the Divine arms are holding you from within your own heart and be comforted in that Holy Presence.

8

Positive Flow Parenting

Now that we have explored what it means to live in the positive flow of life, let's look at how this information translates specifically into parenting. The same underlying energies that we tap into in our effort to feel the positive flow can now help us in our relationships with our children. The reason this works is because *Positive Flow Parenting* is based on each person's actual connection to the universe and not a "one fits all" list of do's and don'ts that wouldn't take into account the unique needs of each individual and situation.

The foundation of our approach is an understanding that our experience here on planet earth is at its roots a spiritual one and not just physical. When we see life as a school where our main purpose is to grow spiritually, it makes sense that we should orient our physical and mental activities so that they will enhance our spiritual efforts. As parents our first responsibility is to make ourselves as capable as possible of living in tune with our highest potential. That is one of the reasons we have spent so much time talking about things that will help "us", regardless of whether we are parents or not. By developing our ability to live in tune with the positive flow we will be most able to act in the ways that will be beneficial to our children.

If you were going to compete in the Olympics you wouldn't just show up and hope that things go well. You would prepare yourself to the best of your abilities. If you don't yet have children or are trying to understand how to relate to children that are not your own, till and fertilize the soil of your consciousness with concentrated and sincere efforts to practice living in tune with the superconscious positive flow. This will give you the best possible training for the Olympian task of parenting. If you already have children then you will be doing on the job training to enhance your current efforts!

While parenting is so life encompassing that it seems like an almost impossible challenge, it really is one of life's greatest pleasures. Don't wait until your children have grown and are out of the house to enjoy them. Each phase of the child rearing experience has its own special moments. Often parents hear about the horrors of infancy, teething, the terrible twos, the more terrible threes, the difficulties of pre-pubescence, the hardships of puberty and the almost unbearable teens: When will it ever stop? For those who look at life in terms of difficulties it never will stop. For those who see each day as a unique opportunity to explore life's potential it wouldn't be any fun if it weren't a challenge!

One of the keys to enjoying life is to live in the moment. Even planning for the future, based on the past, can be done consciously in the present. Rather than seeing life as a struggle that won't end until you are on vacation, or until the kids are gone, or until you retire, live each day with a sense of inner free-dom. You can do this by tying your sense of well-being to the inner spring of happiness in the positive flow rather than the ups and downs of daily life. People who live thinking that they will be happy at some future time find that when they get there they are so used to being unhappy they don't know how to be happy. They have spent so much time living in the negative flow that it will take a great effort to change their orientation. Whether life is dealing us choppy waters or smooth sailing there is always an undercurrent of peace, joy and love available to us if we take the time to feel it.

When we are feeling the inner glow of God-Communion and the corresponding positive energies of living in the superconscious positive flow, we will be bathing our children in the kind of positive magnetism that will charge their lives in the very best way. We have all met people who just feel good to be around. Whether they are aware of it or not, they have in some way plugged into the positive flow and the magnetism of that flow is radiating out so that others can feel it. This is the law of magnetism that we discussed in the last chapter and is key to our approach.

The most powerful affect that we can have on our children, whether we want it this way or not, is by who we are at the core of our being and the way that our inner essence manifests in daily life. The reality of how we approach and react to life experiences, the qualities of energy that we radiate toward life: these are the beacons by which our children will follow us. As we live, so shall our children be magnetically imprinted by our vibrations.

As parents we have a unique relationship with our children. The idea that it is a relationship implies that it is two ways, not just one. Just as we will affect our children we are also being affected by their vibrations. It is important to remember that they are here to teach us, just as well as being taught. If we cut ourselves off from our children by thinking, "Because I am the parent in all things I know more than my child," we may be missing fantastic opportunities. While it is true that we are more experienced in this world at this time, our child may have developed abilities from the past that are far beyond ours. It is by attuning ourselves inwardly to our children from the very beginning that we will be most able to learn, appreciate and direct, as the needs of the moment require.

Since we are so closely tied to our children it is mutually beneficial if efforts are made to harmonize our energies. Many people make the mistake of thinking: I am the adult, the child must change. While there are certainly many times when it is clear that this is true and best, there are also times when a child may be pointing toward a higher view or at least one of equal value. This points to the essential truth that we are all equal as souls. Within the boundaries of responsible parenting we must always respect the individuality of our children. They have every right to see life differently than we do. Allowing for these differences is very much part of the "art" of parenting. The subtle give and take that is necessary for harmonious living is something that must be nurtured.

As the stewards to whom God has entrusted the care and training of these souls we have taken on a holy responsibility. The most basic part of that responsibility is to love them. Just as God loves us no matter what we say or do, as parents we also must try to give that kind of unconditional love to our children. This is one of the ways that God provides us with a built in system for developing our love. As parents this is our number one priority. We must not only love our children, but also do our best to communicate that love. It isn't enough just to feel it, we need to express it. It is through our attempts to express love that we are also increasing our ability to live in the positive flow, for love itself is the foundational substance of the positive flow.

Some parents feel that their many efforts to help a child on a physical level are a sufficient expression of their love. For those who feel that way, I might suspect that they were denied the direct expression of parental love. For once we have tasted the expressed love of a parent no amount of selfless acts can substitute.

At the same time, even though it doesn't replace personally expressed love, we must do everything that we can, on all levels, to give our children the best possible chance to have a good life. I don't mean just the most that we can give them materially. Even more important than that is sharing with them the tools and skills that will help them to make a success of their own lives. That should include the development of specific living skills, as well as, the underlying principles of living in the positive flow.

While we share with our children the best that we have to offer it is hard at times for a parent to not live, to a certain degree, through their children. If there are experiences that we liked as a child or wished that we could have done, it is natural for us to think that we would like our children to have those opportunities. While this in itself is no big deal, we want to be careful that these thoughts don't lead to an unfair imposition of our own desires on our children.

If you enjoyed little league or girl scouts, that's great, but your children may or may not be interested. Giving them an opportunity to try is an act of love, imposing on them is disrespectful. Unfortunately, it isn't always simple to tell the difference. Sometimes your insistence will push them into a direction that will end up a lifelong pleasure, other times over insistence might drive a wedge of resentment between you. This is where we must consult the positive flow. A sensitive attunement to the situation will, with practice, result in a positive resolution of the situation.

Along with our efforts to guide our children we should always carry a healthy amount of detachment. No matter how things go, they won't go quite the way we expected. When we attach ourselves to how things turn out we put a damper on our ability to feel happy in all circumstances.

No matter what area of life we look at it isn't what we accomplish outwardly in life that determines whether life is successful or not. Much more important then "what " we do, is the "way " we do whatever gets done. Even a basically good deed, done with a selfish attitude, loses much of its power of good. A pie that a mother makes lovingly for their child will always be worth more then a store bought pie. It is the quality and then the quantity of our efforts that makes the difference.

One of the most difficult things to do as a parent is evaluate how you are doing. As parents we feel responsible for our children, we want to make sure everything is going to be "all right". Unfortunately, one of the main things that makes life interesting is that we don't know how things are going to turn out. There is, however, something that we can watch for as an indicator of how things are generally progressing: Our child's specific gravity.

J. Donald Walters, in his book *Education for Life*, presents a unique view of how we can understand the essence of our child's vibration and where that will lead. Specific gravity is a term that is used in physics to describe the effect of gravity on different objects of equal volume. It is the density of the materials that makes the difference. Dense materials have a heavier specific gravity, while less dense materials have a lighter specific gravity. This concept of specific gravity is an excellent analogy for what is happening with people.

When a person is positively magnetized their conscious-ness is light. Remember when we talked about being uplifted? When we are in tune with the positive flow we feel an expanded awareness, greater sympathies toward others, we feel more positive and open towards that which life has to offer. When a person is negatively charged they have a contractive consciousness. They are selfish, self-centered, unconcerned with others or the negative consequences of their actions. Their consciousness is heavy and it pulls them down.

Objects having high specific gravity will sink lower when emersed in water than objects of low specific gravity. A person who has a negative outlook – thus a negatively charged magnetic field – will attract negative experiences. A person who has a positive attitude will be surrounded by a positive magnetic field and attract positive experiences. While it is true that we fluctuate daily in the way we feel, each person will return to their natural level of consciousness after releasing the affects of any specific up or down that life brings. Long term changes in a person's specific gravity come from a combination of self-effort and exposure to the inner and outer influences of our life experiences.

Reading a person's vibration can give a much better view of how they will fare in life then any outward sign. We have all met people who we instinctively feel are headed for trouble. Likewise there are those who you "just know" are going to do well. Those reactions come from our intuitive reading of the vibration radiating from that person.

If we really are reading the vibration of a person and not just reacting to what we personally like or don't like about them, we will be able to distinguish between children of a mischievous nature and those with a cruel nature. Pulling the legs off a live frog would be cruel or at least very insensitive, where putting a frog in someone's pocket or in their bed would just be mischievous.

As we become more sensitive in our ability to attune ourselves to others we will be able to inwardly sense how things are gong. When your child is generally happy there is a feeling of contentment that sits under the surface even during difficulties. If your child is not generally happy you will need to search for the underlying reason. It may be something that you are not yet doing in a way that satisfies their needs. It may be a deep-seated discontent from the past that will take time and effort to ease. Just remember that long-term exposure to a positively charged magnetism is the best way to work at the very roots of your child's consciousness.

While parents want to be as vibrationally strong as possible in order to be a positive influence on a child's specific gravity, ultimately, each soul must stand on its own. We can only guide and nurture our children. They must live their own lives, fight their own battles, and follow their own lights.

One of the most difficult things for many people to accept about this world is that all circumstances are neutral. No matter how good or bad we perceive things to be it is only our label that has made it so. If you are hiking up a mountain and it starts to rain you can think: Oh how beautiful or you can think: Oh, what a mess! The choice is yours. Even great tests like terminal disease, accidents or any kind of misfortune can be turned toward one's own benefit if taken in the right spirit. Think of the victories that great souls have achieved because of their unwillingness to succumb to the negative flow even in the direst of circumstances. If we or our children are called to face such tests we must determine to face them with the dignity of spirit that is our natural birthright as children of the Divine.

There is no such thing as pre-destiny. The chips in life are not set to fall regardless of what we do to help ourselves. While we are tied to the past through our karma, we can free ourselves from our past by making the right effort now. These efforts, aligned with the positive flow of Spirit, are the path toward living a successful life and being the best possible parent.

9

Way of the Positive Flow

Living in the positive flow of life is the most central technique of the *Positive Flow Parenting* approach. When we are thinking and acting as a part of that flow, even if we make a mistake, life has an amazing way of somehow turning out all right. Sometimes we are not sure what to do or can't decide if our intended action is the best decision. If we have aligned ourselves with the positive flow and used our God given intelligence with a generous mixture of common sense, the end result will inevitably turn out for the best. Sometimes the best isn't what we thought it would or should be. But with hindsight we can often see how things turned out in just the right way for the highest good of all.

Living fully in the positive flow all of the time isn't easy. While we apply ourselves toward that goal we will have to make some allowances for the fact that some days we won't do as well as others. There are times when positive flow or not, we are going to be extremely upset with our kids. It isn't going to be all hugs and kisses. When little Sally drops ice cream on her Sunday dress right after you told her to be very careful you may begin to think of striking out at her instead of hugging her.

This brings us to another essential part of why we have spent so much time talking about things that relate to understanding ourselves. In the last chapter we talked about specific gravity and how our children will gravitate toward their own vibrational balance according to the particular qualities of energy that make up the current state of their consciousness. Well, it is the same for us.

We all have a specific gravity. It is the combination of magnetic vortexes from our past karma – both from past lives and our past in this life. This current state of our own consciousness must be acknowledged in order to work realistically with the tool of our personality. It is fine to talk about never getting frustrated if you have a naturally easygoing personality, but if you are a person that tends toward impatience, standing around waiting for the kids to get into the car for a trip can drive you absolutely nuts. When you have to turn around three miles from home because Bobby forgot his jacket and you are about to put him on an airplane to Alaska, you just might go ballistic!

Knowing the parameters of our own personality will give us the platform from which we can work to improve ourselves. It will also help us to filter the way that we guide our children. This is another place where self-honesty is so important. We can't assume that the qualities that we find easy to express are the same ones that our children will find easy. Since we hope that others will forgive our idiosyncrasies it is only fair that we forgive those areas in our children. This doesn't mean that we don't work to improve our children and ourselves. It means that we have to take a longer view about self-improvement. Patience and perseverance will be essential parts of all our efforts.

We also need to realize that as long as our perceptions of the world come through our personality, the world will reflect back to us the qualities that we ourselves are radiating. When we think others shouldn't be so critical we are being critical. When we think others shouldn't be jealous we are being jealous. When we see others as loving, so it is that we are being loving.

This doesn't mean that the other person isn't acting the way that we perceive them to be acting. It means that our perceptions of the world are colored by the qualities of consciousness that we are currently radiating. As we free ourselves from the likes and dislikes of the personality and fluidly express the natural positive qualities of the soul, when we see someone expressing a negative emotion we will feel compassion for the unhappiness that it is causing them, rather than putting them down for it or feeling in some way personally affronted.

When our children do things that we don't like we should try to divorce ourselves from any negative reactions that our personality inclinations might lead us toward and think, "Why is my child acting this way? Use this thought to reach out and attune yourself to your child's motivating energies. It is those motivating energies that we want to work with as much as possible.

When we are living in the peace of the positive flow we are much less likely to overreact to the actions of our children. The aura of our good inner feeling will protect us from being stung too quickly by the difficulties of the moment. When a situation does penetrate your peace and you automatically react, be sure that you don't lose complete control of yourself. It is one thing to yell at your child in frustration, it is quite another to swing at them in a rage.

Earlier we talked about finding a basic value system in life. How that system, to work, would have to be relative to the people and circumstances of every situation. If I were to say that good parents never get angry, or that good parents never spank their children, I would be severely shortening the list of good parents in the world. Good parenting, as a practical matter, is about taking what you are working with now and moving forward to make it better – giving our honest efforts to do that which is right. We need the willingness to recognize and admit our mistakes. Remember that until we have perfected our inner selves there is little chance that we will act perfectly in this world.

Is the fact we aren't going to be perfect any excuse for making mistakes? No. Always keep in mind that the actions we put out toward our children, like a boomerang, are on their way back toward us just as soon as they go out. So when we fail or hurt our children, we are doing the same to ourselves. This is how we are held accountable for our actions in all parts of life, not just parenting.

There is an ancient tradition from India, which explains that all of life expresses one of three qualities: elevating, activating or downward-pulling. Elevating qualities expand our consciousness. They are the natural expressions of a soul that is unfettered by limiting attachments. Love, forgiveness, compassion, selflessness, these are all expressions of our higher nature. Downward-pulling or obstructing qualities contract our consciousness. Laziness, deception, lust, selfishness, meanness, these bind us to the world of the senses and connect us to the negative flow. Activating qualities are action oriented. They provide the motion that can lead us forward or backward. They can be positively activating like being smart or lively, or they can be negatively activating like over-serious or meddling. When we see our thoughts and actions in the light of these three qualities we can see which way we are going and which way we want to go.

Since we are all a mixture of elevating, activating or downward-pulling qualities, we need to work honestly with the way things are now as we push forward in positive directions. So if a child has the habit of lying all the time (downward-pulling), they will usually have to go through occasional truthfulness with a selfish motive (activating) before they can get to spontaneous selfless truthfulness (elevating).

70

All of life can be seen in the light of these three qualities. They provide a map that will guide us no matter where we are. It isn't that we have to memorize a list of specific qualities and then try to act them out – although that might be helpful in the beginning in order to see what you are trying to accomplish. So much of what we have been talking about comes under the heading of attunement. When we learn to feel the vibrations that are emanating from all things, people and situations, we can inwardly tell if it is elevating, activating or obstructing. The spontaneous use of this inner understanding is our goal. If lists will help you to get to that goal then use them, but keep in mind that we want to grow beyond lists.

There is a saying: you are what you eat. The idea that we are made of that which we take into ourselves is true on every level of our being. Physically, we are the food and exercise we take in. Mentally, we are the thoughts and emotions that we think and take in. Spiritually, we are the consciousness with which we live and associate. No matter what we are doing in life, until our personal magnetism is strong enough to repel negative energies we are taking them in right along with the positive energies around us.

We will talk more about how this affects us. For now, keep in mind that it is through our awareness of these three qualities of life and how we are affected by them that we can see where we now stand and which way it will be beneficial to go in the future. By developing and strengthening positive habits that support positive elevating qualities we will be increasing our magnetism in the best possible way.

Actually making conscious changes in ourselves and our children is life's greatest challenge. This is where we work with the elemental forces that forged our consciousness into its current state. I am now going to share with you the components of a formula for accomplishing this daunting task. This process is at the heart of *Positive Flow Parenting*.

We can use this formula to release ourselves and our children from the grip of negative energies while we increase our connection to the positive energies in life.

The ***Way of the Positive Flow*** can be defined as**: the continuous process of perception, attunement and experimentation – through the positive redirection of energy – as applied to living in the positive flow of life.**

There are three main parts to the formula. While we look at these components we are going to focus on its application to parenting, but keep in mind, it will also work in every nook and cranny of our lives.

Perception.

Perception means not only observing a behavior with your eyes and ears, but also reaching out with your inner self and trying to feel the perspective and motivations of your child. If a child is lying: Why? Sometimes the reason is as simple as covering up an act that they already wish they hadn't done. In a case like that they may have already inwardly acknowledged their mistake and determined not to repeat it. If we overreact we might undo the benefits that the child has already received from the experience. Taking the time to perceive what is really going on will save us from many mistakes. While you inwardly connect to the positive flow for an intuitive understanding of the situation don't forget to use good communication skills. Keeping your own energy positive while you explore the energies of the larger situation is essential.

Some behaviors that seem simple on the outside are the tip of a deep-seated tendency. It is only through long term attentiveness that we can work with these types of issues. The first important step is to have noticed that there is a problem. Too many parents close their eyes and ears to the realities that are all around them. Even though for years they have noticed things missing in their home it isn't until their child is arrested for stealing that they begin to realize that there is a problem.

And even then, some parents, out of a misguided sense of loyalty or feeling of embarrassment will side with their child against the accuser. I'm not suggesting that people are never wrongly accused. I'm saying that we must be honestly willing to see the truth of any situation, no matter where that truth may lead.

Attunement.

While attunement is certainly the essence of perception, in this case we are talking about attunement to the positive flow. Now that we have perceived something that needs to be dealt with we want to get a solution through our superconscious attunement to the positive flow. This inner attunement shouldn't disconnect us from using our conscious mind to focus our understanding of the situation. But if we use only the conscious mind we will drastically limit our resources.

This is where we apply the techniques of inner connection that we discussed in earlier chapters. Calm yourself in meditation. Feel the peace of the positive flow moving from your heart toward your spiritual eye. Now in that calmness offer up the situation to the universal intelligence. Don't color it with your feelings. Just present it in the clearest light that you can. Then act as a channel by consciously sending positive energy to the situation. Spend some time sitting in the silence. Hold yourself open to a response while staying completely unattached to whether you perceive one or not.

The universal response can come in many ways. Sometimes it is the instantaneous knowledge of what should be done – it can appear in your mind like a flash of understanding. It may happen during your meditation or it may come later. Sometimes our desire to receive an answer keeps us from hearing it. Desire fogs our perceptions of Spirit. At other times it may never be mentally clear to us but circumstances will flow in a beneficial direction solving the situation in unseen ways. As you develop your inner relationship with the positive

73

flow you will begin to see how this uniquely manifests in your life.

Experimentation/Redirection.

Even if you get a clear image or understanding about what needs to be done, proceed carefully. Sometimes the clear messages that we hear aren't the whole story. Let's say you were at a corner and didn't know which way to go in order to find someone's home. You might offer your situation up to the superconscious mind and get the feeling that you should turn right. So you proceed to the right for 10 miles and get lost. Was the guidance wrong? No. You just missed the part about turning left at the next intersection!

It can also happen that our imaginations and/or our subconscious desires can create solutions that feel right because they are based on our desires and not on true inner guidance. Self-honesty and attentiveness to the process over a long period of time will give us the experience to know the true depth of our inner clarity.

Each step of the way we must apply the whole process simultaneously. We need to constantly inwardly observe what is happening and adjust our course as things develop and new insights come to light. The forces of life are always moving. Like a surfer, we must learn to ride the wave of any experience, making adjustments as we move along. If we try to fight the wave it will certainly knock us down and give us the washing machine treatment. If we flow in harmony with the wave just a little effort applied properly can turn the wave's power toward the fulfillment of our goals.

This brings us to the next important point. While there are times when we will need to make a direct frontal assault on a negative behavior in ourselves or our children, it is often more advantageous to approach things from the side or back door. If you are thirsty for some water you can take a baseball bat and bang at the faucet. After some substantial blows you will probably find water in abundance. Of course you will also find that you have done some damage to the plumbing. Why not just turn on the tap? Even if the handles are stiff from lack of use it will probably take much less than a baseball bat to get them working. So it is with people. Rather than fighting directly against the difficulties of negative habits or situations it is far easier to turn on the tap of positive energy to create harmony and the foundation for new positive habits. Once those positive habits have established themselves it is much easier to turn that success toward dealing with negative energies of all types.

It also happens to be true that negative habits don't feel comfortable around positive habits. If we develop positive habits that come fairly easy to us, once they are strong, negative habits won't feel at home. The negative habits may even leave on their own through neglect.

If we constantly hammer at our children to change their ways we may find that we damage them and our relationship with them. Encouraging our children in things they can easily do while we gradually work on more difficult areas is much more beneficial in the long run. Not only is it more helpful to the child but we feel better as well. Our own peace can be shattered every time we have to lock horns with our children. Drawing them toward a goal with positive energy is much more pleasant and effective then trying to drive them from behind with threats or a stick. So as we experiment with ways to move ahead in the direction of our goals what we want to do is redirect the energy of any situation with sensitively applied positive energy.

Let's face it, the day to day interaction between parent and child, to say nothing of life on a larger scale, is like combat. Things are always coming at you. You never know what is going to happen next. The tensions that build up inside aren't easy to deal with. Situations are always coming up that try to steal our peace. It is hard to feel the joy of Spirit when your two-year-old just fell over and is crying at the top of their lungs while dinner burns on the stove. If you have a bad day at the office it isn't easy to exert patience and understanding when you get home and almost break your neck on a skateboard just trying to get in the front door.

While the Saints are truly the greatest exponents of living the *Way of the Positive Flow* I would like to refer to a fictional character who has on the surface developed this technique to a fine art: James Bond. Who hasn't marveled at the way that James Bond is able to improvise his way out of the stickiest of situations? It is truly inspiring to see how he can escape an attacker by falling out of a window, sliding down an awning and landing in the back seat of a taxi to then nonchalantly request that the driver take him to his hotel. James Bond never loses his poise. At the same time he never just accepts the status quo. He always finds in his current circumstances an opportunity to push forward towards success.

Just like James Bond, we want to learn to improvise. Every situation in life has at least a short-term solution instantly available. We must learn to look for opportunities the way James Bond does: in the things at hand. Wherever we are, whatever the circumstances, there are always solutions to be had.

The key to activating this ability can be understood by looking at a discovery that was made during the gold rush years in California. One of the techniques of gold mining, placer mining, utilized the pointing of a water cannon at the side of a hill. The force of the water would break up the soil and wash it down a tunnel. In the tunnel there was a large sluice box that would capture the gold and let the muddy water flow on by. As a mining technique it was quite wasteful, but they did discover something that was worth all that gold to us.

The big water cannons that they used to shoot the water at the hillsides were very heavy. When the miners wanted to change the direction that the water cannon was pointing they would have to hook up teams of horses to move the huge metal monsters.

One day a miner was standing next to one of the water cannons with his shovel. Deciding that the powerful stream of water coming out the end of the cannon was a good place to clean his shovel he raised his shovel up to do so. To his amazement, as soon as he touched the shovel to the stream of water the whole cannon moved. Once he removed his shovel he found that the powerful stream of water was pointing at a new location. Thus it was discovered that a very large amount of energy could be redirected with a small force applied in just the right place.

The *Way of the Positive Flow* involves redirecting the energy of any situation with the application of our inspirations from our inner superconscious connection to the positive flow of life. The application of this technique is limited only by each person's ability to use their positively charged imagination as directed by our inner connection to the positive flow.

Here is an example of how this works. Your toddler, Billy, is walking across the living room floor and suddenly falls down. What do you do? Billy didn't hit his head or injure his body in any way he just lost his balance and fell. Surprised, upset, unsure of what to do Billy looks up at you.

How you react is your first test. If you act like Billy should be hurt then he will probably cry. If you smile and act like it was a joke or something cute there is a good chance that Billy will smile too, and maybe even laugh. If that works – it often does – then you have successfully redirected the energy. If it did hurt enough for that not to work or Billy just didn't buy your reaction for some other reason, then Billy will start to cry.

Now comes test number two: Time to improvise! What can you do? Look for a favorite toy or something new. It can be anything: a sock, a rock or an empty box. Bring it over to Billy and show it to him with great enthusiasm. If you can't find a prop that

77

looks helpful then use your own body. Look Billy right in the eyes and jump up and down like a gorilla! If that isn't your style then use funny faces. Don't buy into the tears yet. You can even tell Billy that you know he isn't hurt and that these other things will be more interesting than crying – if you chose to speak, a smiling cheerful voice is essential.

If Billy still doesn't go for it then get physical. Pick him up and start to play. Hands under the arms bouncing up and down so that the feet touch the floor occasionally is a good one. Flying through the air like an airplane might work. What about giving him a little toss up in the air? (Be careful with this one, if you drop the little guy you will be starting all over again in an even worse situation!) You will quickly learn the types of motion and interaction that your child likes.

If none of these ideas work, move on to hugging and comforting. If that doesn't work then look for an injury that you didn't notice.

Why not comfort Billy immediately? If you feel that would be the correct response then do it. But after a while you probably won't want to comfort Billy every time he gets a little bump. This is where perception comes in. We need to tune in to whether Billy needs comforting or does he need to learn to ignore little bumps. Attunement was the seeking of inspiration – coming up with all the things we tried. And experimentation/ redirection was doing all the things we tried.

Why didn't we tell Billy not to cry? That would have been going against the flow of his energies rather than redirecting them. We encouraged Billy in a positive direction instead of discouraging him. We expanded the energies of the moment rather then contracting them.

You may have noticed that while discussing these ideas I haven't said anything like: at this age you do this and at that age you do that. While I will share some age specific ideas later, this basic formula works for all ages in any situation. The key is how well we can personally apply it. Each parent has their own strengths and weaknesses. Find your strengths and go with them. Use your strong areas to best advantage while you gradually develop the areas that are more difficult for you. This is how we want to work with ourselves, as well as, our children.

The *Way of the Positive Flow* is essentially, living in tune with the superconscious mind through our inner intuitive connection to the positive flow. When we are tapped into the universal well of peace, joy and understanding we can quench any thirst. Even without the infinite potential of our inner connection to Spirit the process of perception, attunement and experimentation, under the guidance of redirecting the energy rather than going against it, is sufficient to bring much success in life.

10

Eight Gifts of Parenting

Gift giving is a common practice in all cultures. The expression of our love and/or appreciation for others is not only symbolized in the gift, but also made manifest. Even more important than the gift itself are the thoughts and qualities of energy that have motivated the gift. The thoughts that we radiate out from our being are an actual force. Good thoughts provide strength to the magnetic field of those who receive them. Negative thoughts – depending on the strength of the thought and the power of the recipient to repel negativity – can weaken others. It is like cheering and booing for athletes. Those forces going toward the competition can actually have an affect on the outcome.

It is easy to think vague thoughts toward others. When we give definite purpose to our thoughts we are committing ourselves to how we feel. Jesus said, "Faith without works is dead." In secular terms it is called: Putting your money where your mouth is.

As parents we should realize that there are certain things that we have signed up to do in order to fulfill our roles . We will constantly be called on to extend ourselves. Those who are not prepared to make this commitment should consider not being parents. If you find you are already a parent and didn't quite know what you were getting into, God has called on you to perform your duty: there is no backing out.

Rather than seeing these parental duties as burdens it is much more helpful and true to the spirit in which they should be given to call them gifts. If we find that caring for our children is like having a tooth pulled, we need to seriously re-evaluate our mental attitude. Even in the most difficult of circumstances it is possible to feel the positive flow of life – if we choose to. That doesn't mean it will be easy, but it is available to us. The law of karma has made the very circumstances in which we find ourselves the most advantages for our spiritual growth. In the school of life no test is given that the student cannot pass. Will our big tests in life be difficult and seem impossible? Yes. Will they be impossible? No.

One of the truths about real gifts is that they are good for both the giver and the recipient. The giver gets the opportunity to express an expanded inner positive quality of consciousness, which is elevating and increases attunement to the positive flow. The receiver gets the opportunity to share in this expanded feeling by opening themselves up to the energy that is flowing toward them. In both cases the participants have the choice of whether to act gracefully in tune with the higher flow of the moment or to contract their consciousness in self-conscious ego awareness. This"good for everyone" aspect of solutions that are in tune with the positive flow is one of the practical ways that we can evaluate solutions that we are consdering.

On the negative side, the giver may choose to think egotistically: How good I am! Or, I wish I didn't have to do this, Oh well, at least everyone can see what a great person I am. Regardless of the giver's attitude the recipient may decide to express negative, or obstructing, qualities as well. Such as: I hope everyone leaves soon so I don't have to share this gift with anyone. Or, If she thinks I owe her anything just because she gave me this gift, she certainly is wrong. When we allow these kinds of thoughts to flow through us we are connecting with the negative flow.

It isn't enough to just do the right actions in this world; we also need to attach the right attitude. Although let's face it, acting properly with the wrong attitude is certainly better than both action and attitude being misplaced.

As we discuss these eight gifts of parenting remember that they should be freely given. While we can hope that our children will love us, make our lives richer and happier, and that they will appreciate our efforts, we can't base the correctness of our actions on what we are going to get back. When we give unselfishly to our children without any thought of obligation on their part we are rising above the limitations of a "What's in it for me?" consciousness.

The Gift of Physical Life

The gift of physical life is where the adventure of parenting begins. In my book, Doorway to a New Lifetime: Childbirth from a Spiritual View, I talk at length about the process of bringing a soul into this world. When we offer ourselves as physical channels for the coming into this world of a soul, into a physical incarnation, we are giving a most precious gift. I have heard some people say that bringing a child into this world isn't such a great thing. There is so much suffering in the world. Maybe it would be better not to have children. Each potential parent will have to decide this for themselves. Keep in mind that it is the challenges in life that push us forward toward our greatest victories. If life was all fun and easy we wouldn't have any reason to strive for improvements in ourselves and our lives. Many have questioned God's judgement in creating a world that includes suffering, but no matter how we feel about it, this physical world is a most advantages place for working out our karma and moving quickly toward reawakening the awareness of our oneness with God. To give that kind of opportunity to a soul seems like a pretty big gift to me.

The Gift of Love

The most essential ingredient for a happy life is love. There is no feeling more satisfying to the soul, both in giving and receiving, then love. The parent/child relationship is uniquely designed to give us the greatest opportunity for the expression and reception of love. When we include a conscious awareness of this truth and nurture it as the most basic value of our relationship with our children, we will find that many mistakes – on both sides – can be weathered.

The Gift of Time

Time is the proof of our caring. When you spend time with your child you are saying: I love you and I would rather be with you than doing anything else. This is one of the most powerful ways you can objectify your love. It is also one of the greatest blessings. Time spent with your children will truly enrich your life. If the lifestyle that you have chosen causes you to be away from your child excessively, taking a closer look at the bottom line reasons for your current choices would be in order. I don't mean that a parent is always being selfish when thinking and acting on their own desires. Kids don't want to be around their parents all of the time either. What we want to do is create a balance that fits the positive flow of the family. Even in evaluating time spent together we can use our formula for success: Perceive, Attune, Experiment/Redirect.

Time is also the prime ingredient for the development of relationships. If we don't spend time with our children, how can we expect to know or understand them? Much of the power of influence a parent has over their children is directly proportional to the amount of time that is spent together.

The Gift of Good Manners

Good manners may seem like a nice thing, but not as important as other items in life. Consider this: Even Tom

Sawyer was given the ability to behave properly when he chose to. That doesn't mean he wasn't a rascal! Samuel Clemens knew a basic truth about life when he created Tom Sawyer: No one likes people with bad manners.

It isn't just an issue of where the forks and spoons should be placed or chewing with your mouth closed, although that is certainly a part of it. I'm talking about all of the basics. Speaking respectfully to others. Not interrupting unless it is an emergency. Not making a ruckus when you go out to eat. Sitting up straight at the table. Being courteous to others. Saying please and thank you. It isn't that we can expect our children to be successful in all of these things all of the time, but if they aren't taught these precepts as a basic value at home they will have to learn it elsewhere. If they don't, they will be socially handicapped and so will you.

How do you feel when you see a child acting with bad manners in a restaurant? Personally, I find it a little embarrassing – not for myself, but for the kids, and even more for their parents. Not only are the parents letting a wide variety of bad habits sprout in their children, they are lessening their own ability to enjoy being with their children – to say nothing of the distraction that it causes to others in the vicinity.

In wolf society a pup that shows a consistent lack of correct behavior is sometimes actually killed by the father. A pup that doesn't act properly at certain times can put at risk the lives of the whole pack. I'm not proposing that we kill kids who don't behave well. But if I were into betting, I would place my money on the reality that a lot of onlookers have had just that thought cross their minds when watching a little brat make things unpleasant for everyone.

Children from a very young age can be taught to behave. This isn't an imposition on their free will. It is a gift that will enhance their lives. The process of developing good manners will help them to begin learning to see how others are affected by their actions. Through the establishment of basic good manners we are giving our children a skill that will benefit them in every other part of life.

The Gift of Self-Control

Through the establishment of good manners from the very beginning we are planting the seeds of a character trait that can serve as a strong support for success in any endeavor: self-control. Learning to harness and guide the energies within ourselves is a prerequisite for achieving our goals. No matter what your child decides to do in life, without self-control, the task will be much more difficult, if not impossible.

Unfortunately, self-control isn't something that you can just give to people. They have to cultivate it in themselves. So we will need to give the gift of opportunities to cultivate self-control. Communicate these ideas to your children from an early age. If they grow up from the beginning with a sense of being in control of themselves they will find life much easier then if they start the process later in life. Self-control is a life long project so don't expect perfection. Practice cultivating self-control in your own self first. Then attune yourself to ways that you can instill these same values in your children.

The Gift of Positive Mental Culture

One of the main ways we can help to guide our children in the development of self-control is through positive mental culture. Because the next eleven chapters go into this in depth I won't elaborate now. Suffice it to say that this is really important!

The Gift of Education

An academic education isn't essential for living successfully in this world. There have been numbers of great people throughout history who couldn't read or write. But next to those great souls who can shine in spite of this lack of formal training there are millions who could advance their lives greatly if they could but read and write.

Some might wonder why I should mention such an obvious thing during today's modern times. The fact is that as I write this book the number of illiterate people in America today is growing, not shrinking. Even with the constitutional right to free public education far too many young adults are coming out of high school without the most basic skills of reading and writing. For this, every parent must take personal responsibility. It isn't enough that we simply send our children to school. It is ultimately our responsibility to make sure that our children get a good education. This is a gift that opens up a world of information and possibilities for our children. Don't leave this area to chance. We will talk more about schools in the chapter on educating for life.

The Gift of Reverence for All Life

Along with these most basic gifts we need to add a reverence for the sanctity of all life. While we can't make our children believe in God or appreciate the beauty and value of the incredible variety of life forms that inhabit our planet, we can communicate our own belief. Not to share your view on these issues is to, by default, preach that they have no value. Some parents feel that they don't want to share their beliefs because it would be an imposition on their child's free choice. Others force their own beliefs down the little throats of their children until it causes choking and rebellion. As with all things: perceive, attune and experiment/redirect. We each will need to find the balance that fits the rhythm of our own lives and the lives of our children. The communication and application of the highest aspects of life should always be at the forefront of family life.

Given the mixture of things that we want to share with our children we will need to mix and match according to how the soup is cooking. This is the beauty of life – its variety. It will, no doubt, turn out different than what we had anticipated in the beginning. If we give our children these 8 gifts: Life, Love, Time, Good Manners, Self-Control, Positive Mental Culture,

Education and Reverence for all life, we will be well on our way to fulfilling our duties as God's Stewards.

11

Positive Mental Culture

What would our children be like if they were perfect people? What would we be like if we reached our highest potential? What is it that we are trying to accomplish in this life? For some, perfection is being the best in the world at something: sports, the arts, business, medicine, whatever your chosen field. For others, perfection has to do with health, wealth, prestige or just the endless enjoyment of pleasures. If we could rub the fabled magic lamp and get our wish from the all-powerful genie: What would we wish for?

Before making that wish it might do us well to look at those who have already received the benefits of a wish similar to our own. Look at the lives of the most successful people in any area of life, who enjoy the type of life that you think would make you or your child happy. Are those people really happy? The truth is that the lure of success in any outward endeavor in life, whether it be material, mental or emotional, never quite delivers the happiness that it promises. The only people who have found an endless well of fulfillment are those who have realized their oneness with the positive flow of life. All others in life have only found temporary shelter in a corner of their consciousness which they have labeled: This makes me happy.

I am not suggesting that there is anything wrong with striving to attain outward success in this world. This is just a reminder that outward success is empty without the foundation of a balanced view of life and an inner connection to the positive flow of Spirit. Something that many people don't realize is that the skills and insights that give us a balanced view of life are the very ones that can help us to most effectively achieve our outward goals. As each soul begins to clean the dust of past incarnations from the window of their consciousness the pure light of Spirit will start to shine through. While each of us, as a unique expression of the Divine Light will shine differently, the basic building blocks of how the Creation is made are the same for everyone. It is from those basic building blocks that we can find the qualities that will help us and our children to achieve our highest potential inwardly and outwardly. The development of these qualities can be called: positive mental culture.

While we use the term positive "mental" culture it is important to remember that it reaches into our physical and spiritual nature as well. The threefold aspects of our nature: mental, physical and spiritual are inextricably intertwined until we become freed from the body at physical death and from the limits of the conscious and subconscious mind when we achieve Self-realization.

In chapter three we talked about how to build a good life. By channeling our God given energies through our will we are building our own lives. The girders holding up the floor of our consciousness are our habits. Strong habits support their rooms well while the areas with weak habits sag. It is through the development of the will and the application of that will toward positive habits that will make our lives most successful. If we want our children to be happy and successful in life, no matter what specific areas they choose to explore, it is the strength of their will – applied through their positive habits – that will bring them the greatest chance of success.

In order to guide our children in the development of positive habits we want to start with the positive habits that they have brought with them from the past. Their strong positive habits we will encourage. To their weak positive inclinations we will apply our creative energies toward strengthening them into strong positive habits. Bad habits, both weak and strong, will need to be approached sensitively. We have already talked about trying to redirect their energies into positive directions whenever possible rather than opposing them directly. When approaching negative habits in others remember this simple phrase from the bible: Unto every thing there is a season. As we become sensitive to the longer rhythms in life we will realize that we can't accomplish everything in a single day. Each area must be cultivated in its own time. Be ever vigilant in your attention, but patient in your efforts.

If you watch attentively you will find just the right moment to share an insight with your child. When my children, Kai and Sabari, were about 10 or 11 years old we were traveling in northern Nevada. Since gambling is legal in Nevada and they had never been exposed to it, it was natural that it would become a subject of discussion. I wanted to communicate to them some of the problems associated with gambling. How for some people gambling can become addictive. We spoke at length about various aspects of the subject but our discussion was strictly theoretical until we happened to find just the right moment.

We stopped in Virginia City where there are a number of museums containing a wide variety of relics from the gold mining era. In one museum there was a scale on which you can stand and get your weight. Kai wanted to try it, so I gave him the necessary penny. When we looked at the place where you insert the penny we noticed that there were five slots instead of one. Looking more closely we discovered that if you put the penny in the "lucky" slot, you get your penny back, thus getting your weight for free.

Well wouldn't you know it, Kai chose the lucky slot. The penny came popping out as his weight was shown on the meter. As soon as the penny popped out Kai's face lit up like a Christmas tree. He reached down, grabbed his penny and proceeded to put place it in front of the slots again. Just before he dropped it into the machine again I stopped him for a moment. Looking at both Kai and Sabari I said, "That is what I have been trying to tell you about."

They both instantly understood the message. They had seen Kai's irresistible urge to try again. To drive the lesson home even more successfully, when Kai reinserted the coin a second time he didn't get it back. If I hadn't been paying attention to the moment I might have missed that opportunity to share a valuable lesson.

Another thing to keep in mind is made clear by a story that is told about Mahatma Gandhi. A woman once came to Gandhi and made a request, "Sir, my son eats to much sugar. Would you please advise him to stop?" Gandhi agreed but asked that the woman not bring her son to him until the next week.

When the woman's son arrived the following week Gandhi made the request to him. As to whether or not the child adhered to Gandhi's advice I can not say. The revealing part of this story comes from Gandhi's comment to the mother after the boy left. The mother asked, "Sir, why did you not tell my boy to stop eating sugar while we were here last week?"

"Because last week I had not myself given up sugar." Was Gandhi's reply.

If we want our children to improve any part of their lives, it would do us well to make sure that we ourselves are following our own advice. While it is true that there are a number of things that adults can do that are not appropriate for children, we must be prepared to live by the standards that we preach.

Adults can stay up later at night than children. Even a very young child can understand and accept this. The reasoning is not complex. We can even strengthen their understanding of this by letting them stay up late once in a while. This will let them experience how it feels to be too tired the next day. It will also help keep them from blowing up their desire to stay up late out of proportion to its real value.

At the same time, if we ask our children to be tidy and we are not tidy ourselves, why should they value our wishes? The lines between some of these acceptable for me and not for you issues can be very gray at times. If we want our children to value our opinions and guidance we must do our utmost to be worthy of their respect. We earn their respect through the example of the way we live. Respect isn't a freebee that comes with the diapers at a baby shower. Example is the strongest form of communication that we can offer our children. Do as I say and not as I do, will only work for a while even with young children. With a teenager, you can forget it!

Try to communicate to your children the "why" of any issue that you aren't sure they understand. When doing this it is helpful to have the child tell you what they think is going on before you explain. You may find that they have a greater understanding of the situation than you had anticipated. This will also help you to avoid them parroting your own words back to you. Then, after you have shared your ideas have your child explain again what they think you were trying to communicate. If your child perceives a genuine sharing on your part and not lecturing, you will be well on your way to having a meaningful exchange.

No one likes to be lectured. People of all ages tune lectures out very quickly. If you find yourself talking **at** your child instead of **with** them, take the time to attune yourself to a new approach. If you practice the perception part of our formula while you discuss an issue with your child you will be able to tell if they are really with you or if they have tuned you out. When your child has disengaged from your efforts to communicate you need to move forward with our formula and attune yourself to new ideas.

Communicating with your child the reasons for a request doesn't necessarily have to be done at the time of the incident. We don't want our children to be in the habit of questioning us on everything we ask them to do. Parents shouldn't need to justify their requests. When a child always resists a parent's requests by questioning them it is a sign of disrespect. At the same time, I have found that children don't always understand what they are being asked to do the first time they hear it. Paying attention to the vibration of a child after you make a request will give you an indication of whether their comments are inappropriate – like an all purpose stall, or appropriate – like a genuine request for clarity or more information. If you aren't sure it is better to err on the side of being polite, just as we hope they will be when roles are reversed.

Another aspect of communicating with your child is that we want to instill in them an understanding that it is on these underlying energies that we should base our actions and not just our desires. If we take our children through the process they will see how to do it and begin practicing it on their own.

If you make a mistake in reading the motivations of your child don't be afraid to admit it to them. Your willingness to admit a mistake and ask their forgiveness will help them to face similar situations in their own lives. It also gives them a chance to express forgiveness. Watching how they handle the situation can be very enlightening. These situations are also good for us as parents. Sometimes parents live in an ivory tower that separates them from their children and the realities of life. These humbling experiences can help to keep our feet on the ground.

When I encourage you to be honest with your children I am not suggesting that you should spill your guts to your child every time you have a problem. Parents who treat their children like adult friends may be giving a child more of life's harsh realities than they need at their age. Adjust your conversations with your children in the light of what will be helpful to them at the present time. Communicate ideas that will strengthen their positive view of life. If we complain to our children about what we don't like in life they will probably pick up the same habit.

Developing meaningful communication with children means speaking with them and not at them. It isn't enough to just share your point of view and how you arrived at it – although you certainly should do that at times. Ask them what they think. Enlist their suggestions on how you might approach a situation – adjust your subject and/or approach to their age. When you get them thinking on your behalf they will be learning to do it for themselves at the same time. You will also find that they often have perspectives that you haven't thought of yourself.

As we look at the specific virtues of a positive mental culture in the next ten chapters keep in mind that all of these qualities are interconnected. Each helps the others toward the balancing of our consciousness. What we are aiming for is the integration of these qualities into the everyday thoughts and actions of our lives. It isn't enough to just agree that these are nice ideas. We must practice the conscious development of these attributes in our own consciousness while we also cultivate them in our children.

Freedom to choose our own path in life is one of the most basic tenants of the American way of life. Yet even without considering the ever-widening strictures of government, people aren't nearly as free to choose their path in life as they think. When we live with desires and habits that we can't control it is those desires and habits that run our lives. It is only through the cultivation of inner freedom from negative desires and habits that we can truly be fee to express ourselves in life as we really want to. Too many people think that freedom is doing whatever you want, whenever you want it. True freedom is knowing that which is right to do and having the strength of will to do it.

   With the development of the conscious application of will through the channel of our good habits we can free ourselves from the past and become the conscious guides of our future. In the coming chapters we will be discussing the ten basic virtues that form the foundation of the development of positive mental culture. When we cultivate these in our children we will be giving them the essential tools with which they can build the life of their choice.

   Who was it that decided which qualities of expression would be considered virtues and which would be faults? Some people think that God just decided that anything fun must be bad. So God made up a list of things that looked like fun and called them the "Don't do these things or you will go to Hell!" list. Thus, many people discount the value of getting to know God. To them He seems like a grumpy old guy who doesn't know how to have a good time!

   This view of God is another classic ploy of the negative flow away from truth. If we check in with those who have proven through the sanctity of their own lives that they were in intimate contact with the Divine, they all – no matter what religious background they came from – agree that God is infinitely satisfying. No one who has achieved union with God has ever come back and said, "It isn't worth it, don't bother. God is boring." In fact, just the opposite is the case. The Saints invariably describe God as intoxicating, indescribably beautiful, all satisfying, ever-new infinite bliss and love.

   The ego through which we express ourselves in this world can be used in two ways. It can be used to indulge in the limited pleasures of the mind and body or it can be used as a tool to focus our energies to reach beyond the limits of the senses into the realm of Infinite Spirit. It is helpful if we understand that while the ego – the soul identified with the body – is generally seen as bad because of its identification with the body and our current personality, it is also the vehicle through which we can

95

focus our energies for our betterment. Until we are consciously aware of our true Self as Spirit, if we want to achieve anything in life it must be drawn through the channel of the ego.

The key to the proper development of our internal energies through the ego is the cultivation of positive soul qualities that expand our identification with Spirit. Otherwise we will be associating with the limiting qualities that identify us more with the confines of the body and personality. Through the strengthening of our positive qualities we will cleanse ourselves from the various negative energies that keep us from achieving our potential.

This underlying view of what we are trying to achieve takes us far beyond the arbitrary values that people give to their thoughts and actions. Acting properly in this world is not just based on opinion. It is based on the laws that control the positive flow toward Infinite Awareness or the negative flow toward limited awareness. In every moment of our lives we are consciously or unconsciously making choices that align us with one direction or the other. As a part of our efforts to improve ourselves and give our children the greatest chance of success in their own lives we want to cultivate those soul attributes that will link us most closely with the positive flow.

We can see the truth of how this works by honestly look- ing at how we feel when we act. When we act in ways that are in tune with the positive flow we feel good at the core of our being. When we live in the negative flow we separate our awareness from the heart to the ego. If we check how we feel in our heart while absorbed in negative energies we will find that we don't feel good. We will find sadness and/or discontentment. While it is true that people can become so enmeshed in their own self- ish actions that they easily ignore the reality of their inner feel- ings, no matter how long the party lasts or how confused we get inside we are never lost. The positive flow will always try to draw us back to greater understanding about how to be truly happy.

As we look toward training our children and giving them living skills and a value system that will really work in life, we need to give them tools that will work with where they are today. It doesn't do much good to talk high philosophy with a toddler or a person who is in the habit of hitting others when they disagree. Each situation must be understood on its own level. Only then can we try to draw things up to higher levels.

One of the great exponents of yoga, Patanjali, outlined ten basic attributes that will naturally shine through the soul as the forces of limitation lose their hold. While we develop our use of the techniques that we have talked about for attuning ourselves to the positive flow we can use these natural expressions of the soul also as guideposts or a map to focus our efforts.

When we develop these qualities in ourselves and our children we are aligning ourselves with the positive flow. Strong positive habits have saved many people from great misfortune. Through the cultivation of positive habits we will be nourishing the soil that can grow a natural inclination to make beneficial choices in life. This is what we are trying to achieve. A positive personal magnetism that draws us spontaneously to acting for the highest good at all times.

12

Non-Violence

One of the greatest expressions of Divine Love that has ever played on the stage of this world is the life of Jesus Christ. His whole life was an exaltation of love and compassion. Yet even he in righteous indignation drove the money changers out of the temple with a whip. Does this mean that Jesus was violent?

We know for certain that Jesus didn't believe that war with the Romans was the solution to the problems of the Jews. He was repeatedly asked to lead a rebellion and he refused. He spoke of his kingdom saying, "The kingdom of God is within you." When the Roman soldiers came to take Jesus into custody one of the disciples cut off a soldier's ear. Jesus immediately rebuked the disciple and healed the soldier. So why did Jesus use a whip on the money changers?

According to each person's vibrational pattern — or specific gravity — we will meet the exigencies of the moment with an expression that is consistent with our basic vibration. That Jesus had complete control of himself was proved beyond doubt by his willingness to accept his role in the crucifixion. He never made any attempt to escape his chosen part. He even forgave his enemies as he hung in pain on the cross. So why didn't he forgive the money changers? Why did he use a whip on them and not the soldiers who oppressed the Jewish people?

There are many facets to questions like these. One of those facets can help us now. In this case, let's remember that Jesus was totally committed to – and able to manifest – God's will at all times. He was fully aligned to the positive flow of Spirit. So that leaves just two possibilities to explain his actions. The first explanation is that Jesus was acting on direct inspiration from God. The second is that Jesus, in his righteous indignation for the worldliness that was being displayed in the temple, lost it for a few minutes.

For us, it doesn't matter which was the case. Both points of view can give us an insight as to how we can deal with our own impulses and those of our children. If Jesus was acting by Divine Command, we can infer that there are times in this physical world when physical force is an appropriate response to a situation. If Jesus just "lost it" for a few minutes, then we can expect that we might do the same at some time: May our reasons be so righteous!

What do we do with the impulse to strike out at life when it doesn't meet our expectations? In order to find our solution we must look to the source of the impulses. Once we find that source we can learn to redirect those energies in positive ways.

The qualities that draw us to people and situations are those that are inclusive, expressing a feeling of shared harmony. Violence at its very root separates us from others: Us versus them, instead of we together or we as one. When we indulge in violence we are closing down our oneness with all life. We are separating ourselves from the object of our anger and denying that all of life comes from the same source.

Expressing physical violence is not a natural expression of the soul. It is an expression of the ego. If the saints went around taking a swing at anyone who got too close they wouldn't be very appealing. Neither are we when we let the mental soldiers of disharmony get control of our minds.

It is helpful to understand that violence is not in itself a causative quality. It is the result of other underlying qualities that have become energized. You can find in the history of all violent acts a stream of negative reactions to life challenges. When we turn to the negative flow as a reaction to any life experience, violence is a possible outcome.

People who just like to smash things are relating to the world as the see it, physical. They want to control it, to have a feeling of superiority over it. Vandalism would be an example of this. Vandalism is often an expression of boredom and negative self-involvement.

Some people who are habitually violent may be mentally ill and in need of professional help. In the case of mental illness, these people have seeds of karma from their past lives that have grown beyond their ability to assert any kind of self-control.

The root of violence and those qualities associated with it, like frustration and anger, is in the thwarting of our desires. When the ego feels that it has been wronged, when life deals a hand we don't like or won't accept, the negative forces say, "I'm not going to take this!" and they strike out. A young child throws their dish across the table because it holds vegetables instead of pudding. A teenager strikes out at a competitor, overcome by frustration during a sports competition. An adult strikes out at a spouse or a child because of some perceived misdeed. These are all acts of violence that spring from a desire for life to be the way we want it to be, rather than the way it is.

Controlling the impulse to anger and its older brother violence is essential for the awakening of our true nature as expressions of Divine Love. Love and anger cannot co-habitate in the same room. When we are controlled by anger we are tapped into the negative flow away from Spirit. There is no telling where we might end up if we ride this wave too far. Indulging in anger and violence is like dancing uncontrol-lably on a precipice; violence can at any time take us over the edge. How many wrongs in life have come to pass from a momentary loss of temper? Far to many!

We must guard ourselves against letting the difficulties of life get control of us. If you ever feel that anger – or any negative emotion – is getting the best of you, quickly remove yourself from the presence of your child. If you can't do that because of safety considerations, turn away from your child until you get control of yourself. Take some deep breaths. Feel that with each inhalation you are taking in peace and harmony. With each exhalation feel that you are expelling your negative feelings.

This is where we learn to redirect our own internal energies. Turn your frustration into a cleansing of your mind and spirit. Consciously connect yourself to the positive flow and fill your consciousness with energy, light and joy. Mentally get a perspective on your circumstances. Nothing in life is so bad that it can't be faced with a certain bit of wry humor. Many of our worst experiences in life will make the best stories once we get through them. Why wait until later to enjoy the moment? If you can bring a smile to the worst of situations you are the victor no matter what happens.

It is important to understand that violence isn't just physical. It can be intellectual and emotional as well. Yelling and even thinking negative thoughts at your children or your spouse are also acts of violence. Whenever we use our words, thoughts or actions to inflict injury on others we are aligning ourselves with the hurtful energies of the negative flow. Many people can attest to the power of hurtful words. The remembrance of hateful words, like a physical scar, can last a lifetime. Actions that are not directed toward a person, but lead to harm of a person, are also acts of violence. An example of this would be the spreading of rumors that lead to harming a person's reputation.

Violence to others can also be done by the omission of actions. If we do not warn others of potential danger when we could have, we have entered into the negativity. If we do not take responsibility for our mistakes and let others take the blame for them, we are also incurring the debt of harm to another.

The expression of violence is a perfect example of how the negative flow cheats us while claiming victory. Not only do acts of violence eventually turn against us through the law of karma, they inevitably do not achieve the result of making things the way we want them to be. Even if we get our way for a short period of time by being violent or threatening violence, life will always change thus depriving us of the gain we sought.

In some people the "no saying" principle is so strong that they are constantly rejecting everything that doesn't meet their approval – which is almost everything! And they often do it as if they were the one that God appointed to place a value on everything. Some people don't even realize that they are doing this. This habit of complaining about everything is so natural to them that it seems normal. Constantly expressing this "no saying" attitude will definitely rub off on your children. While this isn't as bad as hitting your child with a stick, it is like a low grade fever that can eat away at the mental and physical health of your child.

There are many things in this world that have become the "norm" that are not normal. Values in this world aren't made true because many people do them. True values are natural expressions of a soul that is unfettered by the delusions that the negative flow present to us as being reality.

If we want our children to be their best we need to give our best. Sarcastic remarks about others or our children teach that looking at the negative side of others is more correct than looking at the positive side. It also supports an old saying that isn't as true as many people think: Sticks and stones may break my bones but names can never hurt me. While it is true that we need not let the words of others hurt us, the fact is that they can and often do. These hurts are just as real as physical pains. If we teach our children that saying negative things to or about others is acceptable behavior, we are supporting them in the expression of a form of violence.

The more we indulge in negative mental thoughts the more likely we are to have those thoughts explode one day into an act of physical violence. Controlling our harmful emotions or at least learning to release them in a way that doesn't harm others is an essential skill for parenting. If we strike out at our children uncontrollably we become their enemies instead of their bene-factors.

We all need to find those ways in which we can most effectively let off steam. Physical activities are excellent for releasing tensions of all kinds. So is reading an uplifting book or listening to calming, uplifting music. Finding interests that help us to feel more a part of the positive flow will strengthen our positive nature. This will help us to feel so good about ourselves and life that we are much less inclined to get overly upset by life's little ups and downs. These same ideas will work with children of all ages. This is a practical application of the principle of redirecting energies. Playing the right music or getting the body moving in some form of exercise can even work with an infant's energies.

Am I saying that we should never get angry? Well, it might be a nice thing to say but it isn't very likely to happen. For most of us it is not a question of will we get angry, but under what circumstances and how often. Children seem to have a knack for pushing us to the edge of our limits, at which time anger just might pop its ugly head out. To add confusion to the issue, just like in the example of Jesus, sometimes anger is the appropriate response to a situation.

What? I just spent all this time saying we shouldn't get angry and now I am saying that there are times when we should get angry? How can that make any kind of sense?

When your child acts in a way that is detrimental to themselves or others around them, reacting with a gentle smile and a peaceful chat on the error of their ways won't likely be the most productive way to respond. It also won't be a realistic expression of your feelings. Our feelings may not be under our control all of the time, but that doesn't mean that they are always wrong.

There are two aspects to how we should approach our reaction to life's challenges. First, there is how we feel about the situation. Second, is what we should do about the situation. These two perspectives may at times be miles apart. As parents, like a conductor, we are trying to pull together the many different qualities of our children and act in harmony with them. Sometimes harmonies express dissonantly for a while. If we do our conducting well these dissonant passages will, like all good music, resolve into a positive harmonious conclusion.

As Dale Carnegie said, "When life serves up lemons, make lemonade!" This is what we want to do with anger. As much as possible we want to avoid anger through neglect. Just don't indulge in anger. When we develop the habit of reacting to all life situations with a positive viewpoint anger won't often be in our mental picture. When you do find anger entering into your consciousness, try to harness if for good instead of ill. Let your anger help you to run faster or farther. Use anger to channel more energy into your efforts to find solutions to difficult challenges. This is the way that we redirect potentially harmful energies into positive directions.

If you express anger every time your child does something that you don't like your child will be learning: Getting angry at everything that you don't like in life is the right way to live your life. If you save your expressed anger for those moments that need special emphasis, your child will learn that anger is only for times that need special emphasis.

A parent who constantly yells at a child will one day find that yelling no longer commands the child's attention. Then what do you do? Hit them? By saving our expression of anger for those times that really need it, when you use it, your child will take notice.

This is a perfect example of how practical this approach is. Not only will using the positive flow increase the quality of our lives, it will help us to be more effective in our efforts as parents. Here is how it works. Remember our formula: Perception, Attunement, Experimentation/Redirection.

Let's say you have been out driving in the car for awhile with your child. Your child says or does something that you perceive as inappropriate. You suddenly feel angry. What is happening?

Are you angry because of something that your child has just done? Or are you upset because of something unconnected to your child that happened earlier in the day and your child's small faux pas is an opportunity to vent your frustration? If the root of your anger is unrelated to your child, don't take it out on your child. Your child is not your enemy. Looking for the true source of our feelings is a part of self-honesty and the practice of introspection, which we will discuss in chapter twenty. We don't always need to know where our feelings come from in order redirect their energies. If you aren't sure why you are angry it is best to assume that it is not your child.

Let's assume for the moment that the real source of your frustration is not your child. If you aren't too angry to connect inwardly to the positive flow, do so. Try to perceive the source

105

of your anger. Use your inner attunement to understand your feelings. If you don't get an instant understanding that dissolves your negative feelings then seek a temporary solution. Open yourself up to ways that you can redirect your energy until you can look at the problem with a calm mind. Begin by experimenting with the possibilities. Play a soothing tape. Open the window for some fresh air. Sing a favorite song out loud. Think of something funny that happened recently. If necessary, stop the car in a safe place, get out of the car and take a few deep breaths. If your child is old enough you might want to explain that you are feeling upset about something that happened earlier in the day. Enlist your child's help in redirecting your energies. Request them to tell you about their day or what they are thinking about. It doesn't matter what you talk about as long as it gets your energy away from your anger. If your child is too young to have a conversation you can talk to them anyway. Or sing them a song. Use your creativity and keep trying until you find a new direction for your energies.

Children watch parents closely at times like this. They will be learning from your example about how to deal with these types of feelings. So remember, your actions will carry into the future through your children. Consciously choose the qualities of energy that you want to activate as your legacy.

Now let's say that your feelings aren't associated with an earlier situation. Ask yourself if the degree of your anger is consistent with your child's action. Or is your reaction out of proportion to the situation? You could be reacting to the current situation or this current offense could be the last straw of many that your child has been piling on your back all afternoon. Try to figure out what is happening before you act. Reach in with your perception, divorce yourself from any desire to support your feelings of anger and calmly assess the situation.

If we have been living in a vibration of the peace of Spirit, the difficulties of the day won't penetrate deeply into our consciousness of well-being. If circumstances cause us to lose our inner connection to peace we should take the time to reconnect. Life's difficulties look very different when we feel inwardly connected to Spirit.

Now let's look at why your child might have a reason to be unhappy.

People of all ages act in ways that rub others the wrong way for very similar reasons. In this case, your child might be experiencing physical discomfort. This can range from a wet diaper, hunger, thirst, restlessness or having a large teenage body sitting in a small car for a long time. There are also mental reasons like: fatigue, boredom or ill feelings from a previous situation in their own lives. Another reason can be the exploration of limits. Young children are constantly exploring the parameters in which they must live. This is one of the ways they learn. Older children should already know the basic ground rules, but that doesn't mean they won't take things to the edge or beyond.

Tuning in to our children and catching things before they get out of hand should be the first line of defense. There are many possibilities that can lead up to any given situation. Staying attuned to the inner energies of life all of the time will help us to recognize negative currents before our children get swept up in them. If we are in the car and we begin to feel the energies of our fellow passengers aren't going in a positive direction we should try to head things off at the pass. As soon as you begin to detect a negative shift in the energy around you try to subtly apply our formula. Remember, a little energy applied in just the right place can do wonders.

You may have noticed that much of this process is about learning to empathize with how others are feeling. When you are more concerned about others and their feelings then you are about your own you will find it easier to bring out and support the good in others. This positive frame of reference benefits everyone. The natural result of this will be that others will feel good in your presence and be much less likely to misbehave. Thus, you also have fewer reasons to get upset.

The negative flow preaches self-concern. The logic is: If you don't look after yourself, who will? The irony is that it is a philosophy that becomes self-fulfilling. The more that people are concerned about themselves, the less others want to be concerned about them. The positive flow preaches concern for others, subordinating our preferences to those of others. The result is that we increase our good feelings when others feel good. Through this expansive attitude others feel our concern for them and naturally return in kind. Thus, a giving nature gathers friendships with which to share life, while a selfish nature stands alone – sometimes against many.

Remember when we talked about magnetism? If we constantly stay in tune with the needs of our children and energize them in positive directions, negative impulses will be much less likely to take hold in them. In a case like travelling in a car, we should be able to anticipate many of the things that might cause our children to act in ways that we won't like. If we use our creativity before the trip we may not need it as much during the trip. Depending on the length of the drive you can bring appropriate items. Consider food, drinks, games or a book on tape that everyone can listen to. Positive family activities in the car can build many meaningful memories. Try playing games or telling stories. This is a time when the family is together with few outer distractions. Take positive advantage of the situation rather then letting it turn into something negative. When we do this then even on a long trip tensions won't build up and cause your child to feel they must express themselves in a negative way.

If we put our children in situations where we know or can anticipate that they don't have the tools or the abilities to handle it, we are setting them and ourselves up for trouble. I'm not saying that we shouldn't challenge them sometimes. There are even times when it is valuable to push our children beyond what we think they can handle, but not on a regular basis. The saying about an ounce of prevention being worth a pound of cure is certainly true when talking about situations that might make you or your child angry. If we apply our creative talents to anticipating problem areas and developing skills and strategies for meeting those needs, we will find far fewer situations in which we will have to test our determination to avoid anger and/or violence. When we live in the calmness and joy of the soul a non-violent consciousness will be our natural state.

Now let's go back to the car for the final showdown! So now you have tried everything but nothing has worked. Your six year old child has just thrown a milkshake at the front window from the back seat. He was mad because it was vanilla instead of chocolate. Great! You are hopping mad and you have every right to be. If you saw another child do that you wouldn't blame their parents for a moment if they smacked the kid a good one. If you are determined never to strike your child then you are now wracking your brain to find the most profound punishment that you can think of that lies just this side of cruelty. Angry doesn't begin to describe how you are feeling! If this didn't make you angry, you don't need to worry about non-violence, you already have it together! On the other hand, if you don't mind a little sticky cold milk on your dashboard but other things tend to upset you, join the folks who would be livid in the above situation by channeling your desire to know how to deal with things when parenting gets really tough into reading more quickly so that you can get to the chapter on loving discipline!

13

Non-Lying

There is much in life that each of us needs to deeply explore in a very personal way if we want to understand that which is true in life. Truth, like the taste of an exotic fruit, can not be known through someone else's description of its flavor, we must taste it for ourselves.

The only real basis for true understanding in life is personal experience. Yet, can we trust our own perceptions about the way things are? The fact is that life itself places limits on our ability to understand what is actually happening at any given time. Our senses limit us. Society and familial relationships often limit us. Nature limits us in countless ways.

Our ability to perceive and understand what is going on behind the scenes of life's drama is severely limited in more internal ways as well. Intuitive perception is held in check by the many conflicting energies that drive our thoughts and actions. If we want to live life according to a value system that is not arbitrary or limited to mere opinion – our own or the opinions of others – we will need to search the very roots of life itself and ferret out the reality upon which all else stands.

Each of us must find an unquenchable thirst and a life long drive for seeking out truth. When we have dedicated ourselves to this task, magnetizing our consciousness with the vibration of our sincere desire to understand the eternal realities, we will find that the limits keeping us from knowing truth begin to weaken. When that happens, broad new vistas of understanding will form where formerly there was just the darkness of unknowing.

While the conscious mind seeks words and outward experiences for the confirmation of truth, the soul is only satisfied with direct inner communion with truth. This inner experience of oneness is where we can taste directly the infinite flavors of wisdom and justice. It is this inner relationship to truth that we most want to communicate to our children. The example of our own lives – which is the ultimate expression of our own commitment to living in the light of the highest truth that we can perceive in any given situation – will be the strongest force for good that we can bring to bear on our hopes to positively influence our children.

Just as we expect to forgive our children their mistakes, our children are more likely to forgive ours if they can see we are always trying to align ourselves with truth. As we push forward with our efforts, keep in mind that sincerity of effort does not replace the need to act properly in this world. It has been aptly stated: The road to hell is paved with good intentions! The universe is forgiving, yet exacting, when it comes to the creation and payback of karma.

We have talked in depth about attuning ourselves to the positive flow of life in order to directly perceive truth. As a part of this process we also need to work with the conscious mind. Let's look at how the conscious mind relates to truth. Then we can connect this understanding to the superconscious mind.

111

The conscious mind sees life as being solid, firm, and seemingly permanent. From this perspective that which is true in life represents a definite value: yes or no, this and not that, true or false. There are many situations in life where we can apply this simple yes or no formula and get satisfactory results. When you ask someone if they ate an apple they can answer yes or no. One response will be the truth, the other would be a lie. Anytime you want specific information the conscious mind hopes for one correct answer, thinking that anything else would be false. Unfortunately, much to the conscious mind's frustration, life is not that simple.

Take this simple test and see what happens:
1. Is the sky blue? Yes or No?
2. Point to up. Is that the same for everyone?
3. If Mike takes that blame for Tim's mistake in a chivalrous effort to save Tim from punishment: Is Mike's claim of responsibility a lie?

Each of these questions presents to us a glimpse of the complexities that can enter our efforts to align ourselves with truth as it manifests in the world around us. And these are only three questions! The sky is blue: Sometimes. Up is relative to where we are; on the other side of the earth our up is their down. Is telling a lie always to be based on factual issues? In the case of Mike and Tim, is there a higher truth that comes into play when we sacrifice ourselves for the mistakes of others? As soon as we leave questions that have the comfort of mathematical correctness we enter the realm of relativity. And in that realm what compass can we use to guide our boat?

Just as light is the only constant in the physical universe, truth is the only constant in all aspects of existence. But just as light is never static, always in motion, so is truth always moving forward. Truth can not be bound by the efforts of the conscious mind to make concrete that which is ever-expanding. It is only through attunement to the superconscious mind that, instead of capturing and limiting truth, we can express it as it flows through us. This understanding of the fluid nature of truth can then be applied to our practical approaches to living life and guiding our children.

Do not think that because truth is flexible according to the energies of the moment that we can create our own personal vision of what is true in life. We can create our own opinions, but those are only opinions. Truth is not ours to create. We can only chose whether or not we will align our lives with it or not. In those efforts of alignment we can express truth creatively. But if our creativity becomes connected to our personal desires or limited opinions we may be disconnecting from truth. When our actions are guided by selfish desires, even if we do the right thing, we aren't yet expressing the highest possible truth. If we can communicate to our children this inner understanding of what truth is and help them to live in harmony with it, we will be giving them the strongest possible foundation for the building of their character.

Yata Dharma Tata Jaya! Where there is right action – in thought and deed – there is victory. This saying from ancient India should be a guiding principle in all areas of life.

One of the most basic ways that we can align ourselves with the superconscious flow of truth is to always speak the truth in daily life. Try to never let a falsehood cross your lips. How can we do this if we can't yet perceive superconscious truth? Just as we will want our children to do, we start with the facts that the conscious mind collects and files for us. Then we apply the highest standards of alignment to the positive flow that we are able to muster.

If someone asks, "How are you doing?" The fact might be that you are feeling in a negative mood. So you can honestly answer, "Not so great." To turn your reaction to this question into a higher expression of truth for yourself you must instantly shake off your cloud of gloom, change your energy and honestly affirm, "I'm doing pretty good, thanks. How about you?"

You see, truth is always beneficial. Truth is the positive flow. In every situation in life it is possible to see reflections of the positive flow. This does not mean that we should never admit that we are feeling down. It means that we should, as often as possible, redirect negative energies into positive directions. This can be done instantly if we focus ourselves in new directions with enough focus and energy.

If you meet someone on the street and they don't look too good, we don't need to say in the name of truth, "Wow, you really look bad!" That would strengthen the negative flow of energies that they may in fact be feeling. What we want to do is raise their energies toward the positive so that they can shake off those negative feelings. We might say, "It's a beautiful day, isn't it?" or "Oh, what beautiful hair you have!" Sometimes you have to be very creative to come up with something positive. This spontaneous positive creativity is one of the ways we can channel into this world our inner connection to the positive flow. If you can't think of anything nice to say, then stay aligned to truth by following this well worn yet always fresh saying: If you can't say something nice, don't say anything at all. (Be sure to pass this one on to your kids!)

Even when we must give unpleasant information to others it should be expressed with a sympathetic heart. Truth is not always easy to swallow. No matter how bitter the taste, if we communicate and act with a gracious and caring spirit we can bring some positive light even to bad news. When something unpleasant happens to us, like losing a job, it may be factual to say, "I just got fired and things are looking down." But it might be more truthful to say, "Now I'll have more time to devote to my hobby! I wonder if I can make some money at it?" There is always a larger view to every situation. When we can see that bigger picture we will see that life is actually moving in the best possible direction. Even if we can't see a larger good, doesn't it make sense that living with a positive attitude will make whatever hardships we might face in life that much easier to swallow? Sometimes to get to the high rise areas in life we need to go through the slums first. But we won't get through the slums if we stop the car and hang out there for too long.

There is nothing in life that we can honestly call our own. As parts of the Creation all that we have is given to us on loan by our Creator. The only thing that we can in any way call our own – because God gave it to us – is our free will. Even though we have bound our free will with desires and habits from the past, it is ours to direct as we please. Through the development of positive habits and attunement to the positive flow we can regain our freedom.

Some people think of the pioneering days in America as a kind of "Golden Era". While that view might be a bit romantic since early death and disease were also a part of those simpler times, there are a number of qualities that we associate with those times that are worth remembering. Hard working, friendly, willing to help a neighbor in need, these are just a few of the positive qualities that everyone recognizes as a sign that things are going well in society. It is interesting that throughout history the Golden Era's of other countries have also included similar qualities.

There is another quality that fits with good times for society in general. A quality that stands out above all others as the backbone of a healthy society and a healthy soul: The honesty of a person's spoken word. When society can live on a handshake, nay, just the spoken word, and contracts are truly worth no more than the paper that they are printed on, then, virtue is truly alive. Soul's that seriously seek freedom from the bondage of desire can not wait for society in general. We must push forward ourselves, thus serving society by raising ourselves and our children up to the highest path.

When we make a habit of speaking the truth, our whole magnetic pattern is vitalized. It gives strength to every part of our lives. Every time we speak a falsehood we diminish our power to help ourselves and others. The harm that lying does to ourselves is just as great as the harm that it does to others. We undercut our own good efforts in life when we twist things to our own ends by speaking falsely.

These things might seem obvious to many, but if we search carefully we may find that we are not as consistent in our commitment to truth as we think we are. The importance of strengthening our inner self by speaking truth should not be underrated. There are many times that we don't even realize we are diminishing the power of our word. This isn't just about telling the truth when asked a question. What about the times we state we are going to do something and then we don't? I said I was going to clean my room, but I didn't get around to it. I meant to do it, so it wasn't an intentional lie. But I didn't actually fulfill my word. And what about "white" lies? These are the things that we say in order to adjust a situation to meet our desires. They don't really hurt anyone do they? Sometimes we even use them to keep from hurting another's feelings. Doesn't that make them beneficial?

In the case of changing our mind, it is like trying to develop your legs for long distance running. Every time we state our intentions and don't follow through it is like stopping in the middle of a training run. What we want to do is think clearly before we commit ourselves to any given course of action. If we don't want to commit then say, Maybe I'll do this or that. Once we say, "I will", we have given our word. Once given, our word should be our bond. The only time that we should not fulfill our word is when we belatedly realize that our decision was wrong and that following through with that wrong decision would be worse than changing our mind.

This is another reason not to speak out in anger at your child. If in the heat of the moment you give an unfair punishment, you will weaken your word by changing it. When this happens you will have to seek the best way to adjust things. Sometimes you will have to follow through with the punishment just so your child will be in the habit of believing that you mean what you say. Parents who are constantly threatening and not following through lose the power of their word. If you sent your child to their room for two hours when one would have been more appropriate, maybe instead of letting them out of the room after one hour you should take something into the room – possibly even yourself – that will help the second hour pass more easily. Explaining to your child that the punishment was worse because you got angry might help the child to understand that making others angry can make a bad situation worse. Thinking of ways to fix our mistakes and even turning them into a greater good is also part of living in the positive flow!

In cases where you said you were going to do something but changed your mind because you didn't feel like it or something else came up that was more interesting, whenever possible try to follow through with your original plans. This can be done creatively. If you told others that you were going to clean the garage but then decided to go to the movies, do some cleanup before or after you go to the movies. This might seem silly to some people, but when you add up all of the little things that we do to weaken our word and our will, they add up to a powerful weakening effect on our magnetism.

This practice also helps us to think things out clearly before we commit ourselves to a decision. With this clarity of thought will also come a greater conviction that our decisions are correct. That will bring more energy and confidence to our actions. Thus we can see how each part of the process builds upon the next, creating the totality of who we are.

Another aspect of this has to do with always listening to the inner guidance that is available to us. Even though we want to follow through with what we say, we need to listen inwardly each step of the way. If we are guided by intuitive perception to change our plans, we should follow that inner connection to truth.

There are also circumstances beyond our control that may cause us to change our plans. If an unexpected storm arrives and it is not safe to travel, use common sense and stay home. If it is just a little drizzle but you don't like getting your hair wet, maybe you should wear a hat and go anyway. These types of situations must be faced on an individual basis. As you evaluate the options and how you feel about them, be honest!

White lies also diminish our connection to truth. They create a web of falsehood, which is very similar to the way the negative flow itself hides the true spiritual nature of life. When we spin tales that have no basis in truth, we are attaching our creative energies to the negative flow. When the needs of the moment call for a response that doesn't offend, try not to tell even a white lie. Say something that is based in a higher truth, rather then sharing the facts that might be hurtful. If you are invited out on a date and you don't want to go, don't lie, but also try not to offend. Instead of saying, "No, you are too ugly!" which may be true but not a very nice thing to say, try, "Thanks for offering, but I am not available for dating right now." Rather then saying, "I already have a date," when

118

you don't, try, "It is kind of you to ask me, but I'll have to decline."

Coming up with a positive response to the many situations that we meet in life isn't always easy, but it can be fun, challenging and extremely rewarding. When we get into the habit of living this way it becomes much easier through practice.

One of the amazing things that happens when we make a practice of always speaking the truth is that life itself will swing toward the manifestation of our intentions. Just like any powerful magnetic influence, when we have made truth our home we will generate a magnetic power that will attach itself to whatever we say. This vortex of energy will help draw the materialization of our spoken word.

Here is an example of the way this works. If you have made a habit of always getting to your destination on time you will find that things usual work out in ways that help you to arrive on time. People who are habitually late find that life around them conspires to make them late. It is a kind of magnetism. People who always speak the truth find that what they say comes true. This is another good reason to be careful about what you say!

Most children will at some point explore the realms of lying. The best defense against this is to make it clear to your children, from day one, your own dedication to truth. Along with telling them, you must prove your dedication to truth by your actions. As a part of this, talk to your children and share with them the reasons for your actions whenever you think it might be instructive. When we share our thoughts with others they are more likely to share their own thoughts with us. This positive communication will help you to estab-lish how honesty feels when being channeled through your child. If you inwardly reach out and feel your child's vibration of truth during casual conversations you will more easily recognize if they are not telling the truth at some time in the future.

Young children are much more capable of understanding how life works than many adults give them credit for. If we have made a habit of conversing with our children, person to person, soul to soul, asking questions and listening with interest and respect to their answers – along with sharing our own ideas – we will be developing an essential part of our ability to help and enjoy our children. If we explain to our children how truth is beneficial and lying is not, backing up our explanations with our own good example, they will definitely get the picture. This doesn't mean they will not experiment on their own to see what happens, but remember, they are also living our formula: perceive, attune, experiment, they just may not be consciously aware of it.

Some parents might be concerned that a child won't get the correct response from life after telling a lie. Don't worry, truth works for everyone. It will definitely catch up with them, even if not right away. Paying attention to how things are going with your child will help you to stay on top of the situation. When a child starts to lie their vibration changes. If you have been staying in tune with them you will notice it, especially if your child becomes less outwardly communicative. While it is true that as children grow they have more private information in their lives, the privacy of lies and deception have a very different vibration than the privacy of independence. Negativity almost always leaves some kind of signature. The key for us as parents is to refine our ability to perceive these subtle changes.

As parents we can not guarantee that our children will do everything right in life. Our responsibility is to help them along by magnetizing them toward truth with our own vibration and the creative ways that we will come up with to communicate these ideas. The stronger their positive magnetism the greater the chance of their success in life. If a child starts to tell lies, there is a reason. Use your perceptive powers to search for the underlying cause. Attune yourself to the positive flow for a solution. Keep in mind that self-discovery is more powerful than information taken in from the outside. It is often more beneficial to support your child through their own processing of a situation then it would be if you try to impose your view of the situation on them. Experiment with ways to redirect your child's energies in positive directions while respecting their individual integrity.

Through our commitment to truth our connection to the positive flow will become a greater conscious reality. We will find our ability to understand and work with ourselves, our children and all of life, increasing dramatically. It works. That is the truth!

14

Non-Greed

There was once a farmer in South Africa who tired of farming. He wanted to seek his fortune in the world. So he left the farm to his family and went off to find his fortune. After many years of struggle, poor and alone, he died in a far off country.

Back at the farm, one day his son was hoeing in the field. Noticing the reflection of the sun upon something shiny on the ground he bent down to see what it was. It was a diamond! Soon there was no need for the family to farm anymore. They found that they were living on one of the richest diamond fields in the world. Unfortunately their father never contacted them. So they could not share with him the wealth that could have been his.

So many people are searching for a wealth that always seems to be just out of reach. This search can take endless varieties of directions but there is always just one goal: happiness. No matter what a person might call the diamond that they are seeking, wealth, fame, whatever, the reason they seek it is because they think it will make them happy.

This endless search outside of ourselves for fulfillment is what keeps the Creation going. The mind keeps thinking that if I can just fulfill one more desire, then I will be happy. But life is a long hike where every time you get to the top of a hill you find that there is another hill just ahead. Every time you think that you have reached the highest peak you find that there is another taller peak beyond. This goes on and on, endlessly.

If we think about it, the idea that any "thing" can give us happiness is pretty silly. Yet our desires drive us to live as if mere things could actually satisfy our inner most need for joy and fulfillment. What is it about having a new hat or coat that can make us happy? Is there some material with which it is made that exudes the fragrance of happiness? Can a night on the town make us happy? A new boat, car, airplane, house, bike or baseball: can any of these things make us happy?

Some will say that fun makes us happy. What is fun? One person likes roller skating and another hates it. Skydiving is just the thing for some, while others would die of fright! Is there any single outward activity that everyone in the world would agree is fun? Even if we allow for different tastes, what is it about any given activity that makes it fun?

Along with this strange phobia for thinking that any particular thing or activity can make us happy is the idea that the more we do it the happier we will be. Even though we can easily see the falsity of this notion that endless repetition will satisfy us, we still keep repeating our actions in the hopes that it will satisfy us. If we overeat a food we get sick. When we participate in sports the body simply gets tired and stops enjoying the activity after a while. Yet, strangely enough, people often overeat or participate in activities beyond the point of discomfort. So does that mean that a certain amount of discomfort is part of being happy? Are we all masochists?

This whole issue turns on the way we input into our awareness our life experiences. The body is made of sensory pathways that transmit information to our brains. According to our personal preferences, we label these stimuli pleasant or unpleasant. Since some people like onions and others do not, we know it is not the onion itself that determines whether it is tasty or not. So that means each person has their own built in likes and dislikes.

This idea is consistent with our discussion about everyone harboring likes and dislikes from their recent and distant past. So here we are, each with our own set of preferences. That doesn't seem like a problem since the world has such great variety. It would seem that all we need to do is enjoy the things we like and avoid the things we do not like. If we enjoy overindulging in something then go ahead, why not? Whatever you want to do is A-OK.

So, why aren't more people happy?

The problem with this scenario is that it simply doesn't work. The world we live in has a way of constantly turning the tables on us. I wanted a blue ball but got a red one instead. Or even worse, my neighbor got a beautiful blue ball and I didn't get one at all. Maybe we just want to enjoy a nice dinner, but it gets burnt or accidentally spilt on the floor. So we go out to dinner and everything is great until we eat our desert and get sick. Then when we get back to the car we find that we have gotten a parking ticket. And if that isn't bad enough, on the bottom of the ticket it actually says, "Have a nice day!"

It can be maddening at times, this endless hunt for happiness. The real clincher comes when we actually get what we desired. One day, whatever it might be or however long it took to achieve, our desire arrives on the doorstep of our lives. Oh wondrous day! We have arrived! This moment is sooooo sweet. In that very moment of ultimate happiness

124

we find ourselves only momentarily at the peak. In the very next moment our victory is fading into the past. The glory of winning the gold in the Olympics is short lived. The amassing of great wealth leads to great worries. The healthiest body is one day ill. Nothing in this world is permanent. It is just that simple.

Most people accept this up and down adventure as the way things are, grasping at what they can, while they can. Thus, much of a lifetime is spent living in a consciousness of lack. Then, adding insult to injury, some are so driven by their desires that they cross the line of propriety and seek to take that which belongs to another. This grabbing for a moment of happiness leads inevitably to a pit of despair. And so we see the spiraling down of those who are caught by the negative flow.

The only constant source of happiness available to us is attunement to the positive flow of Spirit. It lives right within our own hearts. As long as we search for happiness, like that farmer, outside the home of our own superconsciousness, we will never find the diamond of contentment.

The tendency to seek fulfillment outside of ourselves is like having a chronic illness. It will never go away completely until we are free from desires, which can only be achieved through the attainment of Self-realization. Once we have understood this we can begin to help ourselves. Just like medication when the body is sick, we need something that we can take on a regular basis to minimize the symptoms of our illness.

The secret elixir that will keep us from the clutches of greed is the spirit of giving. When we express this expansive attitude we are attuning ourselves to the positive flow. By making a practice of sharing and expanding our sympathies to others, taking joy in the enjoyment of others rather than our own, we positively redirect our desire to receive. This will not only bring short term gains of good feeling, but it will help us to heal ourselves from our past indulgences.

There are few situations in life that are more nurturing to the spirit of giving than parenting. By the very act of serving as steward to a soul we are setting up endless opportunities for giving. This is one of the reasons parenting is so rewarding. Even people who do not understand this subtler view of what is going on in life are automatically blessed by the fact that parenting forces us to give and give and give. If seen in the right spirit this is never a burden but always a great opportunity.

Just as with speaking the truth, the habit of giving brings about its own reaction from the universe. Have you ever noticed that people with a giving nature are generally happy? Of course a person's ability to feel the joy of Spirit is affected by other areas of consciousness as well, but there is no question that those who are givers by nature or cultivate it until it becomes their nature are happier than those who hoard.

Infants will quickly show their tendencies from the past in this area. While it is true that at a young age grasping for oneself is one of the main modes of learning and communicating, there is an undercurrent of energy that can also be felt in the way babies approach the world. I am not suggesting that we label our children as greedy because we think that they are too grabby with their toys. I am encouraging you to reach in with your intuition and begin to understand the vibration of your child from the earliest stages. As infants, our children are less encumbered by the affectations of a new personality. This is a time when it is easier to sense their underlying tendencies from the past. In order to develop our ability to be in tune with our children it is helpful if we start sensitizing ourselves to their vibrational presence even while they are still in the womb.

As children reach out in their efforts to come to grips with themselves and the world around them it is quite probable that their desire to have something will at some time cross over the boundaries of good behavior. It could be anything from having a temper tantrum to actually stealing something. When dealing with these situations it is important that we find a solution that works for parent and child. If we try to impose a solution that does not work for both, a disharmony may result that will hinder further positive growth.

In the case of a child that steals we want to nip this tendency in the bud as quickly as possible. At the same time, we don't want to blow it up out of proportion so that it hurts our child's self-image. Stealing at a young age isn't evil, it is simply a negative act with negative repercussions. People who steal are not always bad people. They could be basically good people doing a bad thing. Through long term association with negative energies, they may become more powerfully negative themselves which can lead to becoming what we might loosely label as a bad person. If we keep in mind that we are all souls and not these temporary personalities we will be able to see that even in the darkest person there is hidden a spark of the Divine.

What you want to do is explore the situation with your child so that they understand the dynamics of what has happened. From the earliest age possible explain to your child about the positive and negative flows of life, the law of karma and the idea of doing unto others as we would have them do unto us.

Parents who just say, "Don't steal," and punish their child without furthering their education aren't getting as much mileage out of the situation as possible. They also may not be dealing with the underlying reasons why the child stole in the first place. Remember, redirect the energy, don't just go against it. Punishing a child by itself will not be as useful as dealing with the root energies that caused the problem in the first place.

If your child steals something from a store you might want to take them back to return it. Be sure to go with them. Let them know that you support them even though they must face the consequences of their actions. Embarrassment alone may keep them from repeating their actions.

Even more important then the reparations for any single incident are your efforts in helping your child to solve the reason why they did it in the first place. Sometimes people steal things simply because they don't have the money to buy them. If that is the case with your child, help them to earn their own money for times when you can't or feel you shouldn't buy an item. If it is an item that you don't approve of and they stole it to hide their possession of it from you, discussion and possibly some kind of compromise will be in order. If you can't agree with your child on the issue try to redirect their energy in a new more positive direction. If you are successful they will lose interest in the past through energetic involvement in the present.

When we redirect our child's energies in a positive way it is good for everyone. If we just shut them down with a flat no, we are going against their energies. This conflict can cause them to feel the desperation that can lead to stealing or other negative expressions of their frustration. I am not saying that there isn't a time for standing directly against a child's energy. We will discuss this in the chapter on loving discipline. For now, keep in mind that if we stand against them too often, not only will it stop working, we will lessen our ability to communicate with them successfully. This breakdown of communication is one of the most serious ways that we lose our ability to have a happy and healthy relationship with our children.

Once a person has let something like stealing develop from a one time experience into a negative tendency or even worse, a habit, it will take larger amounts of energy to deal with it. Usually there are a number of issues that add up to such a circumstance. Sometimes it is just a temporary weakness or reaction to negative influences. It could also be a tendency from the past that needs to be overcome. This is why constant vigilance is required by parents. If we are paying close attention to our children we can work on these challenges before they get out of control.

It is not our desires by themselves that causes us problems. Even more powerful is our attachment to our desires. This attachment can be directed positively if we seek to attain our desires in an honest way. But sometimes attachment to our desires can be so strong that like a bad dream, they haunt us. When this happens we need to shake ourselves free from the clutches of the desire. The first tendency is to think: Well, I'll just fulfill it and it will be over. But it doesn't always work that easily. If we are talking about a little desire, no problem, eat the ice cream or go to the movie. But if the desire is really strong one scoop or one movie may not be sufficient. What if you can't afford more?

For deep seated issues we will need to pull in all of the resources that we can. It may mean bringing in outside help like friends, relatives or professionals. Do not let a feeling of shame or embarrassment keep you from helping yourself or your child when help would really help. All people have difficulties of one kind or another. If life deals you a hand that you need help with it is your duty as a parent to try and seek help.

No matter what the area of life in which we are challenged we should turn to the powers of the positive flow in order to attain victory. When you feel the tentacles of desire reaching out to enfold you, magnetize yourself with the techniques that we have been talking about. Create such a strong positive magnetism that the little mosquitoes of desire can't touch you.

If we can teach our children to enjoy what they see and do, without the bond of attachment, we will help free them from the negative tendency of greed. It is not necessary to own something to enjoy it. If we can learn to appreciate what we see in this world without a need to draw it to ourselves, gradually we will realize that all of the world is our own. We can enjoy the pleasures of others – less the expense – though others. The best way to approach this world is to say simply, "What comes of itself, let it come." If we can travel through this life without being lured into limiting our happiness by endless desires, we will become ever-increasingly aware of the portable paradise that we carry within our own selves.

15

Non-Sensuality

In the search for happiness all people, no matter their ethnic origin, face the same overarching challenges. On the outside we all look different. On the inside we are all made from the same material – consciousness. Language, culture, social standing, psychological or physiological characteristics, none of these factors change the basic building blocks of the way we are all made.

In the conscious mind our source for information comes in through the senses. We interact with this world through sight, sound, touch, taste and smell.These sensory pathways move through our physical nervous system arriving eventually in our brain. Once in the brain a variety of chemical and electrical interactions take place to store and catalog these sensory impressions for future use. We are seeking to reach beyond the limits of this bological process.

The superconscious mind employs a more subtle method of perception – intuition. It is through intuition that we can perceive the vibrational qualities of life. It is through intuition that we can receive insight into the true nature of any experience, instead of just the "facts" that come through the conscious mind.

People who live only through the senses and the conscious mind are cutting themselves off from a source of undreamed of possibilities. If we do not develop our intuition we are handicapping ourselves. It is like a person who has lost their hearing. Sound still arrives at the listening post of their ears but the sound vibrations do not get translated and passed on to the brain. The love, joy and wisdom of the positive flow is always knocking at the door of our consciousness, but we must learn to hear it if we want to take advantage of its potential for good in our lives. Fortunately, intuition can not be broken like a physical body part; it can only be forgotten or ignored.

Why would we forget or ignore such an important capability? The answer to this question lies on both macroscopic and microscopic levels. In the larger scheme of things it is the battle between the positive and negative flows of the Creation that either helps us to be aware of our true nature and abilities or hides them from us. The forces of darkness are always at work trying to veil the true spiritual nature of life behind the mist of sense impressions. At the same time, the forces of light are just as diligently trying to enlighten us. Glimmers of our true soul potential are constantly being revealed in our lives. The forces of darkness try to convince us that these experiences or perceptions are anomalies and explained by the workings of chance or some strictly physical process.

On a more individual level it is our immersion in sense awareness that keeps us from perceiving greater realities through our intuition. Imagine the full moon reflecting on the still waters of a pond. The moon is the Divine ray of the positive flow that is always shinning on us. The pond is our consciousness. When our awareness is calm we can perfectly see and reflect our highest potential as part of the positive flow.

Now throw a pebble into the pond. The water ripples with outward moving rings. Just one pebble does not disturb greatly our ability to reflect the noon's rays. Now throw a pebble into the water for each sense impression that you receive during just one day. Then imagine all of the impressions of a year, a lifetime or a million lifetimes, Oh my!

You see, our awareness is cluttered up with an endless stream of impressions that reinforce our belief that we are physical beings. This is what creates the false impression that we are only physical. The light of Spirit has become so diffused by our sense awareness that while we can still catch glimpses of it, we doubt it is our true origin.

The power of this world to make us think that it is the sole reality is so strong that we ignore the most obvious signs that contradict that fallacy. What in this world of physical elements can explain love or joy? Where does the inspiration of new thought come from? Are they just a new combination of chemicals in the brain? How is it that people can grow from the mere desire to survive into people who will sacrifice all for others? These higher aspirations do not come from the elements of the physical world, they come from Spirit.

The senses themselves are not the evil characters of this play. They are just faithful servants. It is the part of our consciousness that labels how we react to this world that is the true culprit: feeling.

Here is how it works. There are four aspects to our consciousness: mind, intellect, ego and feeling. The mind is like that smooth pond or a mirror. It reflects that which shines upon it. There is no problem here.

The intellect catalogs that which is reflected in the mind; a tree, a house, a civilization. This is still no problem. Like a library, the intellect is impartial. All inputted information is welcome.

133

The ego identifies our relationship to all of the things that the intellect has stored; my house, your car, his boat. There is now a limiting identification to particular definitions. The ego is the soul identified with the body. We have placed limits on our perceptions. We have identified ourselves with the ripples on the water instead of the whole ocean. Yet even so, we are not yet tied to that point of view.

Now comes the real issue: feeling. Feeling is that which ties us to the things that we experience in this world. I <u>like</u> my body. I <u>do not like</u> his attitude. I <u>like</u> spinach. I <u>do not like</u> carrots. I <u>like</u> this and I <u>do not like</u> that. This is where we become tied to the ripples on the surface of our consciousness. We become bound by our experiences in this world through how we feel about them; our likes and dislikes or actions and reactions. This is how we fully buy in to the belief that we are the ripples on the surface and that there is no ocean.

The success of our attempts to live in the positive flow are directly connected to how we deal with this relationship between what we experience in life and how we feel about it. In the case of the senses we need to understand that the more we identify with the senses the more they will control our lives. As long as we think that happiness will be found through stimulation of the senses we will limit our perception of joy and bind our awareness to the ups and downs of life in the physical world.

The real kicker in all of this is that people who tie themselves to the senses actually experience life less intensely than those who live detached from the senses. It seems logical that if we enjoy something the more we indulge in it the more we will have of enjoyment. But sense awareness is actually diminished through overexposure. With smell you only get a few good wiffs. With taste the first bite is always better than the last. Touch also diminishes in intensity with duration of exposure. Because of this dulling process people who live in the senses are always moving from one indulgence to the next in an effort to keep things fresh and interesting. They seek to arrive at a place of satisfaction that always dissolves before they arrive.

Those who live unattached to the senses find that each experience is vivid, yet not binding. You can enjoy the taste of a fruit but not be unhappy when your are done eating. There is no compulsion to overindulge in order to create a feeling of happiness. Even more importantly, when we untie ourselves from the senses the waters of the mind become still again and we can once again experience the natural light and joy of Spirit.

It is only when the mind is calm that we can perceive the positive flow. That is why mediation is so important. Meditation techniques are specifically designed to calm the mind. Then through the utilization of the inner energies of the spine we can free ourselves from our bondage to past karma – which is our commitments of feeling.

While we work on ourselves from the inside our children will not be ready to consider doing these things until they choose to as they get older. In order to increase the possibility that they will become interested and to keep them from developing habits that will make their lives more difficult regardless of what they decide to pursue, we should nurture them in an environment of non-attachment to the senses. This doesn't mean that we will not enjoy outward experiences with them. What we want to do is transmit inwardly – and outwardly as opportunities present themselves – our understanding that it isn't "things" that makes us happy. Happiness is a flow of consciousness, within us, that we can tap into any time we are willing to make the effort to do so.

Our home life should reflect this understanding. Rather than seeing non-sensuality as a kind of restricting in our lives we should see it as a refinement. It is like the Japanese tradition of placing one item on display for everyone's enjoyment. After the item has been enjoyed for a while it is then replaced with another item. This simple way of enjoying life recognizes that too much clutter lessens our ability to appreciate life instead of increasing it.

Whether we are talking about furnishings, activities, toys, food, music and movies; a simple life is much more calming to the mind and satisfying to the soul then a complex one. Children that are constantly being bombarded with sensory input do not get enough time to assimilate it all. Then they get so used to this constant flow of sense stimulation they feel at a loss when it isn't there. As adults they end up living life the same way. Does that sound familiar?

Most adults realize that you can not just enjoy life all the time. You have to work, make a living and be responsible – which isn't always fun. But underneath the surface there is still that Peter Pan kind of desire for a never-ending, easy going, playful life. The negative side of that desire is just that, a desire to constantly indulge in likes and avoid dislikes. The positive root of that impulse is a soul knowledge that never-ending happiness is not only possible but our birthright. As children of Infinite Spirit we are all born to the infinite potential of experiencing ever-new joy as our reality.

By simplifying our lives not only are we lessening the tendency for over stimulation, but we are also providing time for assimilating and expressing the information that we have gathered.

Children need to spend much more time expressing the creative energies that flow through them naturally than taking in stimulation that eventually dulls their creativity. Young children haven't yet made firm the closing off of their connection to the inner flow through sense identification the way most adults have. The more time they spend exploring and identifying with this inner connection through creative expression of positive energies the happier they will be. Children who spend more time in almost any type of creative expression are invariably happier than those who just sit back and try to enjoy life through the senses. In fact, this is true for adults as well.

Since we can't avoid sense experiences altogether we must decide what type of sense experiences are beneficial and which are not. There is a world of difference between a casual stroll along a peaceful stream while the gentle warm breezes of summer blow through grassy mountain meadows and a walk through the business district of any large city. I am not suggesting that one is always good and the other always bad. I am just trying to point out that life presents us with a wide spectrum of possibilities. In order to find balance in our lives we need to understand how we are affected by various life experiences. With that knowledge we can then make conscious choices about how we want to live.

Our attempts to see life as a flow will help us in this evaluation process. Remember, we don't want to create a long list of do's and don'ts and hope our children will remember the list. We want to give them a way to evaluate each moment with its unique mixture of energies in a way that will help them to answer for themselves the question: What is the right thing to do?

The way we do this is to identify all things by their vibration. Earlier we talked about the three qualities: elevating, activating or downward-pulling. By using these directional signals we can evaluate the energies of any given situation or activity. Then once we know the type and strength of any energy, we can decide how it will affect us and how we feel about that affect.

Energies in life that are elevating help us to feel good about ourselves and others. They expand our interests and horizons. They can be energetic but it is a calm type of energy rather then agitating. Afterwards we feel peaceful and satisfied rather then mentally let down as a reaction to overstimulation.

Downward-pulling energies do just that, they make us feel lower and smaller. Actions that hurt others and places that have low vibrations are energies that make us more sense aware instead of identifying us with our higher self. Low energy is also downward-pulling. Sitting all day like a couch potato would be an example of downward-pulling energy.

Activating experiences can take us either toward elevating or downward-pulling. Games are generally activating. When they are played with an emphasis on beating your opponent they can actively pull us down. When they focus on the joy of wholesome competition, encouraging us to strive for our personal best in a spirit of cooperation, they can lift us up.

The key is learning to inwardly feel the vibration of a place, activity, item or action. When our children learn to recognize these underlying vibrations they will know for themselves what they are working with and how they might be affected by participation.

One year my son Kai tried out for little league and was placed on the team of an overly strict and demanding coach. The coach preached winning at all costs and mistakes were turned into public humiliation sessions. Kai decided to transfer to another team. He ended up having a lot of fun on the new team. His original team did end up winning the season that year. I asked him if he regretted switching. He shook his head with vigor like shaking off of buzzing bee, "No way dad, that guy was a jerk!"

While calling someone a jerk, even privately, isn't the nicest way to describe negative idiosyncrasies, I had to admit that I agreed with Kai's assessment of the coach. Kai had dealt with a difficult situation on his own, making a conscious choice to be around positive energies rather then negative energies. Some people say it isn't whether you win or not but how you play the game. Kai proved through his own choices the reality of that statement. As a parent I smiled inside and gave Kai a good pat on the back.

How affected we are by sensory input from the world at any time is also a question of how strong we are as individuals. The same activity might be no big deal for one child and a disaster for another. That is why we have to individualize our assessment of each situation. Thus the need to be plugged into the positive flow at all times.

Through an attunement to the vibrational texture of our lives we will be more able to see how we are doing and where things are going. A child that is a couch potato or even a book worm may need to get balanced with more activating activities. A child that is rough and tumble all of the time may need to do some reading or drawing. Listening to music can be balanced with times of silence or the sounds of nature. If you take a trip to the amusement park you might want to balance it with a trip to the beach or the mountains. In these ways we seek to balance our lives.

Balancing our lives into a simple flow of harmony is certainly one of the greatest challenges for a family. But it can be done. When the circumstances of our lives force us into complexity we should seek balance in the areas that we can control. If each day of the week is filled with many activities, rather than carrying that active energy into the weekend maybe quiet time would be indicated. Remember, it is easy for the mind to justify complexity when our feelings say, "Oh I really like that, let's don't stop doing that." Or when we

139

ourselves are so used to activity that we have forgotten how to slow down.

An honest evaluation of our lives will tell us where we can simplify. If we live our lives in the fast lane our children will take that as the measuring stick of their own lives. This is not to say that there aren't times when we need to get things moving. If everyone in the house is just sitting in front of the television all of the time, action is definitely indicated. In cases where individuals or whole families are caught by passivity, immersion in intense activity will do much good.

In these ways we can look at each part of our lives to consciously decide what we should or shouldn't do. The alternative is to let outside forces make our decisions for us. Conscious awareness of how we are affected by stimulation of the senses is just the first step. Then we must do something about those perceptions.

If a child has gotten hooked on an activity that can be over stimulating - as sometimes happens with video games - their energies should be creatively redirected. As a parent it is our responsibility to help our children face these issues. The exciting thing about all of this is that once a child starts to recognize these energies for themselves they will realize that they are happier when they act in balance. Then, their own desire for happiness will lead them toward the right activities. When that happens, we will know that we have done our job.

16

Non-Covetousness

It is fairly easy to understand the advantages of not being attached to things that are not our own. In the chapter on non-greed we talked about the problems that can arise when we desire that which is not ours. Not only do we make ourselves unhappy through the consciousness of lack, but we can get ourselves into an even unhappier state if our attempts to gain our desires causes us to connect to the negative flow. In this chapter we are going to look at the way that we relate to things that we already have in our possession. Actually, it is that word possession that lies at the center of the issue.

In the processing of our experiences here on earth, through the ego, we attach a kind of relativity to our lives: my thoughts, your thoughts, my body, her body, his house, my house. These identifications let us know what belongs to whom. On the positive side, we understand that we have responsibility for certain things in this world. We need to care for that which is in our "possession". On the negative side, there is a misconception that often accompanies this sense of responsibility: the thought that things which are mine, are mine.

This little twist on the way we view our lives can create untold suffering for us. Even if we happen to be satisfied with our lot in life – which most people are not – and we do not limit our happiness by desiring things that we do not already have – which few people do – we place a damper on our inner freedom and potential for joy if we become attached to that which we already do have.

Here is an example of what I am talking about.

Through the magic of television the thoughts and feelings of people around the world can be brought right into our homes. As we will discuss later in more detail, this ability to know what others are going through from a distance has opened up new avenues of understanding. Unfortunately, one of the things that news coverage thrives on is disaster. It is almost impossible to turn on any national or local news program without hearing about some extremely unpleasant experience that has happened to someone. There is nothing that producers like more then capturing the tears of agony on the face of a person faced with disaster.

One of the most frequent images in this never ending stream of difficulties is that of a family who's home has been destroyed by fire. There are few losses that are so all encompassing to a family. Not only do you lose your home, but you lose the many irreplaceable mementos that you have gathered through a lifetime. It can be a real shock. The mental anguish on those tear-covered faces carries the impact for which television is always looking. Can you imagine a person losing everything in a fire and smiling? Or laughing?

In 1976, a couple who are close friends of mine gave birth to their son. As you can imagine they were thrilled. Less then a month later their home with literally everything they owned except the clothes on their backs was burnt to the ground by a forest fire. The next morning while surveying the ashes my friend John was heard to say with a smile, "Well, I guess I won't have to worry about fixing those leaky windows now!"

His good spirits amidst what could only be described from the outside as a family tragedy stands in sharp contrast to the sobs of grief that you see on television. Some people might say that John is a very special individual to be able to face difficulties like that. It is true, he is special. But he isn't special because he is alone, he is special because he has freed himself from attachment to that which is rightfully his own.

As it happens, John and his wife Devi were not alone in the testing of their non-attachment. Of the twenty-one homes in the small community in which they live, that fire destroyed twenty. Yet, John was not the only one seen laughing the next day. How is it that more than one non-attached soul could be struck by the same fire? John lives in a community where people are consciously trying to live, all of the time, in the positive flow of life. Non-attachment to that which you already have is one of the secrets to living in the positive flow.

So if all of these folks are so positive, why did all of their houses burn down? Karma is an intricate and often obscure process. For those who live in tune with the joy of Spirit the source of our tests, while important for the avoidance of making the same mistake again, aren't nearly as important as how we deal with the situation now. Certainly some past karma caused this fire to happen. The good spirits with which it was met minimized the negative impact that it might have had and maximized the positive potentials of the situation. Invariably those who went through the experience with a positive attitude saw it as the doorway to a better life instead of a harbinger of future hardship.

Of the people that I know whose homes were destroyed, I am not aware of anyone who tried to save their own home. They were all fighting to save the homes of others. This type of spirit is the hallmark of those who live untouched by bondage to their possessions. They recognize their responsibility to care for that which they have, but they are not overly attached to it.

This view of life and the inner freedom that it brings is so contradictory to the views of the materialist that many simply disbelieve it. They can not imagine that non-attachment to your own possessions will help one to be happy. This is the way that the dust of desire clouds the window of the soul. The soul's potential for infinite joy is confined to the sorrows of attachment.

The attitude of non-attachment should be brought into every corner of our lives: job, home, recreation, relationships, even our own bodies. Everything should be seen for its true reality as a part of God. As such, we do not own or have the rights to anything. We have the stewardship of our responsibilities in life to be fulfilled as we are guided by our inner connection to intuitive understanding.

As our children grow we want them to understand that the reason we act responsibly in the world is not so that we can become more bound to the specifics of our lives, but so that we can be free from those specifics. It is in that freedom that we can experience an inner peace and joy that will be untouched by the ups and downs that come to all lives. Even the Saints are tested mightily. They have all sorts of problems. But they meet each one with an unshakable equanimity that can only come from non-attachment and an awakened awareness of God's all succoring presence.

When we covet our possessions or even the ways that we are used to living, we are the one's that become possessed.

As you explore these attitudes with your children help them to differentiate between positive non-attachment and the negative qualities associated with irresponsibility. Non-attachment is not an "I don't care" attitude. On the contrary, we care very much when we are non-attached. We care about truth. Laziness or lack of attention to our efforts in this world are downward-pulling energies. They represent the negative flow. We need to give every facet of our lives our best efforts, then give the results to God. When we know we have done our best we have fulfilled our responsibilities. Only then can we see non-attachment in its proper perspective.

If a child has been working on a project for some time and gives up before it is completed you might say they are non-attached. You might also say they can't follow a project through to completion. The core issue has to do with which way their energy is going. Is their energy going up or down? When we are non-attached the energy is up, we are moving forward in a flow of positive energy. Quitting a project because it is taking too much effort is a downward moving energy. In a case like that you might suggest taking a break and then continuing on to completion.

Building blocks and legos are a good example of toys that can help develop non-attachment. When something is made and enjoyed for a while it is then taken apart to become something new. Using this as an example when your child is old enough to understand will help them to understand the idea of not being attached to things.

Another thing that can be seen with these types of building materials is how much longer it takes to build things then to tear them down. Children often take delight in knocking down their creations. Mostly it is just fun to watch the blocks go flying. But sometimes there is a note of harshness that can enter the moment. Especially when a child knocks down the efforts of others. Watching for this kind of down-ward-flowing energy and re-directing it is very important. The more a child indulges in negative energies the more they will feel accustomed to them. I am not suggesting that we overreact to every little thing, but attentiveness and nipping negative energies in the bud can save both child and parent much frustration.

Sharing is a practice that when developed early in life will sprout many helpful qualities. The expansive identification with others is an essential part of the maturing process. When we covet our possessions we close ourselves off from others. This limits our potential for happiness. When we cultivate a giving nature we can experience joy not only in ourselves, but also in the joy of others.

Much of what is happening during the maturing process is that a child's ability to relate to other people's realities is growing. In fact one of the best signs of a positively mature person is their ability to relate to and act on the needs of others. The only way that we can develop this in ourselves and our children is to practice it. The perception part of our formula addresses this directly. We want to live in the habit of inwardly reaching out to touch the needs of others.

Very young children are so caught up in their own growing identities that they have difficulty perceiving the needs of others. At this stage all we can do is work with supporting their positive energies as much as possible. Making a habit of explaining what is going on from the very beginning will help us as parents to develop good communication skills. We may also find that our children understand what we are saying much sooner than we might have expected. As a practical overflow of this habit our children will learn to speak more quickly through this direct verbal communication with them. If we share our observations about

146

the energies underneath all life experiences with our children they will grow up with this perspective as a part of the way they think.

As children grow and become more comfortable with who they perceive themselves to be they will begin to reach out and explore the needs of others. We should encourage this as much as possible. Help your child to notice some of the little signals that can point to what will help others. It could be a child that isn't being included in the group activity or a person who doesn't yet have a plate of food. Picking up an item that has been dropped and returning it to the owner is a good one. Make a practice of noticing and pointing out to your children these observations that they might not have noticed. You can even make a game out of it so that there is a spirit of fun involved. This might help to avoid the possibility of this process becoming a negative form of judging.

When selfish people walk into a room they are thinking only of themselves. When selfless people walk into a room they are inwardly reaching out and feeling the needs of others.

People who do not reach out in these ways get caught in the labyrinth of their own ego's and may never fully mature in this life. There are many "adults" running around this world with the small-minded self-involvement of a little child. This lack of maturity is often the result of not having received the necessary training in more positive directions during their formative years. Once a person accepts the status quo of their consciousness and becomes set in their ways it is much more difficult to make changes. Thus we can see the value of keeping the garden of our child's consciousness as free as possible from the weeds of negative attitudes from the very beginning.

It is only through sensitivity to our own mental culture and the development of an intuitive connection with our children that we can monitor these energies effectively. Once we are aware of how things are going we can subtly work our formula as each situation unfolds. This awareness of opportunities to help others can be life changing.

Even in this process of nurturing our children we have to be watchful for over attachment to the way we think things should be going. If everything is not progressing as we think it should, stand back from the situation and see it – as clearly as possible – for what it is. It may take our children longer than we would like to understand what we are trying to communicate to them. There are even some negative qualities that they may express that we will not be able to change in them. In those cases, we don't want our frustration to overcome the good that we are doing in other areas. So stay non-attached while you always push forward optimistically.

As parents it is not possible to be the do all, end all, positive force in the lives of our children. For some parents it is a great test of non-attachment to let others help their children. If you are tested in this way, remember that they aren't your children, they are children of the Infinite. If you become aware of a way in which others can help your child don't let your attachment to them or a false sense of pride keep you from letting others help. We are never diminished by the positive support of others; we are expanded in the knowledge that the universe is responding to our needs through others.

God's Creation is truly ingenious in its ability to throw us for a loop, to provide unexpected thrills and spills. Through the cultivation of non-covetousness we will free our-selves from the clutches of bondage that the things closest to us in our lives can sometimes bring. Through this inner free-dom we will actually increase our ability to appreciate the gifts of life.

148

When we are free from over involvement in our own point of view we will increase our ability to sense the needs of others. Through this greater sensitivity we will not only be able to help others more effectively, we will be able to perceive the effects of that help. Enjoying life with a balanced view through our own lives is fine. Even better is expanding that view to see life through the eyes of all. No longer limited to just one view we will begin to become identified with the infinite view of omnipresence.

17

Cleanliness

The often quoted statement, cleanliness is next to Godliness, is generally accepted as truth. Have you ever wondered why? Certainly many children being sent to wash up before dinner or to take a bath have wondered if God actually feels this way. Of the many precepts that have been handed down through the halls of religious traditions this is possibly the one that the greatest variety of traditions would agree on. Some people have latched on to this precept so strongly as to think that just by making things physically nice and tidy in this world we have done our part in stepping God's way; now the rest is up to Him.

The easiest way to explain the popularity of this saying has to do with health. People have found that when we keep things physically clean we live longer. Since few will argue with the efficacy of staying alive as long as possible, everyone can agree. Adding God's approval may very well be for many simply a convenient way to add authority to their requests for cleanliness. I might have left my own understanding of this subject on the surface of its potential, simply a call to physical clarity, except that I had an experience that opened me up to a much deeper view of cleanliness.

Some years ago I went to a special spiritual ceremony. When I arrived most of the group was already assembled. They were all sitting quietly under a canopy of stately oak trees. In prayerful mood everyone was inwardly communing with Spirit. Being in a bit of a rush to arrive my thoughts were more focused on getting to the ceremony on time then the actual purpose of the ceremony.

As I walked around the corner of a building and came upon the group I was suddenly inwardly aware of the groups vibrational presence. It was like being struck by an actual force. I immediately stopped and opened myself up inwardly to perceive deeply what was going on. As the vibrations of the group washed through my perceptions I was intuitively aware that this is what is meant by the word holy.

Even though I had been on the spiritual path for many years I had never been truly aware of Spirit in this context. Certainly people talk about that which is "Holy" but I had always thought it was more of a sentiment rather than an actual quality of consciousness that could be experienced.

Cleanliness in body, mind and spirit is closely linked to the quality of Holiness. Remember when we talked about the window of our consciousness? How it has been covered with the dust of our desires? When the window is clean the Divine Presence shines through us. That Divinity transcends the idea of cleanliness and enters the much deeper realm of Holiness.

I am sure that all of the people at that ceremony were physically clean. I could easily see that they were wearing clothes they saved for special occasions. The natural setting under a twilight sky was also beautiful. But we have all been in beautiful places with well-dressed people: Physical beauty and cleanliness do not automatically bring us closer to God.

We have talked a lot about the magnetism that all things radiate – their vibration. It is in the magnetic vibration of all things that we can find whether they are clean or dirty. This is another reason that inner attunement is so central to living in the positive flow. Until we can sense these subtle energies we are left strictly with the outward signals. It is easy to tell outwardly when a place is dirty. But there are many places and people that look clean on the outside that are dirty on the inside.

What do I mean by dirty?

I am talking about those qualities of consciousness that limit us from expressing our divinity. Physically it is actions that cause or encourage disease. These are actions that tie us in a downward-pulling way to the body. Mentally it is thoughts that make us more aware of the ego instead of Spirit. These kinds of thoughts encourage separateness instead of unity. They emphasize a feeling of superiority over others and support the taking of personal pleasure at the cost of others suffering. Spiritually it is those things that darken our attunement with the positive flow. When we see all life as material and meaningless we have lost sight of our home in Spirit. Then the dirt of limitations darkens the window of our soul and we find ourselves living in the limiting cage of the ego.

Since all of these levels are connected the most central thing that we can do is to cleanse ourselves in mediation. With the higher practices of mediation we are actually cleaning the astral body by releasing commitments of energy that we have gathered from the past. This inward sweeping action in the spine helps us to cleanse the whole of our consciousness rather than working on one vortex of energy at a time. That is why living in the positive flow helps all aspects of our lives and not just one specific area.

Through the increasing of our inner awareness of the energies around us we will be able to feel the vibrational cleanliness of any given object or situation. We have all met people who make you feel "unclean" just by being with them. Why? Because by being near them we have bathed in the energy field of their vibrations. If we are strong they won't affect us as much.

If we are weak it may take some time to clean their vibrations out of our consciousness.

It is even helpful if we avoid shaking hands with those who we feel have dark vibrations. When we shake hands with others we are exchanging vibrations. If you must shake hands with people you don't know or those that you do not feel in tune with be a force for good instead of shrinking back. If you mentally withdraw, the magnetism of the other person will be stronger than yours and possibly affect you negatively. By becoming a beacon of good energy and sending positive energy out your hand to the souls of others you will protect yourself, as well as, possibly helping others.

It is essential that we do not have a judgmental attitude while we seek to understand the qualities of energy in life around us. If our efforts to feel the vibrations of others puff up our ego's we are defeating our own purpose.

Because of these exchanges of vibration I would caution you against letting just anyone hold your child. Always inwardly feel the vibration of a person before indicating your approval. If you do not feel a person's vibrations are compatible, seek to find a respectful and polite way of avoiding it. While we don't want to negatively separate ourselves from others we need to practice skills of positive discrimination. This is not a form of racial, cultural or stylistic discrimination, which expresses a negatively limited view of outward physical attributes. This is a process of seeing underneath those outward differences to feel the vibrational essence of life, which will enable us to make a positive choice, based on that perception. You wouldn't bathe your child in a mud puddle would you? In that same way we don't want to vibrationally bathe our children in negative energies. It doesn't do us much good to recognize a higher path in life if we don't follow it.

The positive side of this is that when you meet someone who you want to emulate in some way try to arrange to touch them. When you shake their hand try to consciously draw their positive qualities of consciousness through their hand into your consciousness. Do you remember in the bible when a woman touched Jesus as he was working his way through a crowd? Jesus turned and asked, "Who has touched me?" He had felt the energy being drawn out of him through her touch. She believed that by just touching Him she would be healed and so it was true. She had magnetically drawn out of Jesus the healing she sought.

Most people will not, like Jesus, be aware that you are trying to consciously draw inward energies from them. But these magnetic exchanges of energy can be powerful influences on our consciousness. This is one of the reasons that we should carefully choose our associates and those of our children.

Even people who are basically good vibration people can leave us feeling unclean inside if the conversation dips into thoughts that tap the negative flow. We can also make ourselves unclean, and thus negatively affect others, when we express thoughts that are not of the highest nature. This is true not only with the subjects that we discuss but also the words that we use to communicate our thoughts.

Swearing is a good example of this. Swearing as a habit is not beneficial to us. Swear words are even called dirty words. A commonly used remedy for swearing in a child is washing the mouth out with soap. Why is there this instinctive sense that swear words are dirty? Why not just generically bad? Things that are dirty actually coat us with their dirt. When we swear we are coating our vibration with lower energies. This coating attracts other lower energies. People who swear a lot are generally less sensitive to others. They live more in their own egos. Swearing and put down consciousness often go hand in hand.

People who swear a lot can lose their ability to find words that truly describe what they are trying to communicate. In extreme cases you find that almost every word is a swear word. All of life becomes one endless stream of a few words that view life in the basest way. People who swear like this are said to have a gutter mouth.

This does not mean that an occasional swear word isn't appropriate for spicing things up at the right time. Nor am I suggesting that people be prudish about life and unduly offended by the colorful language of others. We simply want to recognize that even within the realm of swearing there is a big difference between an occasional use of the word damn and a regular use of the other terms that are generally considered swear words.

I remember hearing some years ago about a reputedly saintly person who often used swear words. Following their leader's example many of the disciples also indulged in this practice. I have never met this spiritual leader so I can not comment on their "Saintliness", but there are a couple of stories that I can share on this subject that might be helpful.

There was once a saintly soul who felt that he was not supposed to be around people. In order to keep people away he had the habit of throwing rocks at anyone who came too close. He was not trying to hurt anyone. He just wanted to discourage people from approaching. Most of the time people kept their distance. Some people occasionally yelled curses at the saint for his rudeness. One devoted man decided that the saint was his teacher, so when a rock came his way he caught it up and kept it. That night the disciple placed the rock on his meditation room altar. The next morning he found that the rock had turned into gold. In this way we can see that even the rocks - or difficulties - that life gives us can turn into blessings if we have the right response to them.

This also reminds us that life is not always what it appears to be on the surface. This is why we are always seeking to feel the energies underneath our life experiences.

I used to get upset inside when I heard someone swearing with words like, "God Damn it!" or "Jesus Christ!". At first I definitely had a holier than thou attitude. I had a classic "How dare you take the Lord's name in vane!" attitude. I mentally put down those who were swearing in this way. But gradually, I began to see how my reaction was making me negative too, just in a different way.

By applying our formula I came up with a different take on the situation. Now when I hear someone taking the Lord's name in vain I hear the sweetness of God's name. Regardless of where it comes from the name of God reminds me of my positive inner connection rather than the other person's negative expression. This doesn't mean I go around seeking people who act this way. But when it crosses my path their very attempts to degrade life turn for me into a praise of it. I redirect their negative energies into a positive direction.

This is key to dealing with all of the hardships that we find in life. Avoid negativity if you can, but if you can't then turn it into a blessing. It is not always easy but there is always a way.

Negative emotions can also be dirtying to the soul. Jealousy, vengefulness, pride, even over sentimentality; these separate us from others and our basic oneness in Spirit. Any kind of moodiness means that we are being controlled by an emotional vortex not natural to the soul. When this happens we should cleanse ourselves of the mood by increasing our energy flow in a positive direction. With children you can get them up and active. Vigorous exercise can clean away many types of moods. Choosing an activity that emphasizes cheerfulness is one idea. For young children it is hard to play ring around the rosy and stay glum. If that does not work then keep trying. Activities in nature are almost always uplifting. Sometimes just getting up and out of the house will do the trick.

Positive thinking can also change our energy. In younger children audio tapes of happy songs might help. In older children actually verbally affirming positive energy and good thoughts is worth a try.

When my daughter, Sabari, was in the 3rd grade she occasionally was moody during class. Her teacher experimented with a number of ideas to deal with this tendency. The one that helped was asking her to vigorously walk in place saying, "I am awake and ready, I am awake and ready!" Then she would swing her arms to the sides, front and above saying with these motions, "I am positive, energetic and enthusiastic!" These affirmations and their corresponding physical movements were very effective. I even found her doing them on her own at home when she caught herself dipping into a mood.

This last example is at the heart of what we are trying to do. Children will help themselves to do the right thing in many situations if we give them workable tools and show them how to use them.

Habits of cleanliness on all levels should be practiced at all times. Just like dental hygiene the habits of cleanliness of body, mind and spirit that we develop in our youth can make the rest of life that much healthier. Many a parent and child has wished during the later years of life that more attention was given to caring for the teeth. We must not think that these things will take care of themselves. It is only through regularity of effort that we can improve ourselves and help our children. Just like an athlete, we are either getting stronger or weaker. In life there is no staying the same. Through the regular cultivation of these positive precepts our ability to reach beyond our current limitations of consciousness will be greatly increased.

18

Contentment

Of all the virtues that we are discussing contentment is considered supreme. Why? Because unless a person has cultivated the positive qualities of consciousness that we have be discussing contentment is but a dream. When you have contentment you will be, whether you are consciously aware of it or not, manifesting the other virtues of positive mental culture in your life. The degree of relative contentment that we experience in life is determined by our ability to express these positive qualities on a daily basis. Until true contentment is achieved the mind will fluctuate between the various flavors of happy or sad that are generally associated with the human condition.

Most people will admit that they are not content with life. Difficulties, worries and disappointments have kept their happiness in check. Of those who claim they are content with their lives: What does that mean to them? That they have resigned themselves to their lot? That they have accepted that their most idealistic dreams will not be achieved? That the basics of existence having been met, this is all one can expect? Or that the lack of overwhelming pain is sufficient to say one is content?

Without the soaring of the soul in an ever-expanding awareness of the positive flow and its endlessly intoxicating variety there is no such thing as contentment. True contentment is a dynamic state of consciousness not a passive, well it is all over now, resignation. Nor is it an, I will just ignore life attitude.

It is not that people never feel good about their lives. They do. But most people also have periods of sadness and disappointment. This, some good, some bad duality of experience is what makes life interesting. Can you imagine a good story where nothing ever goes wrong? It wouldn't be a very exciting story. At the same time, the soul after many, many incarnations begins to long for a resolution to this never-ending melody. Even an interesting song must eventually come to an end. Contentment is what we will experience when we finally get there.

Along the way, while we develop our inner awareness of Spirit, we will need to adjust the way that we view our lives in order to minimize the way that the world around us can negatively affects us. If a calm mind is necessary for reflecting God's light, then when our minds are made restless by the ups and downs that we experience in daily life we will be stepping back with each step forward.

The times that most people will say they are content is when they have just completed some task or experience. The positive side of this is that after you have exerted yourself mentally or physically – hopefully at a noble task – you can sit down with the feeling of having accomplished something. You feel content. The negative side is when you have over-indulged in something like, well, let's say Thanksgiving dinner. You sit down, stomach bulging, tune the television to a football game and say, "I am content!"

In either case, the one thing that you can say for sure is that the feeling is temporary. When the game is over or when you need an antacid or when your next task presents itself, the feeling of contentment will be replaced with another feeling. So what do we do?

Let me tell you a surfing story.

When I was a teenager I lived in southern California. Like many of my generation in that part of the world I decided that surfing was just what I needed. Even though I fractured my jaw on my first surfing excursion, I had also ridden my first wave and the exhilaration of that ride was greater than the discomfort of my jaw.

Years of effort were necessary for me to get very good at surfing. It is not an easy sport to just arrive at the beach and be good at. One of the difficulties is that you have to get the hang of several essential skills just so that you can have an opportunity to ride a wave. Paddling out while the waves try to push you in is the first step. Once you get out beyond where the waves break you have to learn to sit on your surfboard, one leg on each side, as if you were riding a horse. That might sound easy but if you have ever tried it you know that most people who are just beginning fall off regularly just trying to sit out there.

Once learning to sit on the surfboard you must learn where the right place is to catch the waves. If you sit too far out you will not be able to catch a wave. If you sit too far in they will crash on your head.

Learning to actually catch a wave is yet another skill. Timing, positioning and balance are all essential. Only once you have successfully caught a wave can you try to stand up and ride it. No matter how good or bad you are you will eventually make a mistake and fall off. If you are a beginner falling off will be the norm for a long time.

In the days when I started surfing if you fell off your surfboard you had to swim into shore to retrieve it. Today surfers use a leash to attach the surfboard to their ankle,

160

thus avoiding a long swim into shore. Swimming in for your surfboard was a big part of surfing. It still is for those who ride big waves.

Like most other surfers, all I really wanted to do was ride waves. But in order to do so there was endless paddling, wiping out and swimming. It was exhausting. Sometimes I would wonder why I was willing to put out so much effort. Then I would catch one good wave and all those bad thoughts were washed away in a euphoria that would last for weeks. For those few great rides I would put up with weeks, sometimes months, of struggle.

As the years passed I graduated not only from high school but also from the waves of California to the waves of Hawaii. It was on the island of Kauai that I discovered the secret that I want to share with you. Not that my discovery was new information, it was just new to me.

On the northwestern side of Kauai there is a large bay called, Hanalei. It is incredibly beautiful. It is also one of the greatest surfing spots in the world. At the right time of the year you can ride waves 3 to 5 times as tall as a person for half a mile or more. It is quite a ride!

In order to ride these waves you have to be in excellent condition, know your way around the ocean and be a little nuts. By the time I arrived at Hanalei Bay I was a pretty good candidate, especially in the nuts department. When the waves are big they break so far out that it can take 30 minutes or more of hard paddling just to get out to where you can try to catch a wave.

Once you arrive outside of where the waves are breaking you find that the waves are so big that even though you are out there for the "fun" of it, you can't help questioning your sanity. On those big days, if you got a good ride you were out of your mind with excitement. It is simply the most thrilling thing that can be done physically – or at least that is how surfers feel. If you wiped out you had to survive an incredibly long swim in to the beach while you were being half drowned by the waves. Once at the beach you had to hope you would find your surfboard there. I had two surfboards that were washed out to sea while I was swimming in. One of them I recovered 5 miles down the coast. The other was lost forever.

Surfing at Hanalei Bay took so much effort that I began to spend most of my time unhappy. Paddling out was not fun. Wiping out was not fun. Swimming in was not fun. Only riding waves was fun. And even the fun of riding waves was limited to whether I got what I would consider a good ride. Thus, most of my time surfing was no longer fun.

One day I decided to re-evaluate my outlook. It took me a while to figure out what to do about it but eventually I came up with a solution. I decided that if I wanted to enjoy myself all of the time I had to enjoy everything that I do. That is the only way it was going to really work.

It took me some time to implement this new approach to surfing. Each time I caught myself starting to get negative I looked for some rewarding feature in my current circumstances. The long paddle out became an opportunity to get into top condition and enjoy the incredible beauty of the environment. The scenery, the light on the ocean surface, other surfers riding waves, I absorbed the beauties of each part of the whole.

I had always approached riding the waves with an attitude of harmony rather than trying to conquer them. Now I went even further and gave less worry to my performance and more attention to the wholeness of the ride. When I wiped out on a wave I began to enjoy the ride of being tossed about by the churning waters. I appreciated the power of the waves. I developed an appreciation for the challenge of holding my breath for long periods. Swimming in became a challenge of survival which I began to face with confident strokes.

In these ways I transformed what had become drudgery into never ending entertainment and self-improvement. By living in the moment and bringing a positive frame of mind to every experience I disengaged from all of the negative points of view and enjoyed whatever was happening.

Soon I began to apply this same approach to every part of my life. I realized that if I wanted to be happy it was up to me. As a good friend of mine often says, "If you want to be sad, nothing in this world can make you happy. If want to be happy, nothing in this world can make you sad." It is up to us. Do we want to plug into the positive flow of joy that is always available to us? Or do we want to go with the times? Happy with the ups and sad with the downs.

The key to contentment is consciously making the decision to live in the positive flow of each moment. When we do this we free ourselves from the unpleasantness that we associate with tasks that we don't like. We also will learn not to overreact to the good times, which creates the need for a balancing let down.

Learn to be even-minded and cheerful. This is the goal. Through our good feeling in all situations we will be radiating to our children the very best that life has to offer. Our example will encourage and magnetize them to do like-wise.

During each stage of your child's development you should look for ways you can help them to see the good in all situations. Learning to have a positive outlook even during difficult circumstances is key to being happy in life. As the little ups and downs of youth progress use them as opportunities to train your child in the art of even-mindedness. Help them to laugh when things get tough. If we always buy into their disappointments they will never have reason to reach beyond them. Then, what will they do when they are out on their own?

Little tasks around the house can be used as a testing ground for positive attitude development. If you find your child grumbling about chores help them to redirect their energies. Point out to them that they are making things worse for themselves because of their attitude. Give some suggestions as to how they can look at things differently. Or better yet, ask them to think of ways themselves. Go through the process with them. Nudge them here or there as needed. Ask them to experiment. When they do the results will be there. They may not choose to have the right attitude all of the time but in these ways we will be showing them how to improve their lives if they choose to.

Some children catch on quickly to this and do not have any problems. Others need long term attention. Sensitivity is the key from the parents perspective. Knowing when to push and when to look the other way, when to hug and when to discipline, these questions can only be answered by you in the moment.

Your own solidarity in the peace and joy of the positive flow will provide you with the best possible perspective from which to help your child. As you develop an ever-greater awareness of that flow contentment will fill your own being and spill out onto your whole family.

The soul that is truly rooted in the inner sanctum of Spirit is unshakable. There is no greater power for good that you can bring to your children, your family and the world in general, than the act of living in harmony with the positive flow of Spirit.

19

Self-Control

How many people have started the new year with a resolution to improve some part of their life? I would guess that the number is quite high. Now, how many of us follow through with these resolutions? Need I say more on the subject of our need for self-control?

Not only do most of us have trouble facing the big battles in life, we are constantly struggling with many of the little challenges in life. It should not be hard to eat less, yet people spend millions of dollars each year to help themselves lose weight. We all know that exercise is important, but many of us do not get enough of it. Each of us can see many ways in which we might improve ourselves, yet we often do not act on that knowledge.

When our children become adults will they have the same difficulties as those who have come before them? If you consider that the basic issues in life do not change all that much from generation to generation our children will face the same types of challenges that we do. The only difference will be on the surface of the details. As adults our children will have ups and downs, good times and bad. Life is a school. Even though it may appear that many people are skipping their classes, we are not here on vacation!

If we consider that as time goes by mankind as a whole evolves and learns more about how to live successfully in this world our children will have the opportunity to take advantage of new information as it develops. We are able to use information that our parents did not have available. Yet even with all of this new knowledge it seems like each generation has similar problems. Children write home for more money, co-workers engage in negative office politics, couples argue, teens rebel, retired people lose their purpose, the battle with the bulge is faced on the scale each day, these are underlying issues that each generation must face in their own individual ways. Since there is little chance that we can remove all of these challenges from our children's lives what we want to do is give our children the best possible chance of facing there own version of these challenges successfully. We need to get them in shape for the battle of life.

Let's face it, life is not easy. We can always hope that our children will live without tragedy or hardship but we can not guarantee it. What we can do is give them the kind of training that will help them to face whatever challenges life brings them.

Each of us comes into this life with qualities that we have brought from past incarnations. Some of these qualities will be strong and others will be weak. Some will be helpful positive qualities while others will be hindering negative qualities. One of the great things about living in the positive flow is that while we are strengthening our good qualities we are automatically pulling the rug out from underneath many of our negative qualities.

If we spend our time cultivating positive attitudes, negative attitudes will not have anyplace to hang their hat.

The key is to make the positive parts of our lives really strong. When we do this many of our little problem areas will fall away through neglect. Middle-sized problems will have trouble keeping up – thus becoming weaker and easier to deal with. We will end up having more energy to deal with the big problems in life because the other parts of our lives won't be picking at us all of the time.

Everything that we have been talking about is part of that strengthening process. In order to implement many of our creative strategies by applying just the right energy at just the right time we will need to develop self-control. It is not always easy to hold your tongue when your child does something to irritate you. At the same time, we need to remember that children are just getting themselves going in their new bodies. We need to be patient with them. Through patience we will begin to see the longer rhythms in our child's development, as well as our own.

The key to self-control is building on success. When we have achieved something small we can move up to larger goals. If a weakling goes in to fight a champion it may take a miracle just to survive. We need to consciously build up the strength of our will power, our "Yes!" saying power, before we test it too strenuously. Some parents are worried about being over protective. They feel that a child must see the "real world". But if you ask a little child to climb Mt. Everest they won't have much of a chance. First we need to evaluate where our child is now and then gradually build them up with bigger challenges.

A good example of this is parents who let their young children watch R-rated movies. These movies are rated for a reason. Yet, in the name of not wanting to get a babysitter or thinking that they are exposing their children to the real world – which seems strange when you consider that most movies bear little resemblance to the world as we live in it – they barrage their children with issues and energies that they can not possibly be ready to deal with. By doing this these parents are pushing the chicks out of the nest earlier then their undeveloped wings can handle. (We will talk more about moves later, this is a multi-faceted issue).

One of the binds that many people get into when they determine to take a new course of action in life is that they over do it. On the first day of a new exercise plan in their enthusiasm they go at it too hard and so for the next few days they are very sore. The soreness dims their momentum and in a week or two they have given up. Diet is another area that people are constantly struggling with, as proven by the many products that people buy in hopes of getting around the basic issue of eating less and exercising more.

When we are trying to stop or start a habit there are two main factors at work. There is the part of us that says, "Yes, I want to make this change!" and there is the part of us that says, "No, I like things the way they were!" I want to loose weight but I do not want to eat less. I want to wake up earlier but I do not want to go to bed earlier or sleep less. I want to spend more time with my kids but when I get home from work I'm tired.

These two energies are not just symbolic metaphors. They are actual magnetic forces in our consciousness. This is the law of magnetism at work. If we want to defeat the negative magnets, instead of trying to short circuit them one by one we can in effect weaken them all by making our positive qualities much stronger.

It is the same for our children. As they struggle with learning the ropes in their new bodies they are being magnetically influenced. These influences come from both their past and their present environment. This early part of life, while their old tendencies have momentarily lost some of their power and their awareness is open to new possibilities,

168

is a gold mine of opportunities for transforming their consciousness. If we can help them to develop their strength of mind by applying it vigorously to positive mental and physical activities and a positive mental culture, then this will be the molding stamp by which they live the rest of their life.

With this goal in mind look for opportunities in which you believe your child can stretch just beyond their current abilities. They may not reach their goals all of the time. They may even get mentally or physically bruised occasionally. But this is all part of the strengthening process.

Sometimes they will ask us if they can do something and we will have to say no. Our common sense tells us that it would not be safe. You wouldn't let your four year old climb a mountain or walk to the mall all alone. You wouldn't let a child take a trip with complete strangers. You wouldn't send a toddler into a department store to wander around on its own.

At other times it will be appropriate to say yes and then watch them carefully – like when a child takes the training wheels off their bike. They may or may not be ready for it. If they want to try and you think it is not too risky, let them. Just be there to catch them until they get the hang of it.

When we do this there will be times that our children will find that they were not quite ready for this next step. Letting them recognize and face those situations is also part of the strengthening of their will. We just need to be watchful that they do not get into a situation that is dangerous or where failure would be more harmful in some other way then waiting until they are better prepared.

There will also be times when you make a decision that you wish you had not agreed to. It could be on the side of over protectedness or on the side of too encouraging. At these times it will help to remember that life itself is a partner in our experiences. If we could second guess everything life wouldn't be life. Our positive magnetism will help protect our children from serious harm more often then many people would believe. This is another reason for us to keep our energies positive and strong.

When my son Kai and my daughter Sabari were about 6 or 7 years old they decided to climb a tree in front of our house. Usually there was someone watching them but they were getting to the stage where they wanted to climb by themselves. In discussing it with them I noticed they had placed a board across two of the lowest branches about 6 or 8 feet up. The board wasn't attached to the tree in any way so I explained that it was not very safe. They assured me that they understood what I was saying. Deciding that I would let them climb I went into the house.

Shortly after I went into the house, Sabari, while sitting on the board, decided to change her position. Well, she did change her position, only it was to the ground instead of still being up in the tree. In trying to move she dislodged the board from the tree and fell to the ground. Fortunately she was not hurt. We all still laugh about how perfect the lesson was. She had done just what I warned her not to do – right after I had warned her! But, you know, she will never forget that lesson. After that she always listened to me when I warned her about dangers. She has climbed many trees since that day and never once has she fallen down.

Of course, Sabari and Kai did not tell me right away about their little accident. I heard about it sometime later. There was no need to rub it in or punish her in any way. They had both learned a valuable lesson. Life had given Sabari a bump but she got right back up and climbed again. Parenting is a lot like coaching. You can help them train, preparing them for life in as many ways as possible, but you can not play the game for them.

One thing that we want to be careful of is the tendency to get so into our child's opportunities to grow that we put undue pressure on them. Little league baseball is a perfect example of how this can happen. Some parents take sports incredibly seriously. They can exert excessive pressure on their children to perform. It isn't that we do not want our children to do their best. But their personal best has to do with their own focus and positive efforts not the outcome of the game. Sportsmanship, basic playing skills and just plain fun are the main purpose of sports at a young age. Turning every game into the World Series can bring negative energies into what should be a very positive experience regardless of the outcome of the game.

When a child hears a parent booing a call by an umpire or complaining about the way a coach is running the team, the child is learning that these are correct behaviors at a baseball game and for relating to life in general. Dealing with situations that are not going the way we would prefer is part of life. This is a perfect training ground for learning to react to these challenges with a positive attitude. If we as parents give our children the wrong example, then not only are they learning to reinforce negative attitudes, but we are too.

On the other hand, when our child hears other parents behaving like spoilt kids we can point out to them that there is no guarantee that just because a person's body becomes mature that their minds will necessarily do likewise.

My daughter's baseball team was so positive through excellent leadership that they would cheer for their opponents just as much as for themselves. When they lost a game they took it in stride. For two seasons they did not win one game. But in the third season they were the league champions. This is what giving our children opportunities to strengthen their positive character traits is all about.

I have always loved Samuel Clemens' comment on quitting smoking: To quit smoking is the easiest thing in the world. I've done it a thousand times!

When we are up against a habit that we just can't shake we need to see even our lack of success in a positive light. Instead of saying, "I am a failure." We should say, "I haven't yet succeeded!" It is through this never giving up, always stepping forward, and expecting success just around the next bend that we can really make progress in this area. Isn't that what we find so inspiring about the great adventure stories in life? In the book and movie, *The Right Stuff*, the challenges of the first astronauts are chronicled. Orbiting the world in a space capsule was just the icing – sweet indeed as it was – the real cake was the intensity and commitment of effort that got them there.

It is the same for explorers in all frontiers of life. That is what we were talking about in the last chapter, having an awareness of the importance of the moment, rather than living for a fulfillment at some future time. When I learned to surf enjoying all aspects of the process, living in the joy of the moment, all of life became sweet.

Here is another thing that I learned during that time when I was surfing so intensely. There are some surfing spots where you have to paddle out directly through the surf in order to get out so that you can ride the waves. When the waves are big it is very difficult to get out through the crashing surf. Not being very muscular at the time I often had trouble getting out. Sometimes I just couldn't make it.

One day I started paddling out at the same time as a much stronger surfer. In the beginning I stayed with him stroke for stroke but gradually he pulled ahead of me. I didn't like that. In fact, it made me angry with my failings. Right then and there I determined that I was not going to give up until I got outside the breaking waves. I didn't think: I'll make it if I have to drown trying. That would have left the possibility of failure. I simply refused to accept not getting out there as an option.

I set myself a steady pace and slowly moved forward. When a wall of whitewater pushed me back, and sometimes even off my board, I just got back on and kept paddling. Ever so slowly I got closer to where the waves were breaking. When I started to feel weak in the arms I refused to give in to the tiredness. I mentally forced my arms to keep moving.

After a mighty struggle I finally made it out past the breaking waves. When I got out there I expected to see that stronger fellow who had started with me. But I never did see him. I believe that he didn't make it out that day. After that day I found that once I decided to try I always made it out. I had learned that it was simply a matter, not of body size, but of determination of will.

Once we develop the kind of will that focuses all of our energies we find that there are reserves of potential that we won't realize that we have until we tap them.

Hand in hand with this strength of will must come discrimination. Knowing the difference between that which is brave and that which is foolish is essential if we want to survive our adventures in living. When I say that I always got out past the breaking waves after that day, it also means that I didn't try when my best judgement told me that it wasn't a good idea.

As we encourage our children to explore their potential help them to evaluate the possible consequences of their actions. Sometimes a verbal warning is indicated. At other times a questioning glance will suffice. The only definite guideline is in the area of safety. As parents we must protect our children from situations where they simply can not handle the potential consequences of their actions.

While we have explored these ideas in the realms of sports, which are natural areas of growth for children, these same principles can be applied just as successfully to all areas of life. Many challenges in the academic arena will take stamina and fortitude. Certainly interpersonal relationships need strength of character and even-mindedness. And the business world is rich with opportunities to test our staying power.

Once we have cultivated the determination of will to complete any task to which we set ourselves we will have successfully forged the metal of our will. This sword of self-control can then be powered by the good forces of the positive flow. When we help our children to develop strength of will and nurture them in the ways that it can be most beneficially directed we are giving them one of life's most useful tools.

20

Self-Study

When a child acts in ways that are seen to be detrimental to themselves or others we often ask them: Why did you do that? What were you thinking? Some adults will say that these are unfair questions to ask a child. A child can not be expected to know the "why" of their actions. Especially, in the heat of the moment while an accusatory adult is standing over them. Is it too much to ask a child to stand up and say, "I made a mistake and I am sorry" or "I saw that little toy in the store and I just couldn't help myself, I took it"? All too few adults are willing to expose themselves in this way, why should we expect our children to?

Of all the stories that we hear as children there is probably none more familiar from the annals of American history then the story of George Washington cutting down the cherry tree and admitting his guilt. This ideal of truthfulness is recognized in our society as a cornerstone of good character. No one could plausibly teach lying as the best way to live. Yet, what is it that most children are taught by the world in which we live?

Two of the most common attitudes toward action that are promoted by a materialistic society are; look out for yourself and do whatever you want as long as you don't get caught. If you do not believe that our children are being taught these ideas as a basic value of American culture you do not watch television, go to the movies or read many of the books on the national bestseller lists. Good for you! If you do know what is expressed by-in-large by these mediums you are certainly aware that our society is subtly teaching the ultimate lie: Happiness is to be found in the fulfillment of your desires. This over arching motivating philosophy is what drives all forms of advertising and most aspects of the entertainment industries. Indulge yourself, you deserve it, you are worth it! These are the liturgy of the "you want it? You got it!" society that we live in. So what is a child supposed to think?

Interestingly enough and consistent with our philosophy that solutions are always at hand it is in an aspect of this plethora of American creativity that we can find a golden kernel of truth. There are a number of qualities that have made America so great as a country. One of them is originality. We are a country of people who think for themselves. We come up with new ways to solve old problems. We push the frontiers of that which is thought possible. This tapping of our creative potential as a country has kept us in the forefront of progress in many aspects of life. When we lose this creative edge we will find that it is one of the signs of our country's decline.

We have already talked about the positive flow as the source of inspiration. And that this source can be tapped regardless of a person's spiritual beliefs. Those who deny these higher realities say that creativity is just a whim of life, either you have it or you don't. But those who make that claim are not very scientific in their approach. Have they investigated the subject? Or are they just blowing hot air?

If we want to understand how an automobile works we will study some books and maybe get an instructor to help us

176

start working on cars. Through our direct experience we will discover first hand how cars are made and how they work. This seems like such an obvious line of reasoning, yet there is a most basic part of every person's life that most people fail to approach with this simple procedure: The mind.

I am not talking about the putting of facts and figures into the all consuming gray matter of the brain. I am talking about the way we make decisions in our lives, the impulses that drive our thoughts and actions, our aspirations to greatness and our visits to the depths of despair. The exploration of this vast inner universe is ill attended and left to chance. The only time that most people consider their mental condition is if they are having a problem that causes conflicts with the "norms" of society.

No one thinks twice about teaching their children how to care for their bodies. How many of us give that same attention to the mental health of our children? What about our own mental health?

Learning to understand the way our consciousness manifests as our thought process is one of the most basic tools that we can use for understanding ourselves. Through an honest appraisal of the way we mentally approach life we can come up with ways to improve our lives. If we learn to see ourselves as a disinterested third party might, with complete non-attachment, we can find out what is going on inside our mental process and work with it.

It is the same for children. If we can teach them from the very beginning to explore their minds and impulses, to get in touch with how they feel and how they got to those feelings, they will begin to see how those feelings affect their thoughts and actions. This discovery of how things are working on the inside of our lives will be an invaluable aid for improving the way that we relate to life on the outside. Just as we might use physical therapy to improve a weak muscle mental therapy can be used to strengthen and heal the mind. I am not talking about what most psychiatrists and psychologist do, although there certainly are times when their services are helpful or even essential. I am talking about this whole approach to living that we have been exploring. How by working with the way life is made we can achieve our highest potential.

Society teaches that the self is the body and the personality. But that is just the tip of the iceberg. Because our society has concentrated on the outer parts of life almost exclusively, like a horse with blinders, people think that nothing else exists but that which is directly in front of them.

There is a well-known story told of a man who had five blind sons. One day he asked his sons to wash an elephant. Never having done this before they didn't know what to expect. Each son was given a different area to wash, which they did with due diligence. That evening at dinner the boys discussed their day's activities. When it came to a discussion of the elephant washing an argument ensued as to how the true appearance of an elephant should be described.

The first son said, "An elephant is a big long hose with hairs on it." He had been washing the trunk.

The second son cried out, "No, an elephant is four big thick pillars." He had been washing the legs.

The third son bellowed, "My foolish brothers, certainly you could tell that an elephant is two large walls." He had been washing the sides.

The fourth son was indignant, "You are not only blind, but you are stupid! An elephant is like a rope that hangs from the sky." He had washed the tail.

The fifth son, shocked that his brothers could be so ignorant, said pompously, "An elephant is two hillocks, one small and one large." He had washed the head and back.

The father arrived just as the argument was about to come to blows. He called to his sons in astonishment, "You my sons truly are blind: Not only in your eyes but also in your minds. Can you not see? An elephant is all of those things. Each of you was just washing a part of the whole."

So it is with life, we need to approach life with the whole picture in mind and not just part of it. By developing an overview of the different parts of life that comprise the whole we can see how to blend things together. It is only by considering all aspects of our lives that we can achieve a balance that will bring about inner harmony.

When we make the subject of life's inner workings a part of our everyday conversations with our children they will begin to explore life from this perspective. It shouldn't be only when they are having a problem. Regular discussions will give them an opportunity to ask questions outside the context of a difficulty. This will help prepare them for the future. Their own experiments will show them the efficacy of these truths. They will begin to mould their own approach to life in ways that integrate these ideas into the very fabric of their lives.

Who can say at what age any given child will be able to look at and work with the intricacies of their own mind? Some souls come ready to sprout, just a little water and they begin to grow. Others are like tulips, dormant until the right season, but beautiful when they arise. The thing that we want to avoid is the thought that children can not possibly understand these ideas. We don't want to presume that they do and we do not want to presume that they do not. We rest in the knowledge that it is possible that they do and so we reach out to awaken their latent potential.

This constant looking to the higher possibilities in any situation is part of our own living in the positive flow. It raises us up to be constantly searching for the ways that these subtler truths can be seen. Through our own efforts to awaken ourselves we will increase the chances that our children will do likewise.

Even more important than their ability to deal more successfully with individual areas of their lives, by sharing these truths with our children we will help them to develop a growing vision of the big picture in life. They will see how all of life is connected in subtle ways and their own lives will be immeasurably enriched by this knowledge.

At the very heart of self-study is the exploration of our own personal relationship to the universe. Each of us will need to come to grips with this challenge on our own. As parents we can only encourage and magnetize our children in these directions. As the saying goes: You can lead a horse to water, but you can not make them drink.

The realization that our smaller sense of self, like a bird living in a cage, can one day fly out to embrace infinity is one of the most thrilling moments along the journey. Watch for that moment in your child. Plant seeds of inspiration in their lives. Water them with the gifts we talked about earlier. Then enjoy the blossoming of a soul as it discovers its true nature as Spirit.

21

Devotion to God

God is not a dirty word!

The way that the word God has been batted about in our spoken language would certainly lead an extraterrestrial philologist to believe that the most common usage for the word God is as an expression of profanity.

The common usage of the term that is supposed to represent that which is highest as an expression of that which is lowest is a classic symptom of the disease of materialism that has emaciated our society. Those who are swimming in the negative flow away from Spirit unknowingly use the word God as an affirmation of their separateness. As if only through repeated strengthening can they continue to disbelieve in that which the soul instinctively knows as its true reality.

I could have hedged here titling this chapter "Your Highest Potential" and it would be true. Even amongst people who stand against a belief in God there are few who would deny the higher value of love, friendship and loyalty. Even rank materialist believe in striving for your best. Though these qualities are manifestations of our nature as expressions of God we do not need to label them as such for them to be of benefit. And the principles of *Positive Flow Parenting* that we have been discussing work whether a person believes in God or not. So why not hedge?

If we look to the very best in life, that which is most expressive of our highest aspirations, we inevitably end up with God. I am not talking about a particular description as promoted by any individual religion. I am referring to the concept of an infinite reality that is beyond the Creation and that has made and become the Creation. The fact is that most of the great thinkers and doers throughout history have believed in God. Saintly souls from every generation have confirmed the reality of the Divine Presence.

For those who stand steadfastly against the reality of a conscious, causative force in the universe or aren't yet sure, I ask, "Are you willing for God to exist?" If you are you will certainly receive confirmation of the Divine Reality if you seek it. If you are not willing for God to exist, ask yourself in the name of truth and honesty, why not? We should not confuse a lack of willingness to seek truth for its non-existence.

There are many reasons why people disbelieve in God. But no matter what the outward manifestations of those reasons the underlying causative force is the soul's conscious or unconscious alignment with an aspect of the negative flow away from Spirit. This negative flow is always trying to pull the shade down over the window of our soul. Even people who live exemplary lives can sometimes be caught by the subtle power of the negative flow. Every unpleasantry is used to convince us that God does not exist. Or if He does exist, all of our problems are His fault since he made us the way that we are. Then there is the thought that if God existed He wouldn't allow suffering or injustice. If God really exists why can't I see Him? The bible responds, "To them that have eyes, let them see."

The ways to deny God's existence are many but there is only one path that leads, for those who are willing to follow, to a personal direct knowledge of God: Love. In his book, *The Holy Science*, Swami Sri Yukteswar explains that it is impossible to take one step on the spiritual path without love. It is through the awakening of the hearts natural love that spiritual progress is attained. Jesus said, "Blessed are the pure in heart, for they shall see God."

This awakening of the hearts natural love does not happen by accident. Remember when we talked about the vortexes of feeling, likes and dislikes, that we carry within us? The results of this karma are that we end up with what Swami Sri Yukteswar called meannesses of the heart. These negative commitments of energy harden us from expressing the Divine Love that wants to flow through us. In order to advance toward our goal of reflecting Spirit perfectly we need to consciously act in ways that will cleanse from our hearts these meannesses.

When we act in ways that expand our loving nature we are chipping away at our meannesses of the heart. Utilizing the law of magnetism to help us we can accelerate the process of cleansing our hearts by awakening within ourselves a flow of loving energy. The effectiveness of this is even greater when we connect our individual flow of loving energy consciously with the Divine Flow of the positive flow. In order to do this we focus our energy on an aspect of the Divine and feel our love flowing toward it: Devotion. This is not outward worship but an inward communing with the heart of life itself.

Awakening the hearts natural love is much easier in children. Children haven't yet hardened themselves against openness. By helping them to increase this flow while they are young we not only increase their positive energies but we give them experience in how to access this love in times

183

of need. Even if they discontinue their practices for a time they will always remember how to do it if they decide to try again.

One of the easiest ways to awaken this love is through acts of kindness. Jesus said, "Love thy neighbor as thy self." Helping our children to see that acts of kindness are expressions of love and that we are happy when we give is a basic way to share the idea that these acts can help connect us to the source of love: God.

Music can also be used to awaken devotion. Music that uplifts the soul helps to awaken the flow of positive energy within us. When we channel that inspiration inward and upward toward the spiritual eye we can uplift our consciousness. Even better then listening to music is singing. Participation is almost always better than standing on the sidelines. Teaching your children songs that awaken love is excellent.

Another aspect of this is to not sing just about God but sing to God. We want to feel as if God is the direct recipient of our expressed love. Taken to the next step we will then feel that God is singing through us to God. This completion of the circle allows us to get our ego out of the way and let the Love Divine flow through us.

It is the same with prayer. We don't want to pray with a sense of separateness from God, wondering if He/She hears us. Prayer should be the intimate conversation that is shared between the best of friends or lovers. God knows our heart better than we do. But it is only when we express our love that the Divine Source can grow within us. It is up to us. Our free will is the activating switch. We must consciously decide to let God be a loving companion and guiding presence in our lives.

I have already mentioned this, but let me remind you. This is not about religion. The particular style with which you want to approach God is up to you. Follow the crowd or strike out on your own, the choice is yours. The issue is having a conscious inner experience, not what it looks like or how it is labeled on the outside.

Here is one way of looking at it.

Everyone likes different kinds of food. No matter what kind of food you like to eat you would never complain if someone who likes a different kind of food than you taught your child how to use eating utensils. It is the same with the techniques that we have been discussing. These are the utensils of how to awaken devotion. How you spice that devotion according to your religious preferences is totally up to you. The only time there is a conflict is when a particular religion cuts itself off by claiming sole ownership of truth.

It would be unthinkable not to teach your child how to eat or speak or the basic laws of good hygiene. It is the same with the information that I am sharing with you in this book. These are the principles of life. How religions color them is a different issue. There isn't only one outward source for this information. The key is to explore these issues and experience them for yourself. That is the true test of any course of action.

When we do not share this most important part of life with our children, what are we saying to them? That these issues are not really important.

Another thing to remember is that our children have been drawn to us for a reason. It is not by accident that souls are brought together as a family. Whoever we are, both good and bad qualities, this is what our children have been karmicly drawn to. It is their reward for past actions. From our point of view, whatever is the best of who we are, that is what we want to give to our children. We should not hesitate to give it in the best way that we can even if it doesn't have the affect that we hope for. They have the free will to do as they please in life. We must fulfill our responsibilities as parents by giving our very best and leaving the results to God.

When it comes to the most important part of life, our relationship with our Creator, we need not – in the name of fairness – leave out that which is most precious to us. For in truth it is only once we have acknowledged our relationship to the universe and acted on our belief in that relationship that we have really committed ourselves to it. When we flinch in the expression of our beliefs then either we do not fully believe them or we need to see a higher view of what is currently being expressed.

No matter what your chosen spiritual path you can always feel good about instilling in your child the best qualities that all the religions of the world teach. And devotion is certainly one of them. Awaken within yourself an all-consuming flame of love for God. That will magnetize your children toward interest in their own devotion. Then apply our formula to awakening in them their own expressions of devotion. Spend time with them in worship. Do not compartmentalize this part of life. Let your children see your sincerity of devotion. It will move them like nothing else.

As with all of these areas, awaken interest through attuning yourself to your child. You may have a particular style that you like but your child may prefer something different. Be open and supportive of diversity in their positive expressions. Seek to see things through their eyes and look for ways to help them. They may even open up to you ways of expression that you had not previously considered that you will find wonderfully inspiring.

Each of us in our own way must face God on a one to one basis. This most personal of relationships should be nurtured with the utmost care. When we approach every part of childrearing from the perspective of this heavenly

relationship we will find a depth of attunement and understanding for our children that we never before thought
possible.

22

The Art of Loving Discipline
Part 1

One of the ways to truly understanding non-violent, loving relationships is in the act of forgiveness. That Jesus could endure the suffering of crucifixion without hating his enemies is alone a great feat, but to add forgiveness; that is Divine. Where did Jesus find the strength of heart to express this supreme act of forgiveness? Certainly it must have come from the Ocean of Infinite Love with which he was fully identified.

That same Divine Love is also available to us. When we tap into it we can fulfill our responsibilities as souls and as parents in the highest possible way. It is through alignment with Universal Love that we will be able to express to our children the loving and forgiving support they will need in order to grow physically, mentally and spiritually healthy. Some people think of love as a kind of softness. Many men have been taught that to express love outwardly is weak, not manly. Make no mistake about it, love is the most powerful force in the universe. Through the power of love anything can be accomplished – even the molding of a limited soul into Unlimited Spirit.

Some examples of the strength and enduring nature of love can be seen in the results that the expressions of great

188

love have produced in this world. Historical figures of the political arena are quickly forgotten only to be remembered when we dust off the history books. Then, like reading a tombstone in a graveyard, we can conjure up the past. But great lovers of God and Truth like Buddha, Krishna, Jesus and others are great beacons of love that not only reach through the centuries with the stories of their lives but with the love with which they lived. The love that these great masters of Spirit express is still transforming lives after thousands of years. Having merged their individuality into the Infinite they are ever alive guiding those who attune themselves to their loving emanations.

The transformation of the soul through the power of love can take many forms. It is easy to see how imersion in a loving embrace is an expression of love, but when it comes to disciplining our children, things are not always so clear. Questions start to arise in our minds: How much discipline is the right amount? Is it possible to discipline within the boundaries of non-violence? Do we spank our children? Are we going to train them like some people approach training dogs, giving them a reward for good behavior and punishment for bad behavior? These kinds of questions are as endless as there are situations in life so we need to simplify things to their most common denominator: Our basic nature, our child's basic nature and where we want to go with our efforts.

Let's start with what we are trying to accomplish. We are not trying to train circus animals – even though at times it may seem that way! What we are seeking to do is bring out the best qualities in our children, diminish the negative qualities and give them the life skills with which they can create the best possible life for themselves. While doing this we want to love them and be sure that they feel loved. Pretty simple huh!

Raising a child can in many ways be likened to the growing of plants. There are two extremes in this realm: The wild flower and the hothouse plant. Let's see what we can understand from the world of gardening to help us find a middle ground that will work for each of us.

Some people think that the best way to grow a child is to just let them grow naturally on their own. Let them flower as they will, like wildflowers. Wildflowers are strengthened by their exposure to the elements. Living unrestrained they are free to blow any way the wind blows. This makes them strong and flexible, thus they tend to be healthy, hardy and beautiful.

Of course, there are some draw backs to being a wild-flower. Your unprotected exposure to the elements may lead to an early demise. Those who do survive will be strong and flexible, but are they also able to stand up straight and resist the winds of life when necessary? To achieve a purpose in life we need to be able to harness our strength of will and apply it in the direction of our goals. Blowing hither and thither all of the time may keep us from developing the specific strengths that would be best for our overall growth.

There is no question that this approach certainly has its charms. For those who feel inclined to explore the wild-flower approach toward raising their children I encourage you 100 percent. Just keep in mind the considerations that we have been discussing and pay attention to how things are going.

It will not be as easy as just watching how they grow because there will be times that life will force you to intervene, after all, life is not as simple for humans as being out in a meadow on a beautiful spring afternoon. When something in life comes along to munch on your little one you will probably want to get out there and help.

On the other end of the spectrum is the hothouse plant. Nurtured in an environment that is most suitable for growth the hothouse plant often grows larger and faster than the wildflower. Protected from predators and disease these plants have little to fear from life. They rest safely in the bosom of comfort.

Well, that sounds pretty good! Who wouldn't want to protect their child from harm and allow them to grow large and tall? Free from the difficulties of life our children can explore their own areas of interest without interference. Their minds can blossom with the colors of intelligent exploration.

Parents with a protective nature and the material were-with-all to follow this approach will find it very appealing. Providing their children with an environment that minimizes risk and maximizes opportunities for educational possibilities seems ideal.

Here again I can wholeheartedly support those who want to traverse these grounds. Just keep in mind that plants that are always protected from the elements may find life difficult if circumstances change. When a storm comes and the heat goes off hothouse plants may easily succumb to the cold. Without opportunities to strengthen the immune system disease can more easily be a problem. And without the winds of difficulty the strengthening of the will is less certain.

As you can see, both ends of the spectrum have certain appealing features and some drawbacks. Earlier we talked about building a strong house and how balance is the key to success in the personality area of our lives. So how can I support either of these two extreme approaches? It seems obvious that they are unbalanced.

The seeking of balance in our lives must be sought from the point at which we are now. Only from an honestly understood present can we then move forward in a direction that we feel will be beneficial. If we try to jump way over to the other side in order to achieve balance, in most cases we will be over correcting in a way that we can not control, which increases the chance of failure. Like a tightrope walker, most of the time we will be making small adjustments. As we develop our skills we will find a diminishing of the need for drastic changes.

People who are protective by nature can not expect to be instantly easy going. Those who are free flowing by nature are not likely to suddenly become disciplined and orderly. While it is true that through the strong application of will we can instantly change ourselves in any desired direction, as a practical matter, few of us do.

The balanced approach is to move according to the guidance that you get from your inner attunement to the positive flow. This inner guidance will take into account who you and your child are vibrationally and lead you to a mutually compatible lifestyle. While we develop our ability to perceive this inner guidance let's see if we can gather some more ideas from the garden.

There are a number of valuable tips that we can take from how a master gardener works with plants. The first thing that we notice is that each plant gets different care. Some plants need to be tied to stakes or trimmed regularly. Others are left more or less on their own and only trimmed occasionally. Some plants need shade, others prefer strong sunlight. Watering schedules often differ as well. The depth of planting the seed and the length of time it will take to grow, these are all different according to the individual characteristics of the plant. Some gardeners also believe that while most of the garden needs cultivation and attention, for balance, there should be a part of the garden that is wild and left to grow in any way it wants without interference.

If we want our children to be healthy and strong enough to meet the challenges of life, yet flexible enough to flow with changes, we need to give them the individual care that is best for them. This means tuning into the specific qualities that our child has or needs to develop. Once we have a clear view of where they are now, we can push forward to improve the situation.

Gardeners spend a lot of time working with their plants. It is the same with children. We can't expect to get them into shape in a few minutes. It will take time. Loving discipline is not only for shaping children, it is also for training ourselves to be patient, as well as, persistent.

One of the most difficult areas to deal with is the molding of a child's behavior in ways that do not diminish the strength of their will or their self-esteem. If our goal is to help our children become strong with a positive self-image we can't expect to achieve that result if we are constantly putting them down. This is where our creativity is truly tested. As we work with our children we will be juggling many objectives simultaneously. This is another reason why the central solution to parenting is an inner point of balance and not an outward racing to keep things from falling apart.

The development of initiative and determination are essential. At the same time a strong will can be channeled negatively towards stubbornness and a lack of cooperation. This is an example of the same basic energy going in either a positive or negative direction. This is what we want to work with. As you develop a strategy for working with your child's energy through your attunement to the positive flow keep in mind that you want to strengthen their will while keeping it positively directed and flexible enough to meet a wide variety of circumstances.

Let's look more closely at how this works.

If your child gets upset every time they don't get their own way they are being unreasonable. You will need to come up with ways to redirect their energies so that this negative behavior does not become a habit. On the other hand, if they are generally cooperative but come upon a particular thing that they are determined to have or do that you would not normally give in to, as long is it will not hurt them this may be an opportunity to strengthen their will. Give them a chance to achieve their goal. Even an occasional fit of temper in a young child is healthy. Sometimes we can even inwardly enjoy our child's mischievousness while we outwardly redirect their energies.

Whenever possible use the present circumstances to the advantage of moving energies in a positive direction. Going against your child's energy constantly will over a period of time increase the risk of either weakening them or turning their strength in a negative direction. It will also greatly diminish your ability to guide them. Redirect their energies in just the right way and you will be disciplining them in ways that they don't even realize. As time goes by they will love you more for your attentions, rather than pulling away from you because of them.

Knowing when and how much to intervene in any given situation isn't always easy to figure out. In the case of general good manners, you know what is acceptable to you. Within those boundaries you must insist that your child behave. Once you have set the basic parameters of acceptability, if you do not follow through you will give up control of the situation and your child will become the guiding energy.

Outside of the family circle it is even harder at times to tell when it is the appropriate time to intercede. We want our children to take their lumps and grow strong but we also want to protect them from situations that are beyond their abilities to cope positively. We also want to be aware of the energies that are exerting influence over our children that can turn them toward negative energies and bad habits. A sensitive attunement to your child and the environment that they are interacting with is the only way to tell.

If you are not sure what to do about any given situation and you have the time and opportunity, don't be afraid to consult a trusted friend. Sometimes we are so close to a situation that we can't see it clearly. Even if you do not agree with the assessment of your friend, just listening to them or explaining your concerns often opens up new ideas that you had not before considered.

If your child has a quality that really bugs you, find out if it bothers others. Get some input as a part of your attempts to perceive what is going on. If everyone you talk to says it is a problem you have a strong support of your need to do something. If they don't support it as being a problem area, keep that in mind as you seek a solution. One thing that you want to be careful of when sounding others out is not feeding them negative thoughts about your or anyone else's child. Keep your discussion on a positive note and always present the difficulties from a positive mental outlook. You do not want to spread negative images of your child. You are simply trying to get a wider positive perspective on what is happening.

Even if your child has a habit that others do not find offensive, if it bothers you, something should be done. One of you may need to change. Or it may be appropriate for both of you to change a little. Work with your children to make life harmonious. Let them know how you feel and listen to how they feel. Discuss with them the different alternatives. This should include some of their ideas along with yours. Then show them that you are willing to swing their way and give them an opportunity to show that they care and are willing to swing your way as well. This is much of what we want to teach our children. How to get along with others. It is a process of give and take.

When we take the time to communicate directly with our children, reaching beneath the emotions of any given situation and sharing with them, heart to heart, we will be minimizing the need to fight with them. The real heart of loving discipline lays in avoiding, as often as possible, the need for confrontation. That is why the principle of redirecting energies is so important.

When our children know down to the depths of their being that we are on their side, because of the positive energies that we constantly feed them, they won't want to fight with us any more than we want to fight with them. Through an understanding and cultivation of the ideas that are a part of *Positive Flow Parenting* we will be minimizing the chances that we will need to stand directly against the energies of our children. And then, when those times come and we do need to stand firm, our actions will not be guided by negative emotions but by love.

23

The Art of Loving Discipline
Part 2

Now let's look at the big question: Is it ever right to use physical force on your child? The reality is that most parents do at some time strike their children. Does that make it right? As I mentioned earlier, just because something is common doesn't mean it is necessarily right. On the other hand, when something is common just saying that we should not do it is not likely to make much of a difference. And is it likely when something is as common as corporal punishment that it is wrong in every situation?

Living consciously means realizing that we each need to understand truth personally and make an appraisal of that which is best in any given situation. That appraisal should be based on the highest view of truth that we can see. Whether or not we personally like the view from that perspective is not the most important factor. I certainly wish I could say unconditionally that it is never right to use physical force on your child. But the facts of life are such that there may actually be times when we would be hurting our children more if we do not use physical force.

What about all that talk about non-violence? Consider this: If a child has a tumor on their arm you will let the doctor remove it won't you? Is the pain of that removal violence? It hurts, yes, but the procedure includes no desire to inflict pain, it is an educated attempt to ultimately heal. Thus, it must be seen not as an act of violence but as an act of love.

There are many kinds of bad tasting medicines that we use to help our children. They certainly are not pleasant to swallow. But in the end that ill tasting medicine may save the child's life. Nurses often must physically restrain a struggling, crying child in order to administer a vaccination shot or other medical procedure. In this way we can see that the cure for any particular situation can not be evaluated by a simple view of discomfort on the part of the recipient or the caregiver. It needs to be based on what will actually help the situation.

Each of life's circumstances must be weighed in the balance of who is involved and what is at stake. If a parent chooses to never strike their child and fails to help a child when the proper application of physical energy would solve a serious problem, that parent is failing in their responsibilities. At the same time, if a parent unnecessarily uses physical force on their child, they also are failing in their responsibilities.

Those who find it easy to physically strike out must take pains to curb this tendency. Most people don't have total control over these impulses. If you don't, you must work to control yourself. Physical force should be used very carefully, lest like a sharp knife it cut the doctor, as well as, the patient.

The basis of all forms of discipline, whether they be physical or not, should always come from a calm state of love. The only exceptions to this are life-threatening situations in which you don't have time to do anything but react to the situation. If your child is doing something that may jeopardize their life or the lives of others you must do whatever it takes to remove them from imminent danger. If that means getting physical, then so be it. If your child is about to step in front of a moving car you may not have time to be gentile. In a case like that if your child gets a little hurt or scared in the process maybe that will help guard against it happening again.

Under most circumstances we have time in which to reflect on the situation. Even if you have determined that your child needs to be punished in some way, no matter what you deem the correct punishment, try never to do it in the heat of passion. Let yourself cool off before you act. Even just a few minutes can save you from making a mistake you will regret for a long time.

Forgiveness is the banner by which we should live. After the punishment is over we will forgive our child. So why wait? By forgiving your child before you administer any punishment you will get a better perspective on what is an appropriate punishment. As soon as the child is old enough to discuss the situation ask them what they think is appropriate. You will find that if they are being honest – and they will be if you work on this with them – they have a pretty clear picture of the severity of their actions and will find it beneficial to live by their own judgement. It may be hard to believe but sometimes they will even be harder on themselves then you would have been.

The key to successful discipline is consistency. This is another reason why we don't want to act in anger. Children are keenly aware of what is fair even if they don't like it. If we overreact to a situation we will undermine our efforts.

Remember the quote: Those who live by the sword shall die by the sword. If we make a practice of spanking our children the time will inevitably come when they will try to use it back at us. Think about how you will feel. Your child trying to hit you. Some say that it is a kind of rite of passage when this happens. Others feel remorse that things turned out that way. It is only by careful attention to our actions that we can minimize the chance of our efforts backfiring on us.

No matter what course you try, remember, you need to be willing to change course if things aren't working out as well as you had hoped. If you aren't willing to change course when it seems positively indicated then re-read the chapter on Non-Lying. As parents we may personally prefer one approach over another, but the bottom line is that to fulfill our responsibilities as parents we need to do what works, not necessarily what we would prefer.

The realities are that we may not have as much control over ourselves as we would like to think. Parents who feel comfortable with using physical force will find ample reasons to support their actions. And parents who can't abide by physical force will find support for their view. Earlier we talked about specific gravity. Here again is a situation where the essence of our own magnetic pattern will exert tremendous force over what we do. Since the use of physical force on a child has such potentially dangerous repercussions it is essential that we keep ourselves from reacting in ways that are tied to our own past rather than being rooted in the best interests of the present moment.

To some it may seem that I am supporting parents in striking their children. I am not. I am supporting what works. We have all met parents who never spank their children. Sometimes it works and everyone is all the happier for it. Other times you meet a child that can't behave and is having difficulties in life because their parents haven't communicated successfully the limits of acceptable behavior. I am not talking about asking a child to do something beyond their capabilities. It is just that sometimes a child needs a good whack on the bottom to get the message. Once received, everything is on the up and up.

It might be hard to believe, but there can be a number of reasons why a child actually wants to be spanked. It may be that they are feeling neglected and they won't give up until you give them your complete attention, even if it means pushing you to the point where they might get spanked. If that is the case then you should look at why they feel neglected and consider giving them a hug instead of a swat. It is also true that some personalities are just plain physical, they understand and feel more comfortable with physical forms of communication. At other times it can be the exploration of limits. Children need to and want to know where they stand. If you can't communicate those limits in any other way then at times you may have to do it physically.

There are a number of ways that parents get physical with their children. Spanking is certainly the best known, but there are a wide variety of ways that we can communicate physically with our children without actually hitting them. The least intrusive is to simply hold them in our arms so they can't move or to guide their motions in the proper direction by holding their hands, arms or shoulders. Even a squeeze of the hand or wrist adjusted in strength for the size of the child can be sufficient physical guide to get their attention.

When considering some of the time honored approaches like ear boxing or ear twisting, remember that the head is a sensitive area. There is a greater risk of injury in the area of the head than the well-padded bottom. Even shaking a child too vigorously has been known to cause damage to the brain in ways that a parent might never expect. There is always a risk when you get physical with your child so make sure that you think any given situation is really worth that risk before you get started.

It is my personal belief that you should never use any kind of weapon on your child. A switch, a belt, a shoe, even a newspaper, to say nothing of a fist, these are items that have been used on children. It seems to me that when we remove the discomfort of physically disciplining our children from ourselves by using a weapon it is all too easy to think that we are not really hurting the child. If it hurts your open hand to spank a child on the bottom you are probably spanking them too hard. And if it stings your hand a little it will remind you to do what you can to avoid getting to this point again in the future. Much – if not most – of the time parents are responsible for their children needing this level of intervention by not paying enough attention before the child's offense occurred.

Mental disassociation with the realities of the moment is the prime reason that adults hurt children. They mentally stand back from what is really going on and just fly forward on the power of their negative emotions. When that happens a parent is not acting as an agent for good, but has been caught by the powers of the negative flow.

I am giving this issue so much prominence because it is such a difficult area to get into a proper perspective. At the same time we must keep in mind that there are many alternatives to using corporal punishment, most of the time. Physical force should be a last resort and if you don't have control over your emotions you should never do it. It doesn't matter how mad you are or what your child has done: THERE IS NEVER ANY EXCUSE FOR INJURING YOUR CHILD IN THE NAME OF DISCIPLINE.

The real purpose of any action that goes directly against the flow of a child's energy is not to hurt them, but to shock them, thus short circuiting their current energy flow. If we are paying attention, most of the time we will redirect a child's energy into a more productive direction before this is necessary. But if they get rolling in a negative direction before we can redirect it or if our efforts fail, we may need to use more drastic measures to change the energy. Whatever type of force is used – it doesn't have to be physical – it needs to be applied with this in mind: We only want to stop the current direction of their energy flow. Hurting the child is not what we are trying to do. If you ever find yourself applying mental or physical force to your child with the intent to hurt them, even if their actions were wrong, you must stop and redirect your own energies.

After you have applied the energy necessary to short circuit your child's energies, move immediately toward guiding things in a positive direction. Try not to wallow in the unpleasantness of the moment. Release the tensions from you mind and help your child to move forward toward positive goals.

Now that we have reviewed some of the issues surrounding the worst case scenarios, let's talk about what we are going to do so that it is rarely or never necessary for us to use physical force.

The most affective tools for everyday use in disciplining your child are your voice – what you say and how you say it, body language – especially the eyes, and freedom of choice. Which of these you use or in what combinations must be left to the inspiration of the moment. The only formula that fits all situations is: Perceive, Attune and Experiment/ Redirect. Even short circuiting their energy flow should be seen and used in the light of trying to redirect your child's energies into a positive direction.

It is well proven that the voice is more than just a vehicle for intellectual information. A soothing voice can heal hurt feelings, a loving voice can embrace from a distance, a voice filled with laughter can bring happiness to a crowd. The voice transmits not only audio information but consciousness. It is the quality of consciousness in a voice that you are reading when you perceive the sincerity or lack there of in someone's voice. A parent may not be a good singer but the love that pours through to a child when being sung to is received much more intensely than the tones themselves.

Children are naturally good at understanding the underlying implications of any tone of voice. They intuitively read the meaning even if they don't understand the words. This truth is especially helpful with infants. As our children grow they may become desensitized to these subtleties. It is important to make a practice of using your voice consciously and consistently from the very beginning. If you do your child will have a direct link to what your are trying to communicate. They may chose to ignore you at any given time but they won't have failed to understand the point you were communicating.

The eyes are also extremely good at communicating how we feel and what we expect of our children. If you practice looking straight at your child and saying with your eyes what you mean with your words they will learn to read the eyes without the words. This can be especially useful in public. If your child starts to mis-behave or looks at you to find out what is or isn't acceptable behavior all you will have to do is look at them. With a slight nod of the head, yay or nay, they will know exactly what you are saying even though your lips don't move.

The use of the voice and especially the eyes is a very powerful tool in parenting. If you make a practice of using these tools, when the time comes to use them a single glance or word will achieve the desired results. This only works if you really cultivate it and make your eyes and tongue consistent.

This is much more subtle than yelling or staring daggers. There isn't any knack to reading someone's face when their eyes are bugging out – although I'm not against bugging your eyes out if the needs of the moment call for it! The idea is to develop a kind of attunement with your child that you could swear you know what they are thinking. I can't tell you how many times I have watched the cogs turn in my children's minds and told them what they were thinking. I'm not saying that I do it right all of the time, but it works much more often than coincidence could account for.

I am not talking about reading a person's thoughts like with ESP. I am talking about watching the decision making process going on in another person. When we try to look at life through the eyes of our children we can see much of what logically would be taking place. To that we can add our experience and attunement to the positive flow. These add up to a real feeling for what will be helpful for you child and not just what your desire might be. Loving discipline comes from a desire for the child's welfare and not just our own convenience. By exploring the frontiers of these underlying energies we will steer ourselves clear of needing more physical forms of discipline.

If we look at this issue from a broader universal perspective we can see that when we act in accordance with the laws of truth the results of our actions lead to an ever greater awareness of the soul's freedom to explore the infinite possibilities of life. When we act against the universal laws we are bound by our selfishness into the smallness of the ego. This negative direction limits our ability to roam freely beyond the boundaries of sense consciousness. This automatic limiting of possibilities through our misdirection of God given energies is a universal law, a law that we can use to help direct the energies of our children.

Where did people come up with the idea of prisons? It comes from a universal principle that, as often happens, has gotten drastically distorted through ignorance. The thought of confining people who can't behave in ways that are safe for society or themselves certainly makes sense. The idea of punishing people in ways that re-enforce their negative energies rather than redirecting those energies into positive directions is strictly punitive – definitely not non-violent – rather than rehabilitative. Most prisons are gross distortions of a principle that can be truly helpful for society in general, as well as, for guiding our children.

Whenever we feel the need to exert control over our children we should do it in the spirit of helping them to improve themselves, not as retribution. When we punish our children just because we are angry with them it is punitive. When we punish our children because we love them and they need to learn proper behavior it is an act of kindness. While it is true that these two energies don't always conflict – we may be angry, but they still in the name of love need to be disciplined – we need to guard against those times when our displeasure with the situation distorts the rightness of our response.

There are a wide variety of ways that we can use limits to redirect a child's energies. The key is to figure out what channels will be most helpful to the child. Just sending a child to their room to sulk isn't nearly as helpful as giving them a positive task to do while they are in their rooms. This is where we need to apply our formula to the specific situation.

When a child is abusing a toy we might either remove their opportunity to use it or let them destroy it so that they see for themselves the results of their actions. They may catch on the first time we use either method or we may have to follow through a number of times for them to under-stand. No matter what we are applying this idea to we must be consistent. If we give in to negative energies because we don't feel like putting out the necessary energy to follow things through we will be undermining our own efforts and adding energy to a potential confrontation in the future.

If a child knows they are definitely not allowed to do something, don't ever let them do it. If it is something that is acceptable at some times and not at others they will have to learn what the parameters are. One of the most useful techniques for learning these guidelines is also one that will help in many other areas: Asking for permission. This simple process sets up a system by which a child can learn, not only what they can or can't do in a specific situation, but the basics of good behavior through the use of self-control, application of will toward a goal and respect for parental guidance.

No matter how we apply this idea of limiting a child's freedom remember these two important points: Let your child know that they can increase their freedom of choice in life through the expression of positive energies and never create a limit so great that you have no where to go if things are not yet turning in the right direction.

Giving a child the knowledge that through their own responsible actions they can gain the right to make more of their own decisions isn't just for getting out of trouble. It is also for pushing ahead when things are going well. As a child develops the habit of good behavior and an under-standing of self-control and commonsense, they should be given opportunities to make more and more of their own decisions. The time framework for this will differ with each person and the area of life being considered. The environ-ment in which you live and your own personal comfort level will also affect it. Since one of the goals of parenting is to one day see your child successfully making all of their own decisions the earlier we instill in our children a sense of how their actions can help or hinder their possibilities in life the better.

As we apply the idea of limiting or expanding our child's possibilities and opportunities for making their own decisions keep in mind that there are practical limits to what we as parents can do. In the light of this be sure that you don't turn a small skirmish into a war. Redirect negative energies as soon as you see them beginning. It is much easier to change the energy before ego's and emotions are fully committed. Once you do decide to act, don't limit your possibilities by dropping a nuke in the first volley of the incident. What will you do if the nuke doesn't work?

Life is full of unexpected changes and mixtures of possibilities that we can't foresee. That is why we need to be fluid in our approach. If we practice living in the positive flow and being creative with our application of these techniques we will find ourselves dancing with our children in harmony rather than always stepping on each others toes.

We have talked about specific gravity and how our overall vibration will lead us to act according to it's basic level of equanimity. Part of the basis for the molding of our own vibration is how we were raised as children. If our parents were strict disciplinarians there is a good chance that we will be the same – sometimes even if we determined that we would not be. Through the practice of meditation and our attempts to consciously live in the positive flow of life we will find that we are gradually freed from those past experiences and that we are more able to live in the moment without those bonds from our own past.

If we practice non-violence in our relationships with our children we will be giving them a legacy of positive energy flows that they won't have to change later. It will also be much easier for them to see how all of life can be met in a spirit of non-violence. When we live in this world without thinking or acting with the intent to harm others we will find that life itself will turn towards us with that same graciousness.

The heart of loving discipline is just that, living from the heart. When we feel the love of God flowing through us the negative flow can't touch us. It is the same for our children. If they experience war at home, whether it be between parents, parents and children or between siblings, they will expand that perspective to all of life. When they live in a hive of loving support, even if there are occasional sour spots, they will have been nurtured on the nectar of love that wasn't just offered, but that was also joyously received.

24

Environment is Stronger than Will

According to the law of magnetism, which we discussed earlier, all things in life, both mental and physical, are putting out a magnetic field which expresses vibrationally its particular qualities and strength. Whatever the quality or mixture of qualities – elevating, activating or downward-pulling – that is being expressed will enter our consciousness on a subtle vibrational level. Even if we are not consciously aware of it. The greater the strength of this field the greater its potential affect on those who come into contact with it.

As we practice living in the positive flow we will automatically be increasing the energy of our own magnetism, thus drawing more positive experiences and minimizing the effects of negative ones. Through our increasing sensitivity to these energies we will be able to tell those situations that will or will not be in tune with the positive flow for us. When we use our discrimination in choosing what we want to do in life we are exercising our free will in the direction of that which will benefit us. When we let circumstances roll over us without attempting to act consciously for good we are lessening our attunement to the positive flow and in some cases even aligning with the negative flow. As we consciously engage in this process it is essential to remember that discrimination is not judgement. If we choose to avoid a person, place or situation we do not need to put it down, we just want to recognize that it isn't an energy that we feel is right for us.

The difficulty is that many times people don't realize how much or in what way any given activity or environment will affect them. They think, "Oh, I am strong enough to do this without it affecting me." We need to keep in mind the old adage about how when you peel onions your fingers will smell like onions.

Paramhansa Yogananda put it like this: "Environment is stronger than will." This simple statement covers in a nutshell a truth that when understood will be most helpful to us personally and for raising our children. While it is ultimately true that the enlightened soul is unaffected by environment, until we are supremely strong we must carefully consider what we can or can't handle. Even more important then the issue of whether or not we can handle a situation is the underlying question: Do we really want to? And Why? Why would we want to do something that is potentially harmful or diminishing to us?

Certainly there are times when we, as an example, go along with friends to an event that we wouldn't normally attend. If we feel that supporting our friends is a greater good than the potential harm of the activity we go. But, if they want to go out and get stumbling down drunk, why would we want to go? I suppose driving them home would be a good reason. Better, would be to pick them up when they are finished. If you go in and sit with them while they drink will you be tempted to have a drink or two yourself?

Paying attention to the environments that we subject ourselves to is part of the refining of our higher nature. The more we associate with elevating energies the more elevated we ourselves will become. If we spend our time in places with lower quality energies the chances are they will pull us down.

Many of the activities that people do are not in themselves bad but they have an affect on one's consciousness that may not be beneficial. As we learn to tell the difference between the different qualities we will begin to feel inwardly how we are affected by each. Elevating environments will help us to feel peaceful, joyful and loving. Activating environments can energize us in either expanding or contracting ways. Downward-pulling environments will lead us toward a negative, sense aware, ego limiting, self-involved consciousness. Using our understanding of the directional nature of these qualities to help us evaluate how we will be affected by something is more helpful then trying to make a list that covers every eventuality. Lists don't take into account all of the particulars of any situation. An awareness of these qualities, through intuitive attunement, can enable us to take into account all of the multifarious possibilities of the moment.

If we can teach our children to read environments, people and situations through the value system of these three directional qualities they will be able to know for themselves whether or not to participate. Otherwise they will only be able to decide about things that you have specifically discussed with them. When we have helped our children to perceive these underlying energies we will be giving them an ever-increasing ability to guide their own lives successfully.

The younger the child the more control we will have over their environment. As they grow, share with them your reading of the vibration of the places you visit and the people you meet. This will give them reference points that they can use to tune their own readings of vibration. As they gain independence through the years they will have developed the habit of listening inwardly and observing the vibrations of life around them. Again, it is essential that judgement and an attitude of putting others down or being superior to others, not be a part of this process.

As infants our children drink in every experience without being able to filter them through these reference points. They will react to things that they like and dislike physically, but they have little protection against subtler influences. It is important that we protect them from undue negative energies. When we bathe them in a positively charged environment as an infant we are establishing the feel that they will use as the foundation of their assimilation of life experiences. If this basis is calm, loving and joyful they are much more likely to be well adjusted then if it is harsh and angry. Even avoiding arguments around an infant is a good idea. While they may not understand the words yet, they are quite capable of understanding the tone, volume and vibration of the words.

To those who worry about overprotecting a child consider this: there is no place on earth where the power of the negative flow can not penetrate and work its harmful ways. As parents we need to be constantly vigilant in maintaining the best possible environment for our children. At the same time, a parent who expresses an excessively protective nature is expressing a kind of attachment and fear that is part of the negative flow. What we are seeking is a balance that takes into account the parents, the child and each individual situation. The younger the child, the more protection they need. And of course, children mature at different rates so each child should be introduced to greater challenges at their own pace.

As a practical matter it is extremely difficult in our society to keep our children from being influenced by energies that will try to pull them toward limitation instead of expansion. Since the overriding values of our society are materialistic we will have our work cut out for us just trying to stay even. Each of us will have to evaluate the particulars of our living environment was we work with the flow of life. Just keep in mind that if you expose a weak positive magnetism to a strong negative magnetism the weak positive one will become negative. Understanding how we are affected by our environment will help make this more clear.

Everyone has heard about a child who was basically good but got into trouble because they got in with the wrong crowd. There isn't really any mystery about this, we all know how we can be influenced by others, especially when we are young. An extreme case of this kind of magnetic influence is like what happens when there is a riot. A kind of mass hysteria takes over a crowd and normally law abiding citizens act in shocking ways.

A more common example would be when a child spends time with a friend who likes to take things. Through the influence of the friend the child experiments with stealing. In the beginning they may have tried to persuade their friend not to do it. That not having worked they had to make a personal decision: to stay or to go. Instead of realizing that this person isn't really the kind of friend they want they hang around but don't steal themselves. Over a period of time their familiarity with the situation will weaken their own determination not to steal and they will, depending on their own strength of will and the insistence of their friend, eventually steal themselves. And even if they don't steal themselves, by supporting someone who does and maybe sharing in the spoils of the act, they are vibrationally entering into the negative magnetism of the moment.

If our children play sports with kids who show a lack of good sportsmanship it will be more difficult for them to develop good sportsmanship. If a child associates with others who lie, cheat or complain it is likely that they will also begin to express these qualities. It is the same in every part of life. That is why finding situations that support positive character qualities is so important for young children – much more important than the activities themselves.

The influence of other children on our own is enormous. Peer pressure isn't just a figure of speech. It is an actual magnetic power that will affect even strong willed souls for good or ill. When you consider the school that your child attends keep this in mind. We will talk more about schools in the chapter on education.

The balance between exposure to the influences of the world on our children and the nurturing environment that we cultivate at home is one of the greatest challenges for parents. The activating key is to make as many conscious choices as we can and not let outside forces take control of us or our children. Many parents succumb unnecessarily to the influences of our society. We don't realize how strong this magnetism is to go along with the crowd.

Here is an example that has always amused me. After a movie is over why do all of the people jump right up and squeeze together in an effort to get out? Why not wait until the crowd has dispersed a little? Could all of those people be in that much of a hurry to get out? People just can't help themselves, the crowd starts to move and they do likewise.

Try this as an experiment. The next time you go to a movie see if the impulse to get up and rush out catches you. Make yourself wait until the others have left and watch how your mind resists slightly.

Learning to act consciously in life takes constant vigilance. When your child tries to support a desire by stating that everyone else is doing it, remind them that they are not everyone else, but a unique individual. We need to make decisions on our own, not just because others are doing it. At the same time, that doesn't mean we should always buck the group energy. Children that have trouble blending in with group energies will sometimes throw that same argument at you from the other direction saying, "I am just being myself!" What we are trying to do is act according to the highest truth that we can see in the moment, through a conscious attempt to perceive truth. Each situation has to be evaluated in the light of the current energies that are being expressed. The key is to pay attention and to not live passively. You may have to say, no, to a particular activity many times until one day it is right to say, yes. This honest evaluation of each moment of life as it presents itself is how we consciously live in the positive flow.

We talked earlier about freedom. True freedom is the actual ability to inwardly perceive truth and live in full accord with that perception. Even obeying the laws of our country should be done as a conscious act of cooperation instead of blind following. We need to be ever ready to protect our freedom by standing up for truth. Even if it means getting laws changed. That is, after all, one of the founding principles of our country.

By awakening our awareness of the positive flow and living more and more through the superconscious mind we will strengthen our ability to be unaffected by the whims of society or our own subconscious tendencies. The inner freedom that this brings to the soul allows us to live more in the joy of Spirit and less through the limitations of the senses and the conscious mind.

This understanding of how we are affected by our environment should be utilized to increase the positive energies in our children and to steer them clear of unnecessary negative influences. Whenever you are unsure about the affect that something will have on your child take the time to consciously attune yourself to the positive flow. It is only through developing this as a habit that we can learn to rely on our ability to read situations correctly.

Ultimately any negative environment can be overcome through right attitude and strength of will. As our children grow we want to help them develop the confidence that they can meet successfully the challenges of life. If we have helped them to develop the virtues of positive mental culture they will have the character qualities that can best prepare them for any situation.

Once again let me emphasize that while we attempt to bring out the best in our children and ourselves we must be careful not to be judgmental about things in which we choose not to participate. Even souls that are under the influence of the negative flow are parts of God. If we separate ourselves from them with "holier than thou" attitudes we are limiting our sense of oneness with all life. God is equally present in those who do wrong as those that do right. He just can't express the Divine Qualities through those who choose to live covered with the dirt of ignorance.

So as we seek to refine ourselves, our children and the world in which we live, let us also send the blessing of those efforts to those elsewhere in need.

217

25

Television, Movies & Music

Throughout our discussion I have tried to make it clear that living in the positive flow of life isn't something that can be done passively. It is only when we actively participate in the process of life that we are really living. Otherwise we are just biding our time, waiting for the waves of life to wash us where they will and deposit us on the shore of oblivion when we die. The strengthening of our will and determination to succeed in life, no matter what our specific goals may be, is central to what we have been talking about. And in order to succeed we need to practice making conscious choices.

When our children are faced with decisions in their lives what are the factors that they will consider? How will they process the various considerations? By what value system will they evaluate their choices? As parents it is our responsibility to help our children develop a way to deal with the wide variety of demands that adult life will bring. How can we best insure that they have the tools that they will need to handle life?

In the world of computers it is said, "Garbage in, garbage out." That reminds us that the processing of information is only as good as the quality of the data that is inputted to begin with. While the human mind is certainly able at any time to rise above "garbage in", it would be unrealistic to think that our children will grow up with a healthy view of life if they are constantly bombarded with input that supports an unhealthy view of life.

Over the next few chapters we are going to look at some of the most common sources of input that our society offers and see what effect we can expect them to have on the forming of a child's approach to life. And most importantly, what we can do about them.

Few would disagree that in all of recorded history the most dramatic change in the way people spend their time and understand the world in which they live has come since the invention of television. While at first it was just a novel way to spend an hour or two being entertained at home television has become the most powerful force of communication on earth.

Television, like all powerful forces in life can be used for the betterment of mankind or to its detriment. Some people think that television is inherently evil, bearing nothing but the sins of a decadent world. Others consider television a potential savior, by bringing the issues of the world to each person's doorstep. In various positions in the middle are those who think that there are positive and negative aspects to television. The one thing that everyone can agree on is that barring global catastrophe, television in some form or another is here to stay.

So what do we do about it?

The first thing to do is understand how it affects us. I don't mean just the psychological effects of spending hours watching a box that is affectionately called the boob tube or the idiot box. It is only common sense – which seems to have evaded millions of people – that continual exposure to endless acts of violence, dishonesty, selfishness, anger, lust, derogatory humor and materialistic attitudes in general, would be detrimental to a healthy view of life. We need to look at the way television affects us vibrationally.

Have you ever watched someone watching television? If you haven't, try it sometime. The mental stimulation that arrives at the viewer is incredibly powerful. The television can trigger all of the human emotions and those feelings can be seen on the face of the viewer. This is why people like television. It is totally engaging. It stimulates our mind and emotions. All we have to do is sit back and relax. What a deal!

This total stimulation of the mind and emotions is at the center of what we should be concerned about when discussing television. In the chapter on Non-Sensuality we discussed how the mind becomes agitated by the sensory impressions that we experience each day. And that it is through over stimulation of the mind that we lose our ability to perceive the positive flow of Spirit.

When we watch television we are plugging into a constant stream of stimulus. This stimulus has two aspects: quantity and quality. The quantity is the duration of the exposure and the overall intensity of the programming. The quality is the type of exposure. Elevating? Activating? Or downward-pulling? Since television as a medium is in itself stimulating to the viewer it is activating. But according to how it is used and the programs that are watched it can go in an elevating or downward-pulling direction.

This constant flow of stimulus affects us just the way any sensory input does. The more you do it the more you become desensitized to it, so the more you need to do it in order to get the same satisfaction. It is a lot like drugs and alcohol. In fact, for some people television is almost as addictive, certainly psychologically if not physically. If you overindulge in watching television you can even feel a mental hangover the next morning. And if you are hooked on television and haven't watched for a while you can actually feel a sense of well-being rush through your system as you relax into the viewing mode.

Even more detrimental to the viewer is the fact that by excessively stimulating the mind and emotions we are binding ourselves to a never ending cycle of ups and downs that keep us from experiencing the natural even-minded cheerfulness of the soul. The way to be happy isn't to live in an endless stream of sense stimulation but to bathe in the vast ocean of joy that can only be perceived when the mind is calm. So, it is this subtle effect that television has on our consciousness that is at the root of its potential danger to us.

Does television have any redeeming qualities? Or should we just throw our sets out? Well, throwing the set out is certainly an option that should be considered but let's see if there is a compromise that for many is more realistic.

While we have been focusing on the negative impact that television can have it would be unfair not to look at the positive things that have come from television. Through television the world has become a single family. We are more aware of and able to respond to the needs of all people just through the sheer speed with which we can be informed about circumstances around the world. This ability to communicate quickly with hundreds of millions of people has brought about a change in national and international affairs that has been on the whole for the betterment of mankind.

The potential for television to educate and motivate people for good should not be underrated. Programs that express the best in human endeavors or inform us of our history can be very helpful. Good programming can educate us about ways that we can improve ourselves or inspire us to be more concerned for others. They can entertain us with wholesome adventures, touch our hearts and imaginations with stories of inspiration or they can enliven our spirits with joyous comedies. Any of these can be good uses to which the power of television can be turned.

Like a sharp knife, television can be used to cut away our peace of mind or it can be used to carve beautiful moments of inspiration. The key is to treat it like we would anything that can be helpful but is also potentially dangerous: carefully.

Some people think that you need to let your child watch television so that they will know what is going on in the real world. Make no mistake about it, television very rarely depicts life as it actually is. People who think that television characters are expressing real life need to pull the plug out quick! Even the shows that try to deal with real issues do so in ways that are designed for ratings first. The content is presented by people who want to get signed up again for next season, not by people who are dedicated to inspiring people toward their higher nature. If this seems a cynical view, why is it that you can flip through fifty, seventy-five or more channels on cable and end up saying that there is nothing on?

In the early years of broadcasting television was a family event. Everyone would gather together as a group to watch a limited number of shows. Now many homes have multiple televisions just to avoid arguments about which show to watch. Establishing guidelines about the use of television in the home is essential. Each family must evaluate for themselves which and the number of programs that are considered more beneficial than harmful. Keep in mind the underlying issues that we have been discussing. Don't forget that commercials should also be a factor in your deliberations. Commercials are even more stimulating – on purpose – than most programs. They also preach consumerism as a way of life. They say, "Buy me and you will be happy!" This supports the most basic delusion in life, the thought that any "thing" can be a true source of happiness.

My own personal experiments with the television have shown that life is better without it. One day I just unhooked it from the antenna. When my children were growing up we only hooked it up for special events like the Olympic Games. Sure, we missed a few good shows, but in my opinion life is definitely better without it. And my children didn't feel deprived. For some reason they love to read books. Do you think there might be a connection?

When my children visited the grandparents they were allowed to watch what they knew to be acceptable programs for a reasonable length of time. The parameters of this issue were discussed in advance so that they had no questions to use as an excuse. Thus we avoided, "But Dad I wasn't sure so I asked Grandma and she said it was o.k.." I also reminded them that visits to the grandparents were for visiting with them and not for disappearing into the television. One of the keys to dealing with television is to give children just enough so that they don't feel like it is forbidden fruit. At the same time, give them alternate activities that they find positively engaging and they won't miss it at all.

Once the television was unhooked from the antenna videos became of prime interest. Videos have the advantage that if you are not sure if a movie is appropriate for your child you can view it first. I have found the rating system for movies to be very unreliable. I don't trust them one bit. I have found some R rated movies that are less offensive than some PG and PG-13 movies. There are also some G rated movies that are too emotionally upsetting to young children. So you have to do some selecting. The advantage is that you can.

Movies, whether videos at home or at the theater, should be considered the same way as television. Of course there aren't any commercials during the show, which is a real plus, but movies have even more energy behind them then your average television show. Choosing wholesome subjects is very important and not easy given the general state of Hollywood movie making.

When I took the kids to a theater as they were growing up I would make a big deal of it. We didn't do it very often so it was always something special when we did. We enjoyed it much more than we would have if we went all of the time. This is an important point: when we repeat an activity too often it becomes less enjoyable. We have talked about this before, but it is easy to forget because the senses keep saying: more, more, more.

As your children are able to understand, explain to them your philosophy about television and movies. Explain to them how you make your decisions on what is or isn't acceptable to watch. By doing this they will learn how to evaluate shows for themselves. Once, when my daughter was about 10 years old she went to a birthday party and found herself watching a video that she knew wasn't appropriate. She just went into the other room until it was over. There is no guarantee that your child will do this, but if they aren't told how to make an evaluation, they definitely won't. After that party we learned to ask if a video was going to be shown at the party, thus avoiding future problems.

The whole key here is to act consciously concerning these issues. Don't just figure that you have to go along with what everyone else does. Just because everyone else is watching a particular show doesn't mean that we have to. We want our children to learn to think for themselves and make conscious decisions based on positive guidelines. In order for this to happen we need to set an example and explain to them how we make our decisions. This will allow them to learn the process in a very natural way.

There is another point that people often miss concerning the content of many programs. It isn't just a question of what the subject is but also how it is presented. I don't mean just the obvious lessons that are shown but the underlying way in which the characters act. It is fine to have a plot that leads to the point that stealing is bad or telling the truth is good. But if the characters are obnoxious all of the time through the use of negative put down humor, bad language or disrespect for others, then the positive lesson of the plot is mostly lost. And in fact, because in the end they told the truth or returned the stolen item the negative qualities of the characters are subtly supported. These are the lessons that our children learn by watching television and movies. They are sometimes subtle and sometimes not so subtle, but to think that our children or ourselves are unaffected by theses underlying energies is to stand against the very way that we are made.

Something that goes hand in hand with these issues concerning movies and television is music. I remember hearing a story about a young boy who found a dead body on the beach. When his mother asked him if he was afraid he answered, "No." Surprised by his response she asked the boy why he wasn't afraid. The boy thought for a moment and then said, "Because there wasn't any music."

The power of music to create a mood is one of the ways that the emotions are triggered in the movies. Just by listening to the soundtrack you can tell when something bad is going to happen or that everyone is happy. The music will tell us very clearly whether the story line is heating up or cooling down. Like the spices of a gourmet meal the sounds are dashed upon our minds to create just the right effect.

225

This power that sound has to affect us is just as real as food when we eat a meal. Good food makes us feel light and energetic. Heavy foods leave us feeling sleepy and/or very body conscious. It is the same with music. Good music brings us toward the elevating qualities of life. We feel inspired or uplifted. Music that plays to our lower nature pulls us down, it leads to negative emotions or emersion in sensuality.

If you want to bring out the best in your children expose them to music that brings out the best in them. Songs with strong melodies that express an expanded empathy for the many positive facets of life are far superior to the grinding anger or self-involved materialism that is represented in much of what is called popular music.

Many adults wonder why so many youth listen to music that just sounds like horrible noise. The answer lies in a story about an ancient emperor of China. As any good leader would, the emperor wanted to keep tabs on how things were going in the many different provinces of his empire. His method of determining how things were going was very different than one might expect. Instead of asking his counselors to report on the economic, social and political conditions in each area the king toured his empire on a regular basis. On these trips he asked few questions. He wasn't concerned about factories, crops or schools. He had only one purpose: to hear the music that his people were listening to. Hearing the qualities that were expressed by the music of his people he could tell if things were going well or not.

Music is born through the consciousness of the composer. If the composer is tuned into happiness the music will express that quality of consciousness. If the composer is tuned into sadness or discontent the music will express those qualities. Any type of music can only become popular if it strikes the right cord in the consciousness of the listener. People who feel anger will like angry music. People who feel blue will like the blues. Since this is a book primarily on parenting we can't go into the countless variations of how qualities of consciousness can be expressed in music, but that all music is an expression of consciousness and that it has a tremendous affect on the consciousness of the listener is important to understand.

The music of our society on a whole is very hard and angry. People are frustrated that the wealth of our society hasn't brought happiness. They seek to drown their disappointment in the frenzy of intense sensory stimulation. This is one of the reasons why drugs and alcohol are so popular. People can see that happiness isn't found outside in the world but they haven't yet found the source of happiness inside their own selves. So they seek the false happiness of a temporary high.

In your child's early years, expose them to music that is joyful and life affirming. Teach your children to savor good music but not to overindulge. People who are always listening to music, even if it is uplifting music, are still trying to find happiness through stimulation of the senses. True happiness is found in the silence of the soul. The very best music will help the listener reach beyond outward sounds so that they can begin to hear the inner sounds of Spirit.

Just like with movies, television or the food that your children eat, in their younger years you can control and educate them in good eating, listening and watching habits. As they grow older they will begin to make more and more of their own decisions. Don't be passive in your efforts to educate your child in these areas. It is much more important than many people think.

Another thing to keep in mind is that overexposure to these stimulants tends to make people restless, yet at the same time, passive. As a result, they want to experience things but they don't want to put out energy, they just want to sit back and be stimulated. In this case encourage your child to make music instead of just listening to it. Whether it is singing or playing an instrument, on their own or in a group, making music is much more beneficial then just listening to it. As an aside, studies have shown that students that study music do better in their other subjects as well.

Here is another idea. Pull out the video camera and get your child to make their own movie. There are lots of inexpensive ways to do incredible things with a video camera today. Making movies is no longer just for Hollywood! It is fun, educational and much more productive than sitting passively in front of a screen.

The ramifications of personal involvement in these types of activities reaches far beyond playing a song or making a movie. Reaching forward to develop and express ourselves is an important part of character development. It doesn't have to be music or movies. Any hobby or area of interest that involves us in creative thinking and a positive outflow of energy is tremendously beneficial. This isn't only for children. Adults too will find great benefits through this type of involvement. The feelings of satisfaction that come from our efforts to express ourselves are far greater than the passive enjoyments of being in the audience.

Whatever your decisions might be about the use of television, videos, movies and music, make your choices consciously. Think about it. Observe how you are affected by your choices. Seek a deeper understanding of these issues through your connection to the positive flow and then experiment with your inspirations. It is only by consciously making these decisions that we can take control and be a causative instead of passive force in our lives and the lives of our children.

26

Sports, Books &
Heroes

In primitive societies it is for the sake of physical survival itself that people are driven to develop their abilities of body and mind. Today, we don't need to stalk across the plains and through the forests to find our next meal, we stroll the aisles of our local supermarket. Yet at the same time, there are skills of body, mind and soul that we will find just as essential for negotiating the challenges of today's world as there are for people of primitive societies. Strength of body, mind and will, stamina, patience, determination, courage, humility, enthusiasm, cooperation, patriotism, forgiveness and love: these are just some of the qualities that are expressed by those who live successfully in any society.

As we watch and guide our children's growth it is important to remember that it is the qualities of energy as they flow through a child's character that we should be most concerned with. Strengthening the body can be done in any number of ways and likewise the mind. But remember, just like with religion, it isn't the style that is important, but what we become as the result of our efforts.

The thing that is often forgotten in this equation is that the development of body, mind and spirit can not be compartmentalized. They are always happening simultaneously, whether we acknowledge it or not. Even in sports it is readily accepted that strength of muscle isn't the ultimate factor in being the best. At the highest level of competition it isn't even in the mind where victory is attained. The greatest victories come from the very depths of being, from a person's strength of spirit. This is where the greatest champions achieve their heights.

How can we help our children to become champions of their own lives? There are three main parts to the winning formula: opportunity, understanding and effort.

Providing our children with opportunities to grow is something that shouldn't be left to chance. It isn't enough to just sit back and let our children do whatever they feel or don't feel like doing. Depending on the inclinations of your child they may be interested and motivated in various activities, in which case you won't have to worry about it. But if your child is not interested and motivated you will need to help them. No matter what direction – as long as it is a positive direction – your child chooses to explore, keep in mind that it is in the process of consciously engaging life that we can make the greatest progress in life.

One of the most fertile grounds for helping children develop positive living skills is through sports and other elective activities. Areas of involvement can range from traditional sports like baseball, football and basketball to swimming, horseback riding, climbing, gymnastics, chess, playing a musical instrument, scouting and dance. These kinds of activities can provide scope for the development of basic skills like increasing their energy, focusing their concentration, and learning to cooperate with others and the positive flow of life.

Not only do we want to develop strong muscles and good hand-eye coordination, but we also want to develop the mind and character so that they can function clearly, even under pressure. Each specific activity has its own unique challenges. For football and boxing you need physical toughness. For basketball and soccer you need endurance. For tennis and chess you need mental toughness. For dance you need physical grace. For horsemanship you need balance and an attunement to your animal partner. And yet, since all human activities are the product of the basic qualities that make the soul, every activity provides a basis in which our children can develop a balanced approach to life.

The key lies not so much in the activities themselves, but in the understanding that we bring to bear on those activities. Sometimes it can be a question of how to improve a skill specific to the activity. At other times it may be an aspect of understanding oneself or others. But in all cases, these are the grounds where our children learn how life really works. This is where they learn how to learn, and how to apply and develop what they have learned. This is also where they come face to face with their own desires and the desires of others.

While it is true that many of life's lessons must be learned on one's own, giving our children a framework in which to process these challenges is an essential responsibility of parenting. During the activities that our children participate in they will be exposed to a cross section of positive and negative energies. These energies and attitudes come form both their peers, their teachers and their coaches. How they process these energies is something in which we want to participate.

We all know how impressionable children are. A positive or negative experience during formative years can have a lifetime affect. It is not at all uncommon for a high school or college coach to become a friend or enemy for life. We don't want these experiences to go by unnoticed. While it would be nice to think that our children will automatically share anything important with us the fact is that they often don't. It is only through time spent in conscious communication with our children that we can learn what is going on in their lives and how they feel about it. Through the act of listening and supporting, as you would with any friend, you may earn the opportunity to help them.

As a part of this idea of time spent, and an important part of the perception part of *Positive Flow Parenting*, it is essential that we know what is going on during practice sessions or rehearsals, as well as, during games and performances. As a youth soccer coach I noticed that even on the first day of practice many parents just dropped their kids off. While it is true that neither kids nor coaches really want parents looking over their shoulders all of the time, it is important that we as parents know what is going on during these sessions. Once we have a feel for the way things are going it is appropriate to back off a little.

There is no mystery about what our children are being taught when coaches or parents preach winning at any cost. Or when they make fun of the losers and condone unsportsmanlike conduct. Good sportsmanship should be foremost of the things that our children learn in any activity. If that isn't what they are being exposed to, we need to weigh the pros and cons of the circumstances and apply balancing energies. In the worst case scenario we should consider removing our children from the situation.

When my son, Kai, was twelve he had a soccer coach that couldn't control the boys and allowed them to complain all of the time. The coach also let the players use bad language. Since I attended many of the practices I was well aware of the situation. After discussing the situation with Kai we agreed I would talk privately with the coach. Unfortunately the coach just couldn't see the points I was trying to make. It didn't help that his son was the star player of the team and the boy with the worst attitude.

My first inclination after talking to the coach was to take Kai off the team. But I didn't feel good about him missing the chance to play soccer. There was no other team to which he could transfer so we sat down and had a chat. Kai and I discussed the situation at length and I warned him against being influenced by the negative energies of the other kids. Kai felt that he could handle the situation and so I felt that unless he began to show signs of not handling it he should stay on the team.

The next season Kai informed me that if he had to have the same coach he didn't want to play. It came totally from him. Fortunately we found a team with a great coach and he had one of his very best soccer years. Not only did he do better in soccer that year but he understood very clearly the difference a good coach can make. It was a lesson well learned, not because I tried to force it on him, but because we were both paying attention and trying to flow in the right direction. The thing that really made the difference was that we both made an effort to perceive what was going on and experimented consciously with our highest understanding. Kai learned to mentally reject the negative energies of his teammates instead of entering into them, while I learned to let go a little and let him grow up.

Effort is simply the putting of one foot in front of the other in order to move toward the achievement of one's goal, be it mental, physical or spiritual. As parents we need to monitor the efforts of our children as they push forward in life. If we notice that they are falling behind we will need to find that subtle application of energy that will motivate them in a positive direction.

It is through the application of will that we achieve anything in life. Whether it is a team or individual activity each person must try to do their best. This conscious effort to do one's best is one of the most important perspectives on life that we can share with our children. While we have all heard that it isn't important whether you win or lose but how you play the game, the fact is that there are many people in the world today who believe that winning is the only important thing. Our children will no doubt encounter people who approach life that way. How will they act when acting properly means losing the game? Or later on in life, what will they do when the proper action may mean losing a job?

While we can never know the results of the game until it is over we do know that if we have trained hard and practiced doing our best we will do our best when we are tested. And if we fail the test? Then we train some more, until at last we attain victory!

One of the best ways we can inspire our children toward their highest potential is through reading. Books are a doorway through which each person can explore life's possibilities in their own way and time. For those who learn to read almost anything can be learned, any place visited and any type of adventure lived.

Through the power of the imagination books can have just as powerful an affect on our lives as the outward experiences that we have. Because of this it is important that we monitor the books that our children read. We can use the same criteria that we apply to movies and music. Books that express the positive flow of life will reinforce the energies that we are trying to nurture in our children. Books that support the negative flow will work against our efforts.

Consider the subtle ways in which many books speak of good actions while supporting generally "worldly" attitudes. Excessive concern with looks or popularity is better replaced with efforts to help others or to attain a difficult – but positive – goal. In an effort to face the issues of the day many books spend more time wallowing in the sensationalism of the problems then they do in exploring solutions. It is helpful to remember that avoidance is the least interesting but often most effective way to deal with many of life's potential problem areas.

Our goal should be to teach our children to tell on their own which books they should read and which they should avoid. In many cases it is plain to see by the subject matter or the vibration of the way it is being presented what the contents of a book will be. Of course you can't always tell until you are part way into a book, so then we should teach our children to put down a book that has turned in an excessively negative direction. I am not suggesting that we be fanatical about this, but there is no question that if we apply a little energy to this area we can do much good.

At the same time, there is an aspect of this that we can apply much energy to that will bring even larger rewards. It starts by reading to our children when they are too young to do it by themselves. Once they learn to read it is helpful if we make a practice of reading the books that they read. If you can't read all of the books your child reads then have them recommend to you some of their favorites. Read them and then discuss them. Don't limit your discussions to favorite parts of the plot. Seek stimulating conversation on issues that will enrich both of your lives. It can also help if you read some of the books that your child didn't like. Find out what it was that they didn't like. Ask them why they read the whole thing if they didn't like it. In other words, have a meaningful conversation.

Many adults think that children can't speak intelligently in these ways, but very often children can. And even if a child doesn't yet, they will learn to over time and your efforts will hasten that reality. Most importantly you are sharing a part of their world with them and expressing your desire to hear what they think. It is only when you have proven through your consistent efforts that you are interested that your children will share their thoughts with you.

Be sure that these conversations don't turn into you telling your child what to think. Your goal is twofold. The first purpose is to genuinely hear and understand what you child is thinking. The second is help them discover ways of coming to a positive perspective about things on their own. If we share how we came to a particular point of view they will soon discover how to do it for themselves.

As we discussed earlier, it is in the example of how we ourselves live that we will most affect our children. This applies to both our outward example and the magnetic qualities of our consciousness. So it is essential that we take care of our own development while we also try to help our children. Since we can expect that we won't be perfect it will be helpful if we expose our children to the examples of those who we feel exemplify the best qualities of life. Those examples will inspire us and our children.

It is natural for all of us to look up to people who have been successful in life. Who hasn't found the story of another person's life inspiring and thought: It would be great to be like them. Or felt: This person's effort to overcome adversity has inspired me to do the same in my life. It is very common to hear a child say, "I would like to be just like so and so." Unfortunately, the names that are most often heard in conjunction with that type of adulation are not the ones that we might hope for.

When surveyed about who they look up to most youth will most commonly provide the name of a sports star, movie star or rock star. Why? Because that is what they are exposed to. And if you think about what those people's lives usually represent it doesn't paint a pretty picture. If the best our children can hope for is a lot of money that will provide them the financial ability to indulge their ego's, their senses or their desire for fame and power, then they are being seriously short changed.

The great people of all times have proven that the victory of a good life is won on the day to day efforts at living in harmony with truth and not just attaining fame and fortune. No matter what the area of endeavor or the economic strata of the individual, it is the strength of character and application of creative intelligence toward noble goals that inspires future generations. These are the true heroes of mankind and they are the ones to which we and our children should look for inspiration.

Heroes are a natural and important part of every person's desire and effort to attain their highest potential. It isn't just because they provide good stories; they also radiate vibrations of success. When we seek to attune ourselves to great souls we can actually draw their blessings into our lives. This is true not only for the saints but also for great scientists, artists and leaders. No matter what field of human endeavor we look to, by seeking an inner attunement with those who have excelled we can magnetically draw on their success to improve ourselves.

The individual lives of the great men and women of all times are the history of mankind that our children should study. Through an association with the very best that can be expressed in this world our children will seek their own highest potential. Great will be the day when the list of our society's heroes is turned from flashes of temporary social notoriety to the annals of individual greatness that live through the centuries. When our children list those who have served mankind unselfishly, those who have conquered adversity to help others, those who have dedicated their lives to God, as their heroes, then we will know they are striving for the very best that life has to offer.

27

Educating for Life

One of the most amazing things about the human spirit is that it can rise above almost any hardship. We have all been inspired at different times by the stories of those who have risen from poverty, neglect or even abuse to the heights of success. As inspiring as these examples of greatness are few would suggest that we subject our children to unnecessary hardships just so that they can be strengthened by overcoming them. Yet when we look at the current state of education in America today we find that most children are being severely challenged and handicapped unnecessarily by the schools to which they attend.

We have talked much about how our children are affected by their environment and how important it is for us to make conscious decisions about what we expose our children to. Yet, the place that they will spend more time then anywhere but the home is often left to chance. While our government does guarantee the right to a public education it doesn't guarantee the quality of that education. If we send our children to school in the hopes that they will ignore or avoid the unpleasant and latch solidly onto the things that we think are important we are simply throwing the dice. Maybe in the past attending any school at all was considered such a great plus that the quirks of any particular school or instructor were unimportant in comparison to not going at all. But today that isn't the case. Today we live in a time of choice. We can make decisions about our lives and those of our children that were more difficult years ago. Though it isn't always easy, it is important that we educate ourselves about our choices and make these decisions consciously.

Let's look at some of the areas that we should be most concerned about when considering our child's career as a student. Keep in mind that it is the nature of a child to learn. Children are natural absorbers of information and impressions from the world in which they come into contact. Through the processing of that information changes take place in how a child relates to the world. Something that is often overlooked is that children learn from the totality of their environment and not just from individual areas of the experience. They don't just learn facts and figures from the lessons of the day. They learn about themselves, others and how all of life fits together. That is why the whole of the environment in which they learn should be carefully considered.

The most important factors to look at – whether talking about pre-school, elementary, high school or college – are: the overarching philosophy of the school, the consciousness of the teachers, the consciousness of the students, the physical environment of the school itself and then the course of studies available.

Some schools have a stated philosophy and some do not. All schools have a philosophy that they manifest through the attitudes, actions and vibrations of those that guide the school staff. Understanding the driving energies behind the leadership of a school will help a parent to evaluate the possible effects on their child.

239

This is usually easier to see in private schools. Private schools tend to advertise those attributes that they do best or think that parents will appreciate. In this situation it is the parents job to figure out if the advertising is a realistic expression of the schools day to day reality or just window dressing. This usually means going to the campus and meeting school staff. What parents will be trying to do is experience the atmosphere or vibrational presence of the school. Reaching out with our formula and perceiving the underlying energy of the school is essential. Seek inner confirmation of your feelings through attunement to the positive flow. Ask inwardly for guidance and experiment with ideas that come to mind about how you can deepen your awareness of what it would be like for your child to attend the school.

Try always to include your child in the process of deciding which school to attend. Children are naturally very intuitive about their environment. While it is true that children can also be wrong in their initial reaction to a new environment, it is in the best interests of your relationship with your child to communicate that you care about their preferences and reactions even if you have to go against them.

With public schools, the size of the district and the quality of the people in leadership positions have a great effect on the states general mandate to educate. Large districts tend to be much more impersonal. Politics often play too important a part in what gets done. The everyday realities of the students are often the last issue to be dealt with. Most importantly, many schools, because they are afraid they will offend someone, are unable to fully engage whatever philosophy it is that they really believe would be most helpful.

One of the biggest tragedies in education is that in an effort to achieve equality for all students mediocrity has become the standard. This shouldn't be a surprise to us since the same approach that is applied to most public education has been an outgrowth of the American approach to manufacturing all kinds of products. Why shouldn't it work with students?

The automobile industry is a perfect analogy. At first, each inventor was all on their own. Having no previous experience in the field they had to develop their ideas hit or miss. Once the basics were worked out each successive car and model was improved over the previous one. When Henry Ford came along and developed the assembly line cars were built in ever-increasing numbers at more affordable prices. Seeing this success with automobiles the same techniques were applied to all forms of manufacturing.

As we all know, it is the mighty dollar that drives industry. In their efforts for increasing profits each step of the manufacturing process is studied in an effort to streamline efficiency. The utmost attention is given to cutting the cost of materials and the time and labor that it takes to process them. Once peak efficiency is reached through honorable means manufacturers have to decide if they are willing to decrease the quality and safety of their products to increase profits. History has shown that many are. This is what began the decline of the once untouchable American auto industry.

This same relationship of dollar expense to unit of finished product has found its way into the American educational philosophy. Cities are faced with educating increasing numbers of students with fewer dollars per student. What is the chosen solution? Use assembly line techniques and exchange quality for quantity. This willingness to accept, as the basis of our societies value system, dollars and cents instead of people is at the heart of how the negative flow has pulled us away from values that bring real meaning to life.

As long as the school budget has priority over the individual needs of the students the results of our education system will be not only scholastically mediocre, but even more importantly, we will be teaching our children that money is more important than people. I am not suggesting that throwing money at education is the overall solution to the problem. Practical solutions to most of our challenges in life are available to us. The real question is: Do we truly want to solve our problems?

The solutions to the issues surrounding money in our society are not at their roots economic. Nor are they social or political. They are spiritual. I am not talking about outward religious affiliation. I am talking about the true inwardly motivating energies of the people that make up and lead our society. People who grow up caring about others will generally do the same as adults. People who grow up thinking only of "I and mine" will continue the same way when they grow up, unless they are positively influenced along the way. Systems of government, economics, education or even religion, will never solve the problems that we find in this world. The solutions to all human difficulties have come through individual people. People who have attuned themselves – whether consciously or unconsciously – to the superconscious solutions that are always available. As long as there are caring people, willing to give of themselves so that others may prosper, almost any system will suffice. When selfish self-interest prevails, no system can truly succeed.

This attitude of giving and caring on a person to person level is what our schools should be teaching. It starts with the leadership and guiding philosophy of each school. It has been found true time and again that the philosophy of centralization and control only works to a certain practical level. Once that control goes too far it starts to diminish productivity. A case on point is the assembly line. It has been found that the people on the line can come up with solutions for day to day challenges before others who work in some far off office even know there is a problem. Good leaders are able to reach across these boundaries and touch the "every day man". It is through this true sense of personal relationship that teachers and students alike are inspired to do their best.

No matter how good or well intentioned any system is, it is the people applying the system that will determine the quality of the end results. Have you ever considered how teachers are trained? What about support and training after a person has become a teacher? While progress is being made in this area the fact is that teachers mostly learn to teach after they have become teachers. Once having become a teacher they get very little feedback about ways they can improve. And in the public schools systems, once a teacher is in place it is very hard to get rid of them even when it is known that they are not very good at their job.

Whew! Now that I have gotten that out of my system let me mention that there are many dedicated teachers around the world who are trying their very best under difficult circumstances to help the children that pass their way. These heroic efforts have made the difference in many lives. Because of the success of these teachers we know that their individual efforts can and do make a difference. Remember, it is people that are going to make the difference in your child's education. Otherwise you could just set them up in front of a computer and say, "Learn!"

Teachers not only communicate information about the subject at hand, they share attitudes about life and qualities of consciousness. If a teacher is worn down and cynical about life they will be passing that energy on to the students along with the math lesson. If a teacher tends toward anger or other negative emotions, that will be passed along with the history or science lesson. If a teacher brings a positive energetic attitude to class that expression of energy will be an important part of the lesson as well.

While we can't expect our children to like all of their teachers the overall vibration of a teacher can have a big effect on how things will go. And since each school is like a family the school will tend to attract teachers of compatible vibrations. Getting a feel for the vibrations of the teachers will help us to evaluate the school on a whole.

Teachers who are attuned to the positive flow of life will have the time and interest to know your child individually. This kind of attentiveness is essential in the younger years. Some students that have difficulties in school can be helped simply because a teacher took the time to be aware of the individual needs of that child. Attitudes about how to approach life from a positive point of view are extremely important and a good teacher not only expresses these positive energies in their own life but also helps to bring them out in their students.

When you meet teachers in a school look for good open and friendly communication skills. Look, inwardly, underneath the smiles to feel if they are genuine. Most importantly notice how they treat the students. Do they communicate eye to eye with respect and caring or are they distant and controlling? By looking for these qualities in the teachers you can get a feel for what your child will be absorbing at school.

Without positive role models along with the reading and writing our children may be learning that negative character qualities are normal rather than just common. They will be learning that it isn't how we live but only the immediate outward result that counts.

One extremely common misconception about education is the idea that it is possible to separate academic education from character development. It is thought by some educators and parents that the mind alone can be cultivated at school and that issues of character can and/or should be dealt with elsewhere. The reality is that life just doesn't work that way. Child prodigies are a good example of how this philosophy can go wrong. It is often seen that when a child excels in one particular area and that gift is cultivated to the exclusion of the whole person that child can grow up to find life outside of their chosen field to be very difficult. As we talked about earlier, balance is the key to a healthy life. Good teachers are able to tune into their students and help them to be aware of their attitudes and flows of energy. Then they can help the student to bring those energies into balance while they cover academic and physical education.

Along with the outward efforts and the magnetic qualities that the teachers project will be the vibrations of the other students in the school. Children of all ages exert enormous social and vibrational pressures on each other. Sometimes it is very subtle and at other times it is right up front. Learning to deal with these swirling energies is also part of a child's education. While we want our children to be comfortable socially we don't want them to be drawn into negative directions that will cause them harm. Certainly every school is going to have those students who get along and those who don't. The main thing is to monitor these energies and make sure that they are challenging but not overwhelming. Take the time to find out what types of problems are foremost with the students of the school that you are considering. Asking the principal and/or local law enforcement is a practical approach to getting answers to questions that many people don't really want to talk about. Getting all of this information will give you an up front idea of what your child will be facing if they attend the school.

One of the best things that we can do is choose a school where the parents of the students have the same basic values that we do. I am not talking about racial, cultural or religious values. The real issue is an attunement to those common positive qualities of the positive flow of life that people of every background can experience in common if they choose to do so. If the parents of the other students in the school are seeking the same positive values for their children that you want for yours you will be able to feel much better about the interactions your children will have with their children.

If you are trying to cultivate positive attitudes in your child and they spend the day at school with children whose parents are reinforcing negative attitudes it will be much more difficult for you and your child. While it is certainly true that no school is going to be perfect, that doesn't mean we should be fatalistic about it. There are more educational options available today then ever before. Unique and specialized programs of all kinds have sprung up to meet the individual needs of students and communities. The key for us as parents is to reach out and find out about these opportunities and plug our children into the very best situation available. When you can't find the right situation already up and running, band together with other interested parents and help create the right situation.

While it is essential that a school be academically qualified to teach whatever your child needs and it is certainly preferable that the school have nice facilities a well, these outward measures of quality can never replace the reality of individuals caring about other individuals. Human values will always be the most important thing that schools can communicate to students. As long as we grade students only according to their test scores and not according to the positive qualities of their character development we will be failing to educate the whole child.

The true purpose of education is to prepare students for life: Life in its many facets. Not just issues of the mind, but also of the body, emotions and spirit. When children are given the basic tools for success in all parts of life they will be more able to deal harmoniously with the countless challenges that life will bring. When supplied only with the facts, figures, names and dates of history, students will graduate from school without the skills to manage the totality of their lives.

It is by educating the whole person that we can really bring about the kind of changes that will help not only each child, but also the world at large. When people are understood not by the color of their skin, their religion, their cut of hair, the value of car or their home, but by the qualities of spirit that are manifest in their lives toward their family, job, community, country and the world, then we will be able to say we have shared the values of a good education.

247

28

The Early Years

The principles of living in the positive flow that we have been discussing apply to all people no matter what their age. At the same time it is easy to see that at different stages in each person's life different qualities or needs might be uppermost. While all people need love, a baby needs to be hand fed while a teenager doesn't. Pre-school age children need a lot of directing, college age children don't. During each stage of a child's development parents should be particularly watchful for the needs of the moment as they attend to the broader needs of a lifetime. This balancing of momentary and long term needs is a dance that can only be performed on an individual basis through the constant application of our formula: Perceive, Attune, Experiment/Redirect.

Many people make changes in the way they relate to others according to the age of the person they are interacting with. So they approach their relationships with children differently than they do with adults. This perspective can be very contractive. It places an unnecessary barrier – age – between the adult and child. It also lends an air of superiority to the adult. The idea that an adult is superior to a child just because they have survived longer in this world is a notion that has no basis in truth. All souls are equal in the sight of God. The particular skills that we might develop at any time during our lifetime are only little decorations that temporarily adorn the tree of our life.

The true basis of this sense of superiority can be found in the ego's tendency to always bolster its self-image. This ego consciousness separates us from others of all ages and from our ability to perceive our oneness with all of life. People who can relate to others without this sense of ego find that they are much more successful in their relationships with others of all ages.

Of course, when an adult relates to a child there is a natural tendency to guide and protect. There is nothing negative about that. Just because all souls are equal doesn't mean we don't have different roles to play. But the way to manifest our caring most successfully is to respect each child as a soul first and then serve their needs from that perspective of respect.

This idea of respecting our children from the very beginning is extremely important. It sets the tone for the way we will relate to them all through life. And it will, in itself, save us from making many mistakes. For if we don't radiate respect to our children as a matter of habit we may fall prey to the infamous generation gap. Once that wall goes up it takes much energy to bring it back down again. And besides, one of the greatest pleasures of parenting is the closeness that you feel to your child. Why lose that most precious relationship through a false sense of superiority?

Having reiterated that these principles of right living are not age based it is at the same time true that they need to be applied sensitively to the needs of the moment, which can often be understood by the age at which they commonly occur. If we want our child to express a more loving nature the things that we try to do with them at the age of three will be different than the things that we might try at the age of ten. So in this way we can see that age does affect the application of our methods if not the principles themselves.

Through the rest of this chapter and the next three chapters we are going to be exploring some thoughts on specific age groups. While I will be presenting these age groups in cycles of six years each remember that each person is different. These time periods are just for giving a general lay of the land. Don't box your child in by labeling them according to their age and the stage that is associated with that age. We can use these stages as broad guidelines but each person and situation is individual and has many facets to it. Attune yourself to the specific underling energies of each situation and you will be more able to perceive the realities and solutions of the moment then if you try to project what is happening because of the stage or age of your child.

When I mention specific situations the goal is to give you an idea of how this works, not to give you a specific solution to your situation. The real solution is your own personal application of our formula and not how others apply it. Not that we can't learn from the successes and inspirations of others. We can and should draw on ideas no matter where they come from. But in the end we must live our own lives with the uniqueness that makes each life special.

If you think about the changes that occur during the first six years of life it seems almost impossible that a body and mind could develop so quickly. One day you meet a squirmy little infant and six years later you have a person who is incredibly able to function in this world: amazing! The sheer volume of mental and physical growth during this time is so astounding that we sometimes forget that the emotional and spiritual patterns for this life are also being formed.

One of the keys to helping our children in their development through this cycle is to understand that they are so enmeshed in the process of entering this physical world that it is through the physical that we can most easily communicate whatever it is that we want to share with them. We certainly can't expect to talk philosophy with a two year old. But we can communicate our point of view to them through the way that we relate to them.

As an example: If we want to communicate the idea of sharing, rather then trying to explain it, just do it. Even with an infant you can share things like food and toys. If a toddler grows up with sharing as a part of their daily life they won't need to be taught it later. They will have it as a natural part of the way they live.

During the earliest years there is no substitute for time spent. It just makes sense that the more time you spend with your child the more you will be attuned to their needs. They will also feel the support of your presence. This loving attentiveness is the foundation of your relationship with them. While this holds true throughout their childhood and beyond, during these earliest years it is most essential and enjoyable.

Those families who have two working parents should seriously evaluate how having a child will affect their lives and how their lives will affect their child. Infants who spend eight to twelve hours a day, five days a week, in childcare facilities have a vastly different experience than those who spend their day with a parent. I am not saying that there isn't a time and place for childcare. Just take the time to be aware of the affect that the childcare environment and that much time away from your child will have on them during these formative years. There is a tendency for some to let others raise their children. Childcare, television, babysitters, these have become the parents for all too many children. In some cases young children are left for hours on their own. Is this what we want for our children?

If two incomes are necessary for the family then options should be considered. It could be anything from waiting a few years before having children, choosing a less expensive area in which to live, changing work schedules or finding a way to work at home. Some parents band together so that they can help each other with childcare in their homes rather than working more hours to pay for it. Whatever you decide, keep in mind the affect it will have on your child's formative years. Seek with all honesty to find the solution that best fits the needs of the whole family. Consult the positive flow.

Once you have your infant in hand, along with spending wonderful hours holding and cuddling them, you will also get to feed and diaper them. And since they haven't yet learned to talk they will be using the most basic modes of communication – crying and smiling.

It has always amazed me the variety of things that an infant can communicate by crying. The intonation of the cry is directly connected to the physical and emotional needs of the child. That an infant is trying to communicate and not just making noise is an important distinction to make. Listening to the underlying vibration of your child's cry is part of your early training in the perception part of our formula. If you aren't sure what your child is trying to communicate while crying you should double check the basics of comfort and safety before you assume general grumpiness.

While you may not choose to respond to every call of your child, being aware that your child is trying to communicate their desires or feelings is important. At this stage a child is far more aware of what is going on around them than they can communicate to us. Understanding this should help us to listen carefully for the deeper layers of their needs and inspire us to nurture them not only physically, but also mentally, emotionally and spiritually as well.

Just as we will need to find a feeding schedule that meets their physical needs we should feed the other parts of their being as well. Uplifting music and slow flowing motion are easily digestible by most children during this time. Reading to very young children is also helpful. Not only for their learning to speak but for the time spent and the vibrational benefits of the material read. Singing to and eventually with your child is also very beneficial. These shared experiences may not be remembered specifically later in life but they are the bedrock of good feeling that will shape your child's view of the world. The more time they spend in vibrations of good feeling during these early years the greater will be the chance that they will develop a healthy view of life.

While we want to stimulate our children in positive ways we also want to give them an overall sense of calmness. That means having times of quiet and cultivating an inner sense of calmness even during activities.

I have noticed that many parents feel the need to constantly bounce their infants while holding them. While there are times when this can be beneficial, if it becomes a nervous habit it is more a sign of restlessness than of attentiveness. It can also unintentionally be a subtle way of sending the "always stimulate" message. This constant stimulation is something that babies become used to and then through habit, demand. This is the beginning of the entertain me consciousness that many children develop.

I have noticed this same tendency in the way some parents feed their infants. As soon as the child makes a noise the parent sticks a bottle into their mouth. Even a little baby takes time to digest their food. If new milk is constantly being mixed in their stomach with partially digested milk the curdled results can often be found on the shoulder of the feeding parent.

Developing a schedule of feeding that allows the stomach to be empty of food before it is filled again will minimize the possibility of problems. I am not suggesting that you starve your child, I am just saying that a sensitivity to what is going on in the child's body will help both of you to be happier. Not mixing liquids or solids that are not compatible is a good idea. If you create an explosive combination in your child's stomach you will both pay the price later.

Some of the most common problems that infants have are digestive. Try to find foods and a feeding rhythm that works for you and your child. Then stick to it. That regularity will help you both. Regularity will also help with sleeping patterns. There are some infants that are just plain uncomfortable in their little bodies so we need to accommodate them as best we can. Finding a regular pattern of feeding and sleeping will be beneficial for all concerned. Remember, you are setting the parameters of your child's life at this point. If you set a regular pace with sensitivity to their needs they will most likely respond in a positive manner. If they don't you need to apply our formula until they do.

Reading up and sharing ideas with your friends will help you with ways to solve some of the challenges that come up, but always let your attempts to resolve difficulties be ultimately guided by your inner attunement. Through practice your inner view of life will lead you to unexpected solutions that fit your exact needs. Often you will come up with solutions that others may not have thought of.

One thing that you want to be careful about is coming up with solutions that are unnecessarily difficult. As an example. Some parents resort to driving their infants in the car to get them to sleep. Certainly that works for many. But do you really want to create a pattern where if your child has trouble getting back to sleep at two o'clock in the morning you have to take them for drive? For me, those types of solutions are last ditch efforts. Admittedly, that's what it takes sometimes. But apply your creative efforts and attunement to the positive flow before you give in to patterns that you don't feel comfortable with or that are unnecessarily difficult.

Remember that proverbial ounce of prevention. Try to avoid situations where your child would want to be awake at two o'clock in the morning. If you keep them busy before bedtime and then give them a full belly the chances are they will want to sleep. You see, attunement with the positive flow also means looking at things from a practical point of view. Don't expect a miracle when common sense will suffice.

All of our efforts to create a comfortable and nurturing environment for our child should include the positive reinforcement of their best qualities. Surrounding them with a happy home life with a minimal amount of negative energies is the most effective way to keep their vibrations – and our own – high.

The early years of a child's life are so challenging that many parents let their own energies get depleted. Thus they rise more quickly to anger and frustration. Being attentive to your own energies is also an important service to your child. When you can't give your best because of fatigue or loss of your sense of well-being for any reason, do what you can to remedy the situation. Remember way back when I talked about how your vibration is the strongest influence that you can bring to bear on your child? These early years are the most trying physically. Stay in shape. Meditate regularly. Keep a positive perspective on life. And don't forget, people have been surviving this for a long time, you will too!

Having a child is not like having a disease. This is one of the most natural and rewarding experiences that we can have in this world. Rather than seeing it as a trial, see it as a blessing. Even during those most difficult hours of the night when you are exhausted and you hear the little one calling you, remind yourself that God in the form of your child is asking for help. It is an honor and a privilege to be called to duty. Smile as you trudge dutifully into the dark night.

Once you have survived your child's infancy the nights will be more restful and the days will be more challenging. Be calmly active and actively calm. Bring your attunement to the inner flow of life to all of your activities. Your toddler will be on the move, reaching for everything in sight. During each phase you will be laying out the rules of conduct. Depending on your child's nature you will be experimenting with a wide variety of techniques for communicating the needs of the moment. This constant interaction is the way you both learn to harmonize your relationship. Learning when to be strong and when to be yielding is an individual challenge. That is why you must learn to find your solutions through attunement.

There are three things that young children need in abundance. The first is lots of love. The second is lots of wholesome things to do. And the third is lots of clarity about what they should not do.

The first two we have already discussed. Now let's concentrate on the third. When I say lots of clarity about what they should not do I don't mean sending negative energy – through excessive controlling, criticizing or yelling – at them all of the time. What young children need to know is what the basic rules are and if there is any flexibility in them. If you make it clear to your child what the rules are and stick to them, things will go much more smoothly than if you are not clear and consistent. We have already talked about this, but it is so important that we are consistent, it can't be said too often.

Parental consistency needs to be active and positive rather then passively or actively negative. As an example. The other day I was in a grocery store and a three year old child was sitting in the seat of a shopping cart grabbing items off the nearby shelf. The mother told the child not to do it about fifteen times. Each time the parent replaced the item on the shelve the child immediately reached out to grab it or another item. I couldn't figure out why the mother didn't just give the child something she could hold or simply move the cart so the child couldn't reach anything. Instead the mother repeatedly told the child not to do it in a weak nagging type of voice. This form of parental absentmindedness reinforces negative behaviors in children. Through attentiveness it is possible to minimize the times when we have to go head to head against the will of our child. Once a child knows that we mean what we say they will respect what we say even if they don't agree with it.

If we let our children poke at us with whining energy or the ignoring of our instructions we are setting the tone for the way they will relate to us and others. It doesn't mean we have to be a drill sergeant all of the time, but clear, directing positive energy will give our children a sense of security about the world in which they live. If we establish definite guidelines from the beginning and stick to them our children will not only learn to behave they will be happier.

Children are not happy by accident. They are happy because the environment in which they live nurtures their positive nature. Whether we are seeking to keep them safe, educate their minds, build their bodies strong or awaken their higher spiritual nature, it is through consciously focused energy in the direction of their best interests that we will be most successful.

Stay awake during these early years. They are both the most exhausting and the most precious of years. You will probably never again spend so much time with your child. Know that your efforts during this time will help to carry them through a lifetime. Enjoy!

29

I've Got a Feeling

One of the most basic ways we can communicate our love for a child is by hugging them. While this is true for all ages it is especially important to establish this physical form of expressing our love during the early years. Fathers and mothers should spend many hours holding their children. As the children grow, along with hugging you can add different types of play that are physical. This physical closeness is one of the most powerful ways to communicate to your child that you care about them.

As your child grows the way that you relate to them will naturally change but it is important not to let those changes turn into a lack of physical contact. People of all ages need to be hugged on a regular basis. By maintaining a physical closeness with our children we will be more able to help and support them when they go through rough times. Without that physical contact it is much more likely that our children won't turn to us except in the most dire of circumstances. Keeping open lines of verbal communication is also a part of this equation. Even more important than being able to talk with our children is the development of a bond that reaches beyond intellectual agreement. We want to establish a reservoir of loving support that is so deep that our children will trust that we are on their side no matter what happens in life.

While there is an inborn attachment that comes from the physical act of parenting, that bond can be damaged – and even broken – if we don't pay attention to what affect our actions are having on our children. During the first six years of life our children are so small and dependent on us that it is fairly easy to maintain a sense of closeness. As our children reach farther out into the world during the ages between six and twelve it will become increasingly difficult to balance their dependence with their growing independence. The key to success in this area is support.

As our children grow they will be balancing their lives according to a mixture of the guidelines that we give them and their own tendency to strike out on their own. Each child's nature will be different but the basic process is the same for all. As parents we need to recognize these polarities. As our children begin to explore the world and its possibilities we need to make sure that we don't diminish our child's awareness of our support by constantly pointing out their flaws.

One of the things that we can easily see from the way life works is that it always takes longer to build something up then to tear it down. It is the same with our child's awareness of our support. For every time we come down hard on them we need to lift them up a hundred times or more. This is one of the reasons redirecting a child's energies is so much better than going against them. Children during this time of their lives are extremely sensitive to feelings and their more subtle form, vibrations. When they feel the storm of anger or criticism howling at them they will remember how it made them feel far longer than they will remember what caused the storm. If they spend much of their time as children mentally protecting themselves from negative parental energies – even if those energies are genuinely meant to be helpful – as they build their sense of self-identity the bulwarks of self-protection will be part of their construction. And all too often, these walls can separate child from parent for a lifetime.

In fact, during this second six year cycle it is through feeling that our children can most easily be reached. As their sense of self-identity grows they will become intensely aware of how they feel about things. Encouraging them to feel good about themselves is part of helping them to build a sense of self-worth that will be resilient when life gets rough. It will also increase their ability to resist the negative influences of others.

The goal of parenting is not to keep our children forever dependent on us, but to help them become successfully independent. Even more important than any specific skill is a positive sense of self-worth. This positive feeling can help our children achieve whatever goals they set for themselves. It will also help them to cope with the many times that life – whether it be through people or circumstances – will make the attainment of their goals more difficult. Attentiveness to these underlying issues is another reason why *Positive Flow Parenting* is so helpful.

Because our children are so aware of their feelings during these years it is the perfect time to help them recognize how their happiness is affected by how they feel. And most importantly, what they can do about feelings that they want to get rid of, while cultivating feelings that they like.

All of the techniques that we have talked about to help us be in tune with the positive flow can be utilized by our children. As you seek to help your child understand their feelings and channel them in positive directions guide them in looking for the flow of these energies through their consciousness. Once they begin to watch their internal energies they will begin to integrate that knowledge into the way they relate to life. Sometimes it will be so natural that neither you nor they will realize it is happening.

One of the best ways to insure that your child will be happy is to keep them busy with positive activities. If our children grow up with plenty of wholesome activities, balanced with times of quiet, they will be much more likely to carry forward in life with that same pattern.

What we are trying to do is help our children to understand that it is the quality of their energy that will determine how happy they are in life and not just what they are doing. One of the ways we can work with these ideas is by letting our children help around the house even when that help sometimes hinders rather than really helping. If they start this when they are very young they will develop a comfortable sense of being involved. This not only instills in them a sense of responsibility and the discipline of fulfilling regular duties, it helps them to realize that they are a part of the family. This identification with a larger picture than just the fulfilling of their own desires is an important part of expanding their consciousness.

As soon as a child sees the activity as a "chore" the level of enjoyment often diminishes dramatically. One thing that can help is to do household activities with your child rather than sending them off to do chores on their own. I have found that when they see me helping too life doesn't seem so unfair.

Looking for the fun in life when it seems hidden is also another trick to living in the positive flow. Even taking out the trash can be made into a fun adventure if we set our imagination to it. It isn't that we want to give our children the impression that everything in life is fun. What we want to do is help them to realize that even the most unpleasant experiences can become more pleasant if we bring a positive frame of mind to them.

Sometimes we need to think the way Tom Sawyer did when he had to whitewash the fence. He didn't have the least bit of interest in doing it himself. To Tom it was a chore. When he attached a lure of fun to it he soon had all of the neighborhood kids paying him to do his work. That is the kind of creativity that we need to bring to the activities of our children. Almost any activity when presented in the right light can be made into fun. The creative potential of the positive flow can present unexpected possibilities to any situation.

What you want to do is find a routine for your child that provides the balance between fulfilling and exhausting. The regularity of a routine is very helpful for children. It keeps them on an even keel mentally and provides them with an outward sense of purpose. It also gives their rapidly growing bodies a rhythm with which to find some sense of stability.

Keeping a sensitive ear to your child's energies is an important part of how you can help keep your child's life in balance at this time. Even though a regular schedule is helpful for most children there are times when everyone needs to break free from the regular demands of life and just let go and relax. Even young children can become stressed if their schedules become too demanding. There is always a chance that your child will be one that needs more free time than the average. That is why these ideas must be applied on an individual basis.

The main thing is that your child is allowing positive energies to flow through their lives. As long as the energy is positive the details are not nearly as important. Once a child learns to work with their own positive energies it is easier to turn those energies toward a variety of wholesome activities.

263

All children will experiment either consciously or unconsciously with negative energies. This is completely normal and healthy. Just as they might explore a new playground each child will explore the possibilities of their various emotions and qualities of energy. This exploration will be a combination of their reactions to their environment and their natural inclinations from the past.

The challenge for parents is to not overreact to a child's explorations. This doesn't mean we should let them run rampant, but having a look at what is available is certainly part of a curious mind. When your child explores negative directions be particularly sensitive to not diminish their positive self-image. Seek ways to help them understand the ramifications of their actions not only as to how their own happiness will be affected, but also how their actions affect others.

If you find that your child's energies are going in a negative direction look for the influences that might be causing it. Sometimes negative energies come from an internal struggle. At other times they are the result of environmental influences. In most cases negative energies can be redirected in a positive direction with the application of some creative inspirations. This positive redirection of the energies is one of the main challenges of parenting. Just remember that the more we use it the easier life will be for all.

Another part of the parental balancing act is to accept that your child is all too rapidly becoming less dependent on you. It seems only yesterday that we were changing their diapers and now they want to go off on their own to places that we have never been. How can this be?

Exactly how you deal with their growing independence in terms of specifics will depend on both outward circumstances and your own inward sense of what is acceptable.

As I have mentioned before, be sure to share your evaluations with your child. Don't leave them in the dark about why one thing is acceptable and another is not. While "Because I say so!" might be the appropriate response if your child has been badgering you and you want them to stop, the goal is to develop a relationship with our children so that we can explain things to them and have them begin to understand for themselves how to evaluate the situation.

One caution in this area is that we don't want our children to always associate these explanations with what they can not do. Tell them also why activities are good. In this way they will be able to understand what makes up a good activity and not just what makes up unacceptable activities.

Because the mind is so open during these early years it is far easier for children to learn a wide variety of subjects that adults find more difficult. Foreign languages, math, musical instruments, working with computers, these are all easier for the youthful mind to absorb. Use this openness to new information to your child's advantage. By exploring many intellectual possibilities at an early age you will be giving your child a head start in all aspects of their education. And most importantly, in their ability to access the learning process itself.

These years of your child's life are some of the most exciting because they now have the physical abilities and the language skills to do an endless variety of activities with you. Don't let this special time fly by without enjoying it to the fullest. One of the most enjoyable things that you can do is learn something new with your child. No matter what the area of interest our children can help us explore life with a fresh view. They can also remind us that we have skills that may have become rusty!

When I was a child I learned the basic moves of chess. I never really studied it but I could in the most basic way say that I could play. My son discovered the game and joined a chess club. At the age of twelve, after only a few months of playing, he was pressing my abilities to their limit. Needless to say he thoroughly enjoyed beating me. The really fun part was that I enjoyed it when he beat me too. That doesn't mean I didn't try my best. One of the great breakthroughs for the soul of both parent and child is when we can enjoy life through the enjoyment of others. Parenting is an incredible opportunity to smile through the smiles of others.

During this time of life our children should be both very productive and carefree. Let their idealism fly high. Don't worry so much about teaching them the harsh cold realities of life. They will certainly get their share of mental and physical bumps during these years. Try to never let the difficulties of life interfere with their sense of security and well-being. These should be happy years, filled with times of exploration, exhilaration and love. If we can share these years with our children with a conscious effort to be a part of each other lives we will find that we have formed the basis for a lifetime of sharing. We will feel as every child should feel during these years, that life is good.

30

By My Will

All throughout our discussion we have come again and again to the importance of addressing the underlying energies in our children rather than just the specific outwardly apparent actions. This is similar to what I mentioned about the differences between Western and Eastern styles of medicine. Traditionally, western medicine treats symptoms while eastern medicine treats causes. With children, what we want to do is strike a balance that deals with the symptoms in the short term, yet, reaches to the causes in the long term.

People often wonder at the rebellious nature of teens. Many are satisfied to find an explanation to this tumultuous period of life in the hormones of puberty – the physical transformation from a child's to an adult's body. While certainly this physiological process is a factor, to see the substance of this time as being only physical is to see the symptom rather than the cause.

This age period is the time when each person is called upon to discover their own unique nature and learn to stand alone to face life's challenges. No longer able to hide behind the protective skirt of childhood, during the teenage years each person must to come to grips with their own sense of power to guide their own life.

Why is rebelliousness such a part of this time for many? Why do some teens slide through this period without much difficulty and others with great struggle? Understanding why children rebel against much of life during this time is key to understanding how *Positive Flow Parenting* can really make a difference in the lives of both child and parent. But, to get to the reason for rebelliousness we must first reach back to the cause of these transforming energies in the body and mind.

Earlier we talked about how the energy from the universe that sustains life enters the body through the medulla oblongata at the base of the brain. From there the energy is distributed to the body through subtle energy channels in the spine. These energy pathways are the channels through which activation of the various processes that keep the body going are controlled. Along with activating our body's physiological processes, like assimilation and elimination, they can also activate our mental and emotional energies.

In order to start the onset of puberty the energy centers that are responsible for the physical changes at this time of life must become activated. When this happens, as the body begins its physiological transformation the soul gains greater access to the power that is available to us for relating to life. In the orient this energy is called Chi. In India it is called Kundalini. No matter what you call it, it is the awakening of this energy that ultimately propels us, through the power of its magnetic attraction, to the achievement of both outward and inward goals.

As souls advance on the spiritual path the awakening of this inner energy and the ability to focus it positively is essential for the attainment of Self-realization. The reason

268

that this energy is awakened to some degree in all people at this age is because it is linked to our sexuality. Thus, because our sexual energies are awakened at this time, so also is the power to achieve our goals in life.

As youths begin to feel the bursting up of these energies they are often at a loss as to what they are and what to do with them. It is like a strong water pressure flowing through a hose that no one is holding. The end of the hose just flops around wildly while the water streams out in all directions. If you take a firm grasp on the end of the hose you can guide the water in useful ways. For teens, it is essential that these inner energies be channeled in positive directions. When they aren't, one of the results is rebelliousness.

What happens is that teens start to "feel their oats" and look for ways to express their energy. The direction that their energies eventually flow are most often determined by environment. That is why environment is particularly important during these years. When a child is very young, even if they go a little astray they don't usually get into too much trouble. But during the teen years, a little too far astray can get you killed.

What we need to understand is that these energies are natural and good. Instead of worrying about them or resisting them, we should embrace them for the great progress that can be made during these years.

One of the things that make this time so difficult for teens is that it isn't clear to them what is going on. Sure, they see that their bodies are changing, but people rarely talk about the other aspects of these inner changes. The totality of this process is little understood by most people. The whole issue is usually chalked up to that catch all subject, sex. And so, as our society supports a very strong interest in things sexual, this is the direction to which most youth end up putting much of their energies. It isn't that a growing awareness of sexuality is bad. It is just that instead of making that growing awareness something noble and loving it is most often turned toward lust. Remember, the negative flow encourages us to think in terms of fulfilling our desires and not caring about the full repercussions of our actions. If our children spend years of their lives with frustrated sexual fantasies or the fulfilling of those desires physically at too young an age, positive results are rarely the outcome.

In the chapter on non-sensuality we talked about how focusing our attention on the senses causes the mind become restless and lose its ability to reflect the joy and peace of spirit. This restlessness of the mind not only lessens our happiness but it keeps us from being able to focus our energies on other goals that we might wish to attain.

The way that we access this inner energy is through our will power. We have already talked about how important it is to develop our ability to channel our energies through our will toward the achievement of our goals. The awakening of self-determination through the power of the will is essential at this time of life.

How can we help our children to take advantage of these years to increase their chances for inner and outer success in life? The most central solution is the application of our formula. Let's explore some ideas about how this might work.

One thing to keep in mind is that our children need supervision. I don't mean that they should never be alone, but we should be aware of where they are and what they are doing. As they grow and show their reliability in making responsible decisions we can gradually loosen the reins on them. When you think about how many hours of the day some children are left to their own devices it is no wonder they often get into trouble. You see, children need to be guided in how to channel their energies positively. Once that is done they can fend for themselves more safely and happily.

Activities that encourage children to awaken and channel their physical and mental forces in positive directions are essential for this period of life. While each child might have a different preference of activity the essential thing is that they are challenged. They must be interested and motivated to push forward in the gaining of greater control over themselves and their abilities to succeed. Try to find activities that your child is really interested in and help them to dive as deeply as possible into those activities.

Sports are an obvious choice for many, but intellectual interests are important too. The key is involvement. Doing things. Not just sitting around and watching the world go by with the thought that it owes you something. When teens are actively involved in what they are doing they won't care if an adult supervises it or not. It is only when they are feeling restless that they will even give that a thought.

Variety is also a healthy part of this time in life. Giving our children a taste of the many possibilities in life will widen their scope of interest. Travel, hiking in the mountains, visiting museums, the theater and other places of interest, these are all different ways that we can provide our children with positive directions in which to channel their energies and explore life's possibilities.

Even more important than seeing what others have done is to have our children do things themselves. Hobbies are a great way to channel and grow creative energies. They can be done parent and child or just the child. Helping our children seek out experts or clubs to help them with their interests is another way that we can increase their opportunities for success.

If you find that you are having problems with your child during this time remember that it is through their application of will that they will find the most satisfaction. When they are channeling positive energies through their body and/or mind rather than seeking to simply sit back passively and enjoy, they will be too busy doing good things to feel bad. Much of the time it is just that simple.

One of the things we are trying to do is help our children understand that it is not only in the feeling of accomplishment that we will find happiness. An even deeper sense of good feeling can be found when we help to bring about happiness in others. When we channel the power of good toward the benefit of others, we ourselves are benefited far more than if we think only of our own happiness. This should be the basis for helping our children learn how to relate to others, including those of the opposite sex. If our children grow up with the habit of thinking about the happiness of others they will have a naturally positive platform from which to launch their interactions with others.

Providing children with opportunities to mix with those of the opposite sex in supervised settings can alleviate many of the problems that are associated with these exploratory years. Group activities that have a purpose which is not just social, but helpful to others, is much better then situations that are just social. Helping to clean up the neighborhood as a group is one example. Or it could be helping to run a booth at a church carnival or decorating a hall for a special activity. Activities that involve doing things side by side rather than facing each other, like at a dance, are very important. These side by side activities will provide opportunities for discussion and interaction that can help develop social skills without the overt sexual overtones that you find at a school dance. Mixed groups of young people who share an interest in any positive area of endeavor are much better than letting our children socialize on street corners at night under the aura that no one is looking.

While our children are growing more and more independent it is essential that we keep the lines of communication open with them. The only way to do this is through time spent together. We can't expect our children to just show up at our convenience and spill their innermost feelings. We have to keep our relationship dynamic with them through positive interaction on a regular basis.

For many parents their child's teen years are a real struggle. Parents feel they are losing control of the situation and they don't know what to do about it. This feeling of loss of control comes from fighting the flow instead of going with it. As our children grow we want to control them less and turn toward respectfully influencing them. If we have practiced *Positive Flow Parenting* from the beginning, by the time our children are in their teens the ebb and flow of our relationship will have become something quite natural. They will be in the habit of confiding much, if not all, of their feelings with you. They will know that you support them and that you encourage them to think for themselves.

If you are having serious problems with your teen, you can't expect to make things better all at once. First you need to honestly perceive the practical realities of the situation. Once you have a clear sense of what is going on, which usually necessitates an honest understanding and acceptance of how things got to where they are, you can then seek attunement to potential solutions. If communication has deteriorated too far it may take outside help to rebuild the bridge of positive communication. Without good communication the healing process can not begin. When good communication is reestablished you can then experiment with the creative ideas that come to you through attunement to the positive flow.

Certainly it is easier to say, "Just use the formula: Perceive, Attune, Experiment/Redirect" then it is to actually do it. But what is the alternative? If we don't make an effort to fix that which isn't working we are left with that which is broken. Far too many parents become estranged from their children during these years. This is when the generation gap can creep unnecessarily into family relationships. No matter how difficult it may be to heal an ailing relationship with your child it is always worth the effort. As parents, in the most basic way, we signed up to try when we became parents.

While our children make these leaping steps toward adulthood their increasing self-reliance should be seen as a positive and not a loss. As they stand more and more firmly on their own two feet you will find that you are able to enjoy them in new ways. You will no longer find a defenseless baby when you look into their eyes, but an increasingly confident person that you can rely on to do their best.

When your child graduates from high school and you stand by them for those timeless photos, take a moment to be thankful for the ups and downs, for the tears, the joys and the sharing of love that is expressed so uniquely by the relationship between parent and child. This is also what we signed up for and it can be very sweet.

31

What's it all About?

Quite often the years of childhood go by without much thought about where it is all leading. Each step is taken as it presents itself and upon completion the next step is addressed. The final six year period of the first 24 years of life is the time when our children can finally look at the world through the eyes of an adult and put together the pieces of their understanding. This mental process of putting things into perspective is a completion of the maturing process that all too many people leave out of their lives.

It isn't a question of whether or not a person goes to college or not. It is an issue of self-study. This is the time to really get to know who we have become as the result of our reaction to the environment in which we were raised. Most importantly, it is the time to develop a clear understanding about the way that we want to consciously approach the rest of our lives.

For many students these years are filled with the compiling of increasing amounts of questionably useful information and indulging in the many strange customs of college life. Those who don't go to college find themselves facing the pressures of adult life – which they may or may not be ready for. The freedom of being out on your own during these years can be both exhilarating and frightening. One of the things that makes this time difficult is that many still don't know where their lives are going or what they want to accomplish. Even more importantly, they need to come to grips with the question of life's purpose. What is life all about?

This is the time for parents to encourage their children to take a deep hard look at the world and how they see themselves fitting into the larger scheme of life. Certainly much of the groundwork will have been done, but sifting through to the core of one's deepest feelings doesn't happen overnight. These are the years when our children will begin to take full responsibility for their views and actions.

During these years a person's capacity for reasoning through the issues of life can be one of the most powerful ways to explore the possibilities. Thinking things out is certainly a longstanding tradition during this time of life. Late night discussions, reading different philosophies, exploring various intellectual possibilities, these are all natural progressions of the forces that were set in motion at birth.

If our children rush right out into careers, relationships and childrearing before they have come to grips with who they are as individuals and how they fit into the larger scheme of life, they may find themselves – who knows how many years in the future – down a dead end road wondering, "What happened?" When, if they had taken the time to sort things out in the first place, they could have saved themselves a lot of grief. This certainly isn't something that we can do for them. Nor should we want to. But we can help by supporting their efforts to seek a deeper understanding of their own nature. It is only through that personal process of self-examination that they will be able to find the path in their own lives that will bring out their highest potential.

And after all, isn't that what we want for our children? We want them to explore their very best – to reach for their star. Not in an egoic sense, but as a part of the fulfilling of the best possible purpose that they can bring to life.

As they reach for an understanding of where they can best push forward in life try not to limit their possibilities by dwelling on the limits that have pushed up against your own life. It is all too easy for a parent to think that their child's goals are not practical or so difficult to achieve that it would be foolish to try.

We are all bound to some degree by the view of life that we have lived. That is why they say in India: It is a blessing to be born into a religion but a curse to die in one. This doesn't mean we shouldn't follow a particular path until the end of life. It reminds us that we shouldn't limit our understanding of life by only looking at one view. No matter how beautiful our own view of life might be, there are always other views just as beautiful. We hinder ourselves and others when we lock ourselves into a single positive view of truth.

Like any good teacher, we should hope that our students surpass us in their successes. If we have done our job well there is every possibility that our children will excel in ways that we haven't. Most important will be how our children live, rather than the specifics of what they do. If we have schooled them well in the ways of the positive flow they will have the tools to make much progress toward the achievement of their goals.

One of the things to keep in mind during this time is that your child is no longer a child. Some parents can remember a particular moment when they came to the realization that their child had grown up. For others there is just a gradual dawning of the truth. Unfortunately, for some parents and their children that understanding never comes and the parents treat their adult children as if they were still and always will be a child. If we let ourselves be trapped by this limited view of our children we will not only hold them back, but ourselves as well.

While it is true in our society that during this time all children legally become adults, people responsible for their own actions, it is also true that not all souls consciously take on these responsibilities at the same time. And in fact, some people go through all of life without ever taking conscious responsibility for their actions, while others seem to act with conscious self-control from a very early age.

These variances in the time and way that each person progresses along the path of life should be taken into consideration as we adjust to the growth of our children. Realizing that they, as well as we, are always growing and changing in our understanding about life is one of the reasons that we need to be flexible in our relationships. As our children spend more and more time away from home we shouldn't assume that we know "where they are coming from". That is why, if we have established good communication habits from the beginning, we will always listen outwardly and inwardly to what our children are saying before we share our thoughts. Keep in mind that when our children tell us their thoughts they are not always asking for advice. They may be fishing for ideas or they may simply be sharing. Test the waters before you start to pontificate on what your child should be thinking or doing. It never hurts to make sure that our children are interested in our ideas before we share them. That is one of the ways that we can show our respect for them.

Many children go through a period of time where they do not share their thoughts with their parents. The different cycles of communication that a child goes through often have little to do with the parent. They are just part of the child's personal processing. If such a cycle should come upon your relationship try to balance it with other forms of togetherness that keep your bond strong. There are no pat answers for when and when not to intervene in your child's internal affairs. As long as your child's energies are not excessively negative, give them a long leash. If they are negative, what you need to do is seek options through your attunement to the positive flow. Remember the guideline of redirecting the energy rather than going against it.

There are few challenges more difficult for a parent then when you see your child going in what you perceive to be a wrong direction and, for whatever reason, you seem powerless to help them. This is a time when we must remember again that this is not "our" child, but God's. And in all cases, we can do one of the most centrally beneficial things no matter what the circumstance might be, we can pray.

Some people think of prayer as a last ditch effort. But prayer is more than just trying to save things in the last moment before disaster. Prayer is the conscious channeling of positive energies toward the object of prayer. If we pray for our children we will be acting as conduits for positive energies to flow toward them. We may not be able to perceive the results of those prayers objectively in all cases, but if we practice praying for others through the years we will find that good things do happen to those for whom we pray.

As our adult children are finishing their formal years of education and moving toward new opportunities we should look for the positive ways that we can grow into our own future. Each phase of life is a doorway to the next phase. Your children will feel much better about their own future if you feel good about your own. A sense of confidently moving forward to a positive future is one of the most helpful energies that you can radiate to your adult children. That

279

positive outlook will encourage them to be positive about their own lives.

Actually, this positive perspective on life is one that we want to cultivate from the very beginning. During each part of your child's life encourage them to see the positive side of every situation. By living in this positive frame of reference all of life looks better – even the storms.

One of the best ways for people to "find" themselves is through periods of intense selfless service. When we sink ourselves fully into the task of helping others our preoccupation with our own needs and desires becomes weakened. This lessening of self-involvement frees the mind to expand its horizons. We begin to see that helping others, in almost any useful way, is the foundation of any path that leads to a fulfilling life.

When we live attuned to the positive flow of selfless-ness rather than the negative flow of selfishness we are actually vibrationally changed and the whole magnetism of our consciousness is lifted to a higher level. Through this finer attunement to that which is good in life we can see more clearly the path that we should follow in order to live in tune with the positive flow of our own lives.

It is also in the person to person exchange of caring that we will find the essential truth that it is human, people caring about people, values in life that are really important. If science increases the length of our lives just so we can hate and mistreat each other for a longer time, what is the use? Making the world a better place is not done through the proclamation of governments but through the countless individual acts of caring that can only come from each individual person doing their part.

Sometimes people think that there is just one right place in life for each person. If a person can find that place they will be happy. While it is true that a person who has an artistic temperament is much more likely to be happy doing something creative rather than something repetitive, if we don't learn to bring the consciousness of happiness to whatever we do, we won't be happy even if we are doing just what we think we want to do.

It happens, more often than not, that when people do what they thought would make them happy they find that they aren't as satisfied as they expected to be. The truth is that it isn't what we do that will make us happy, but the consciousness with which we live. When our consciousness is right we will actually draw to ourselves the opportunities that are best suited to our natural abilities or the areas we need to develop. These opportunities will also be in tune with the kinds of experiences that will help us to grow spiritually. This is what we have been talking about all along, living life in harmony with the natural forces of life that are trying to help us.

Along with serving others there is also a need for all people to know themselves from a more internal perspective. In combination with a college education it would be helpful if our children received, as a part of their educational training, opportunities to seek understanding in silence and meditation. The issues of highest import in life have to do with each individual's relationship with God. Now that our children have the faculties to address these issues on their own it is important that they do so.

By this time in their lives we will already have shared our own views with them. Now is the time for our children to make their own decisions about God and the spiritual life. If they are not clear about how they stand on these issues they would do well to spend some time consciously grappling with the subject. Even if your children do feel comfortable with the specific spiritual path that you have been following, this is a perfect time in their life to find deeper understanding through direct personal perception.

There are many spiritual retreats around the country that provide the environment and guidance that is necessary for a successful retreat. While it would be nice if our children learned about and participated in retreat types of activities during their younger years, all too often they don't. Using a retreat as a time to intensely introspect and relate to Spirit, now that your child has the skills of body and mind to do so with conscious intensity, can be a life transforming experience. If you have never been on a retreat I recommend that you try it.

It is common for people to wonder why God doesn't reveal Him/Herself to us. If you check in with those whose lives have shown that they were in intimate contact with the Divine, they all say that we must activate the relationship by consciously seeking it. Along with helping your child go to college, help them have the opportunity to spend some time at a spiritual retreat. And not one that just talks about teachings, but one that helps people to personally relate to Spirit through prayer and meditation.

By the end of your child's first twenty-four years of life you will have nurtured them from seed to maturity. They will be ready to face the challenges of life on their own. Our stewardship as parents will have fully blossomed into the loving relationship that is unique to parent and child. Like war buddies, we will be able to share with each other the stories of years gone by. And in the camaraderie of those memories we will also be able to touch again the moments in which we have, together, tempered our bond in the fire of life's challenges. This is a bond that holds so much reward that no matter how difficult the road has been it is always worth the journey.

32

Living Life in the Positive Flow

As we develop our ability to live more and more in the positive flow of life we will find that we are able to move through the challenges that life presents us with an evenness of mind and spirit that we had in the past only hoped was possible. The feeling of well-being that comes from being in tune with the universal forces of good are the true source of all happiness. It is in a conscious connection to this universal well-spring that we can best serve our children and hope that they too will seek to align their lives to the positive flow.

If we have created a nurturing environment at home our children will feel an affinity to the ideals by which we have lived even if they choose to call them by a different name. And that is the real goal. Not so much that they should see life in terms of the same shades of color that we see, but that they have found their own personal relationship to life in which they feel comfortable. This will allow them to move forward toward the fulfillment of wholesome goals.

Keeping the energies of a family in balance is another part of parenting. It means not only keeping tabs on each individual and their needs, but also blending them in a way that supports a feeling of harmony in the fabric of the whole family. When each person thinks only of themselves and their own needs, harmony can not exist. When each family member is concerned for the others, not only is there an aura of peace in the family, but the individual needs of each person are found to be met much more easily as well.

This truth also works on a larger scale. A family will find its needs being met more easily when the family as a whole is concerned with helping others and not just its own needs. Doing service projects as a family is one of the ways that families can not only expand their sympathies, but also work together, shoulder to shoulder, and deepen their bond through helping others.

This also works for communities, states and countries. When people of any size group think only of their own desires they become ingrown and contracting. That aligns them with the negative flow. When groups align with the positive flow through caring for others, expanding their sympathies to people all over the world, we find that the whole world is our family and the planet earth our home. This broader view of life is essential if we want to be healthy and happy as a society.

When we bring these higher ideals into manifestation through our own actions and the lives of our children we are helping to uplift not only ourselves, but all of mankind. Sometimes people think that their own small efforts to improve life are not important, but it is only through the countless small efforts of many individuals that great things get done.

Seeing all of our actions as being connected to these broader realities is one of the perspectives on life that differentiates our times with times of the past. Now that science has shown the underlying unity of life through seeing life as energy and not matter, whole new vistas of understanding are opening up. This opening up of new potentials started dramatically in the 20th century and is continuing to build momentum now that we have entered the 21ˢᵗ century. During the last century we went from the era of the horse and buggy to the space age in a period of about 60 years. Amazing!

This change from the age of matter to the age of energy is not only on a physical level but also on a level of consciousness. People on an ever-broadening scale are seeing the whole planet as their home and the people of all races and cultures as their larger family. This unifying of our world into a harmonious whole is one of the great challenges of our times. It is a goal that must be met for the sake of future generations. Each of us should do our own part in the ways that we feel inspired to help toward this larger goal. Certainly sharing this larger view of life with our children is a part of what each parent can do to help.

We have talked at much length about how it is when we expand our consciousness that we are aligning with the positive flow. With this expansion will come an ever-increasing awareness of how the underlying energies in life work and how we can use them for our own good and the good of others. This subtler view of how life works, on an energy level, and even more deeply, on a consciousness level is the key to *Positive Flow Parenting*.

For a scientist to work with an abacus today instead of a computer would be considered by most to be quite limiting. With parenting, if we just use our habits from the past we won't be able to make as much progress than if we free ourselves from the limits of the past and embrace the opportunities that the greater understandings of today can offer us. Through the process of attuning ourselves to the positive flow we will find that we are no longer bound by the confines of the body, mind and emotions. We will be able to use these parts of our being as tools to become increasingly aware of our larger reality in Spirit.

285

One of the most difficult things for many people to accept is that it is in understanding and consciously directing the totality of our lives that we can most effectively parent our children. Parenting is much more about who we are as people than specific techniques of interacting with children. The more we change ourselves for the better the more we will be helping our children change for the better. If we have developed our own ability to live in harmony with life itself we will be much more able to perceive and act positively for the good of our children.

When we have learned to live on this more subtle level, as we interact with our children we will be more concerned with the level and quality of their energies rather than the particulars of what they are doing. If they are in the grips of negative energies, like selfishness, boredom or grumpyness, we will try to redirect their energies toward caring for others, creative activities and cheerfulness. If they are having a difficulty with their friends or at school we will help them to seek the solutions to those situations through attunement to the positive flow.

As we work with ourselves and our children on ways to utilize our attunement to the positive flow we will find that all of life changes its hue. Instead of finding a world of troubles we will find a world that is full of opportunities. Instead of wallowing in self-pity when life's disappointments come, we will move forward with enthusiasm for future successes. Instead of loneliness we will experience an abiding love that is always available to us within our own hearts. As we tap into this universal well of love we will find it flowing through us to our children.

The job of being a parent is never over until the end of life. As we grow older and our children meet the world on their own terms we will have opportunities to deepen our relationship with them in new ways. Be ever flexible in the way that you relate to your children over the years. Don't be bound by habits of the past. As you grow, let your children grow.

While we help our children to develop the mental and physical skills for material success in this world, let us also remember that without the skills for living life happily, outward success will be empty of satisfaction.

Think about it for a moment. If your child were to become a successful businessperson, but ruthless as a part of that success: Would you be happy for them? If your child grew up to be a doctor but lost their sympathy for the suffering of others because of what some people might call professional detachment: Would you feel that they had become truly successful?

The outward trappings of success that our children might acquire during their lives can not be the measure of our success as parents. The true measure of success is to look at the qualities of consciousness that they have cultivated. Are they humble and friendly by nature? Are they even-mined and cheerful most of the time? Are they calm and joyful as they meet life's challenges? Are they respectful of others and sensitive to the needs of others? Do they live with vitality, meeting each day with enthusiasm? Are they dependable and persevering in their actions? Are they practical and orderly? Do they live with an aspiration to achieve their best? Is the value of personal integrity at the foundation of their thoughts and actions? These are some of the signs that will tell us how our efforts have turned out.

Working with the qualities of consciousness that flow through us are the real challenges in life. Will we ignore them and simply seek outwardly for a pleasant journey through this world? Or will we dig deep into our hearts and find the strength and courage to deal directly with these most important issues in life?

As I have mentioned, we can't live life for our children. There is no guarantee about how they will live their lives. The only thing that we can really do to help them is to do our best in establishing them in positive energies. When we live our lives to the best of our ability we are, as a part of that effort, giving our very best to our children.

For some people the ideas that I have been sharing about living in the positive flow may not seem concrete enough. Working with invisible energies may seem vague and hard to understand. It was the same when electricity was first discovered. Being unseen many people just couldn't quite believe in it. But when they touched it, they could believe! It is the same with living in the positive flow. You must touch it. Perceive it. Live in it.

As I told you in the beginning, don't take my word for it. Experiment with these ideas and techniques that we have been discussing. Calm your mind and dive into the silence of your soul. There you will find all of the confirmation that you need in order to believe that these techniques actually can work.

As you move through life, free yourself from those ways of thinking and acting that hold you back from achieving your very best. Sometimes we think that we are too set in our ways to change. That is only true if we let it be true. It is never too late in life to make meaningful changes. In just the twinkling of an eye we can free ourselves from incarnations of past habits if we make the effort.

In fact, much of what life comes down to is effort. Are we going to jump in and get something accomplished or are we going to just wait on the sidelines and hope for the best? *Positive Flow Parenting* is about jumping in and getting consciously involved with life in order to change our lives for the better. Just thinking about these ideas is not enough, we need to act on our knowledge. The really exciting thing is that the more we delve into the possibilities of living in tune with the positive flow of life, the horizons of our potential keep expanding until we realize that there is literally no limit to what we can achieve. The only limits lay in our unwillingness to try.

As you walk along the path of parenting, no matter how rocky the trail may be, remember that each experience in life has been given to us as a gift. The gift of opportunities to grow closer to the infinite love and joy that resides at the heart of all life. Thus, all lives are linked in the dance of life that flows from Infinite Spirit. Let us join with our children in a celebration of that truth and share our lives with them by living each and every day in the positive flow of life.